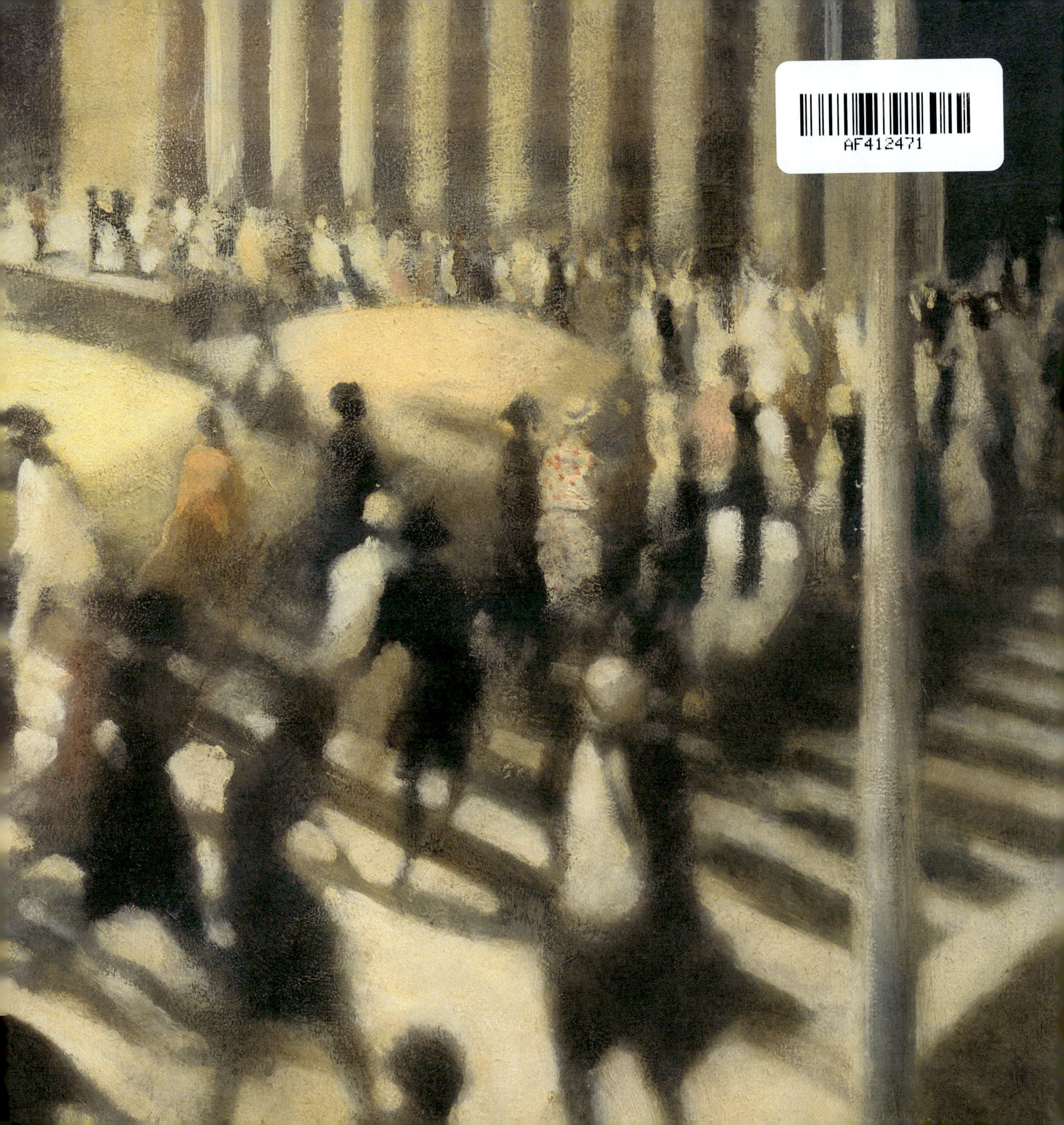
AF412471

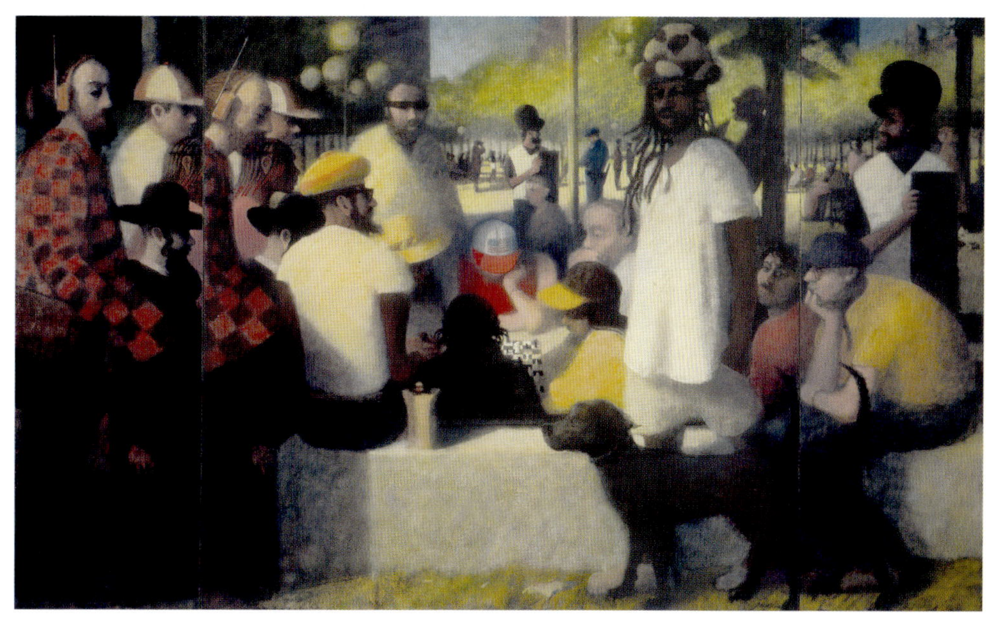

Bill Jacklin's New York

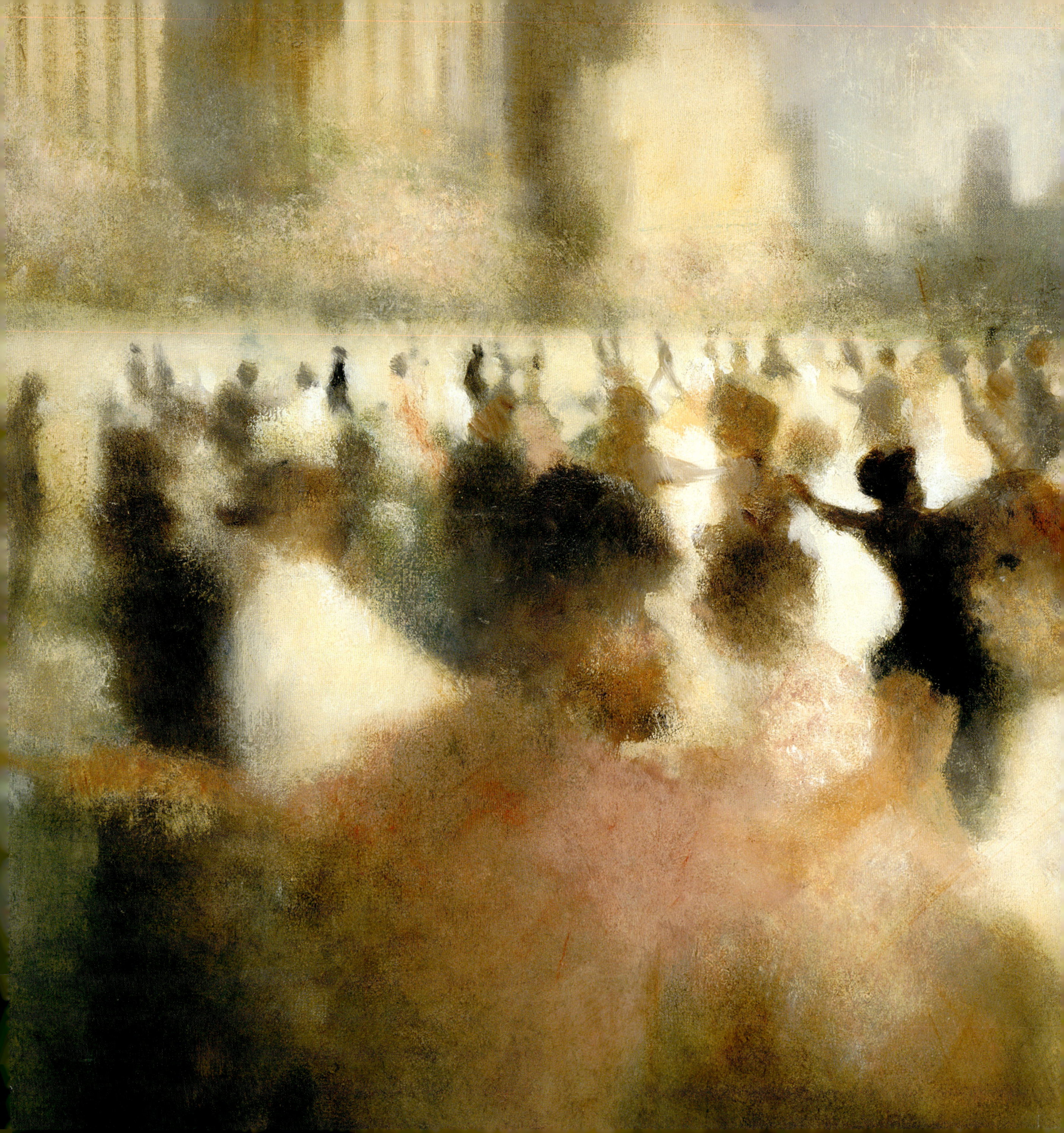

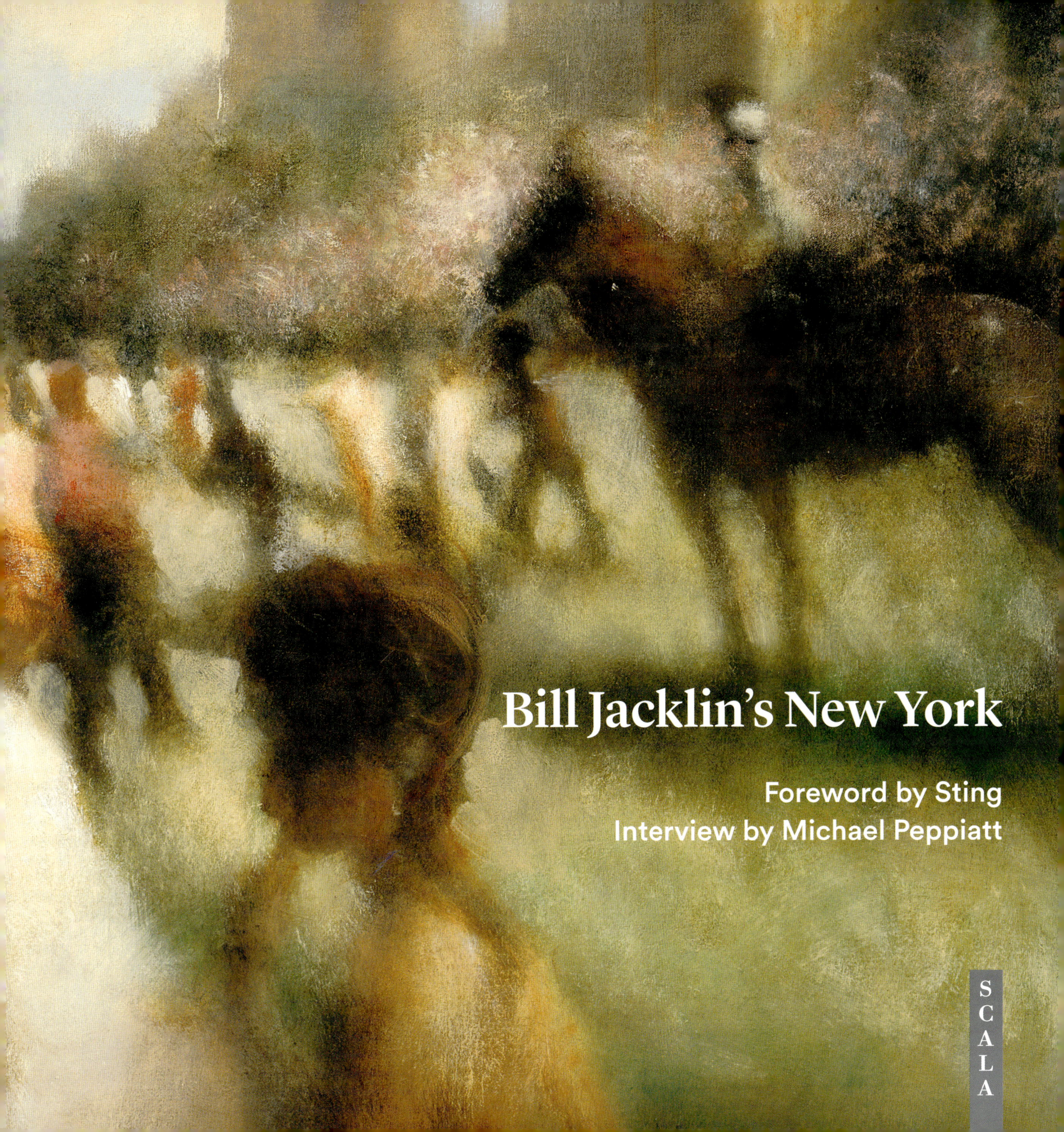
Bill Jacklin's New York
Foreword by Sting
Interview by Michael Peppiatt
SCALA

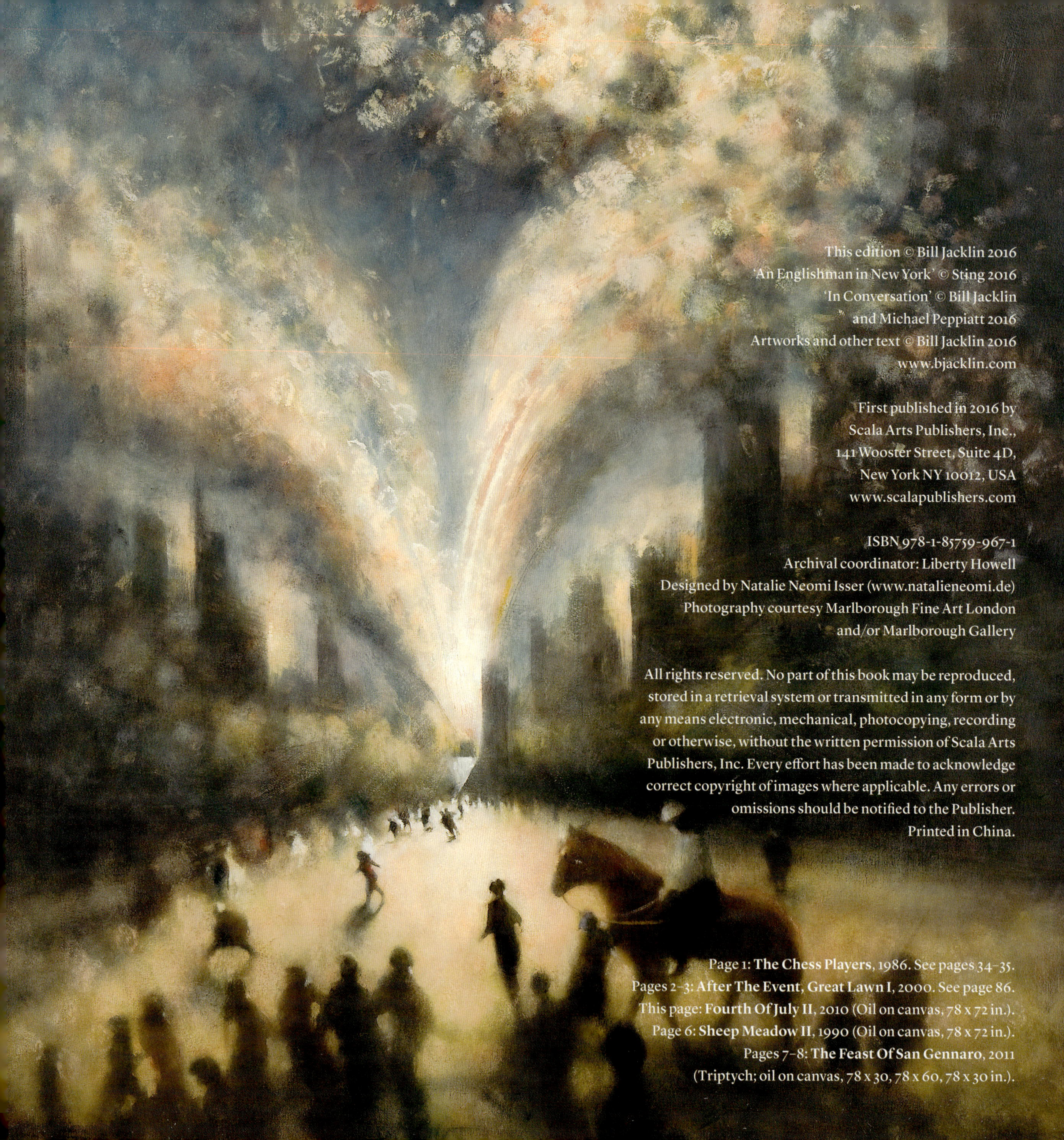

This edition © Bill Jacklin 2016
'An Englishman in New York' © Sting 2016
'In Conversation' © Bill Jacklin
and Michael Peppiatt 2016
Artworks and other text © Bill Jacklin 2016
www.bjacklin.com

First published in 2016 by
Scala Arts Publishers, Inc.,
141 Wooster Street, Suite 4D,
New York NY 10012, USA
www.scalapublishers.com

ISBN 978-1-85759-967-1
Archival coordinator: Liberty Howell
Designed by Natalie Neomi Isser (www.natalieneomi.de)
Photography courtesy Marlborough Fine Art London
and/or Marlborough Gallery

Page 1: **The Chess Players**, 1986. See pages 34–35.
Pages 2–3: **After The Event, Great Lawn I**, 2000. See page 86.
This page: **Fourth Of July II**, 2010 (Oil on canvas, 78 x 72 in.).
Page 6: **Sheep Meadow II**, 1990 (Oil on canvas, 78 x 72 in.).
Pages 7–8: **The Feast Of San Gennaro**, 2011
(Triptych; oil on canvas, 78 x 30, 78 x 60, 78 x 30 in.).

Contents

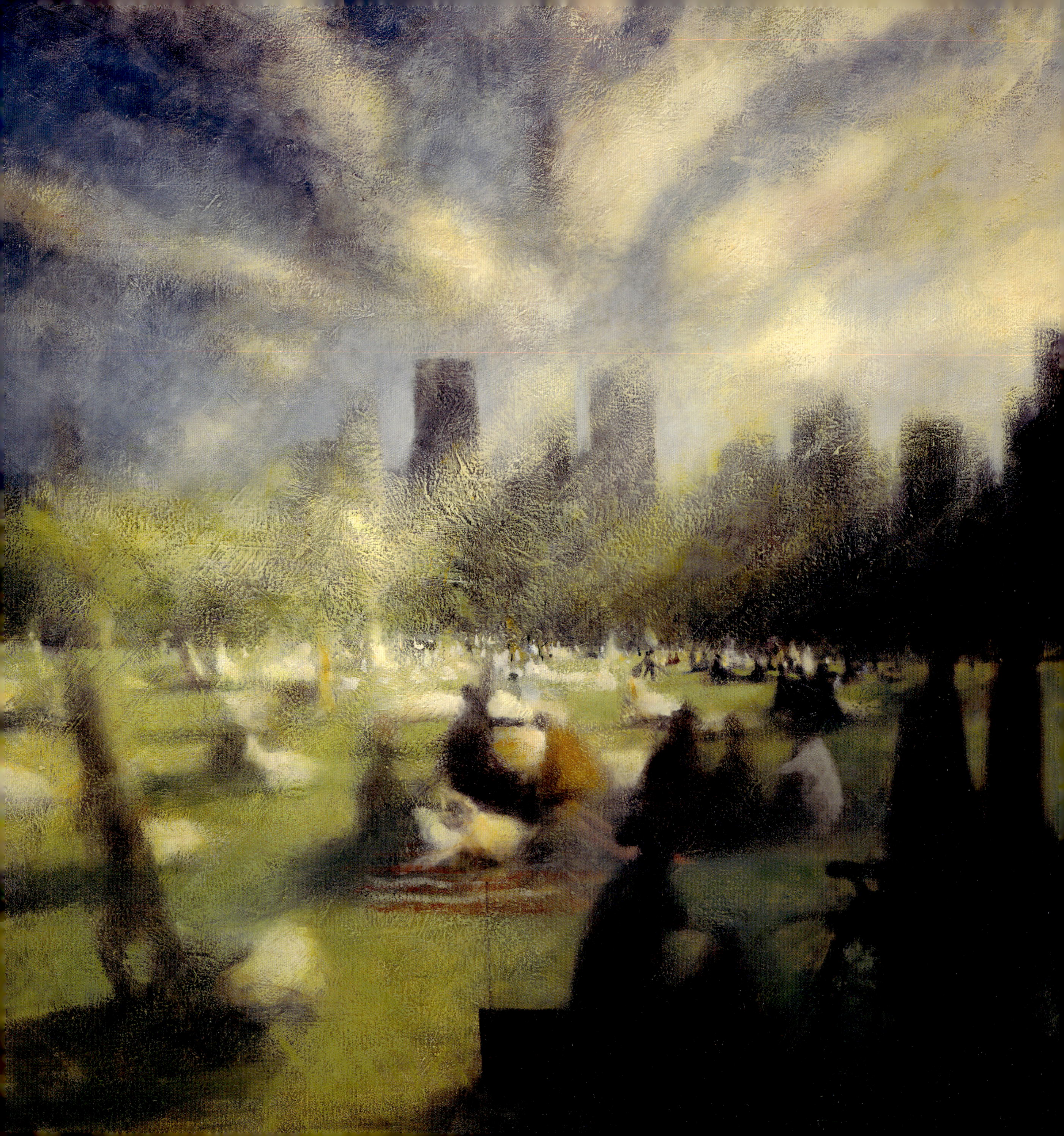

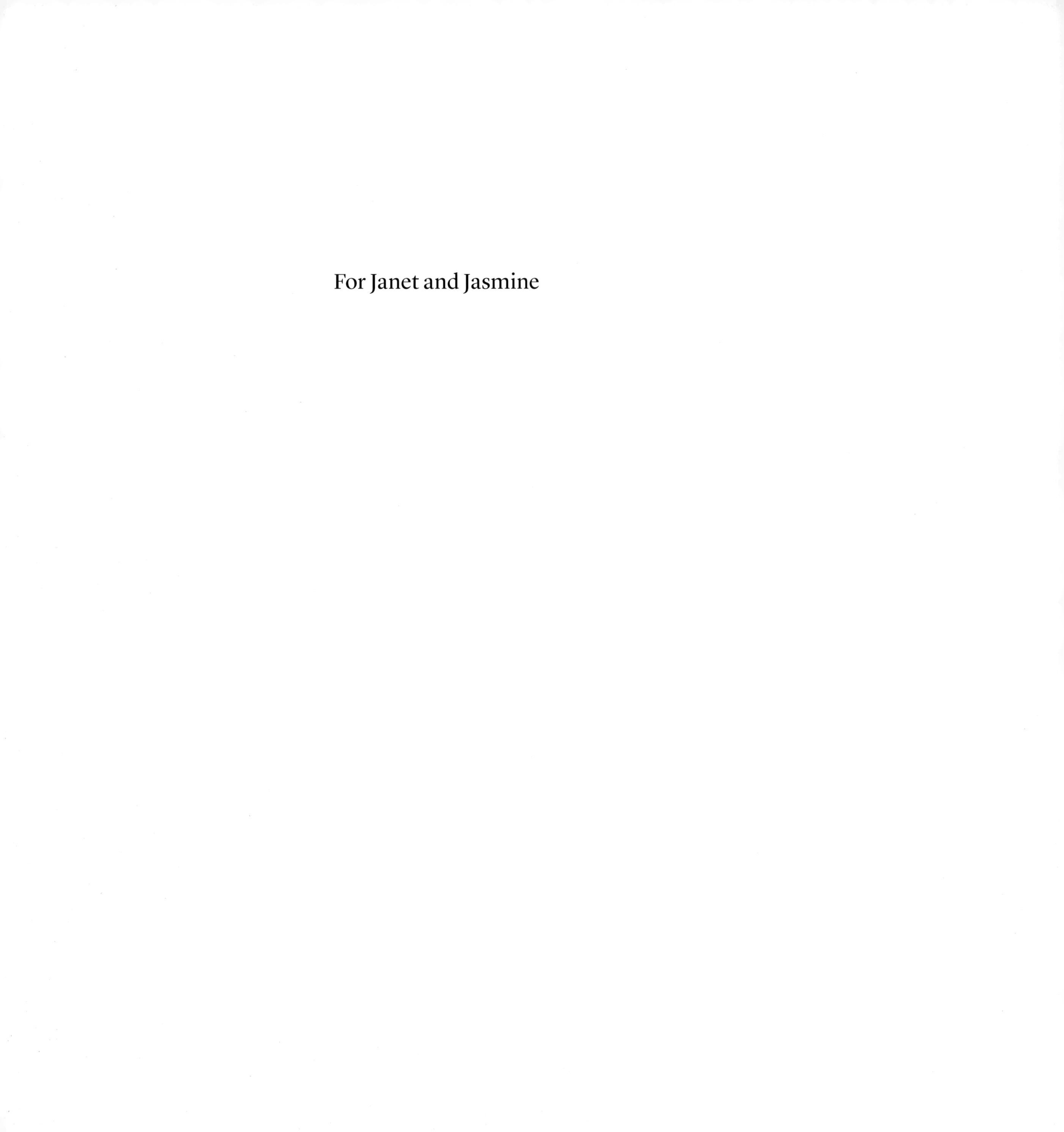

For Janet and Jasmine

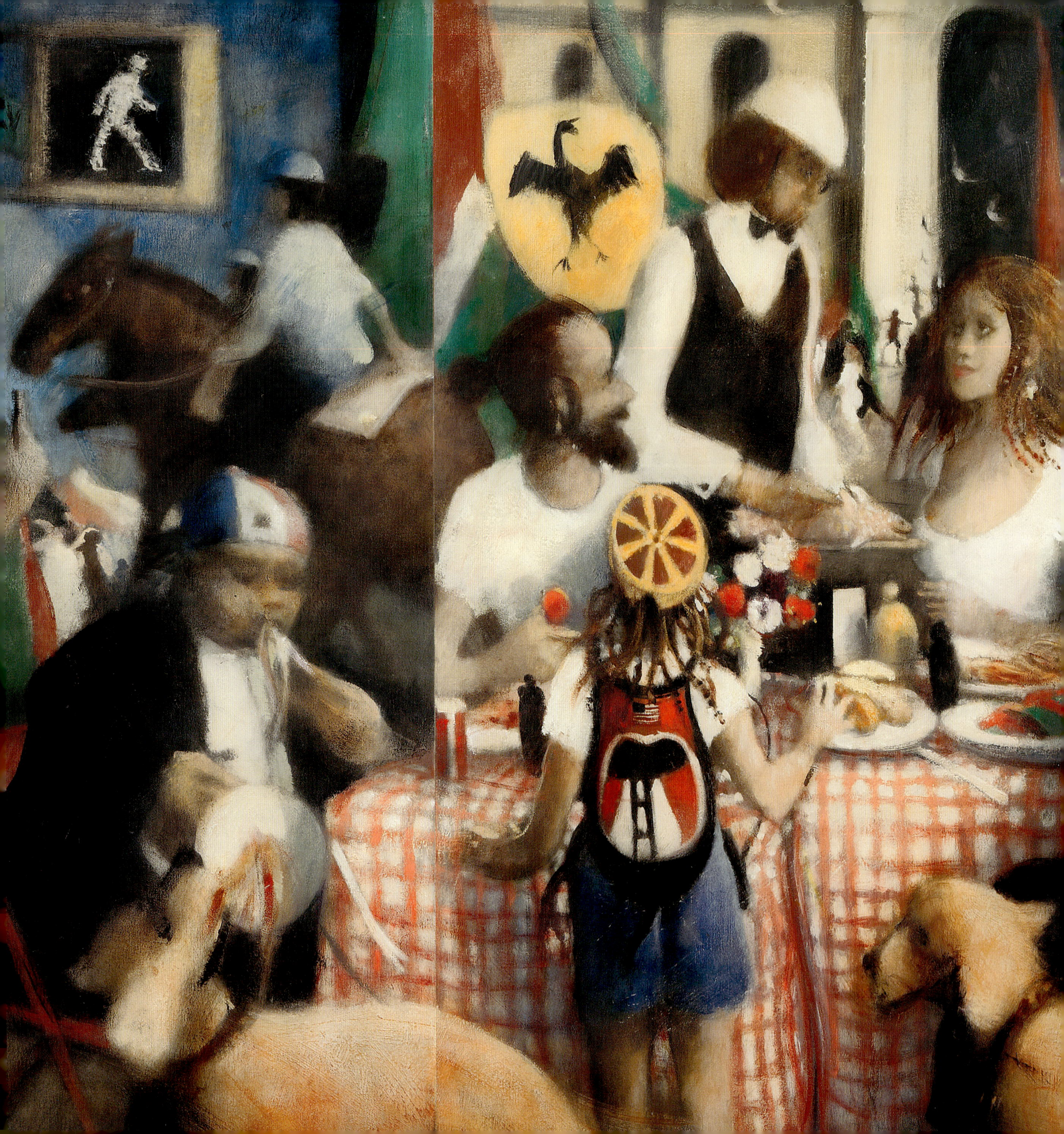

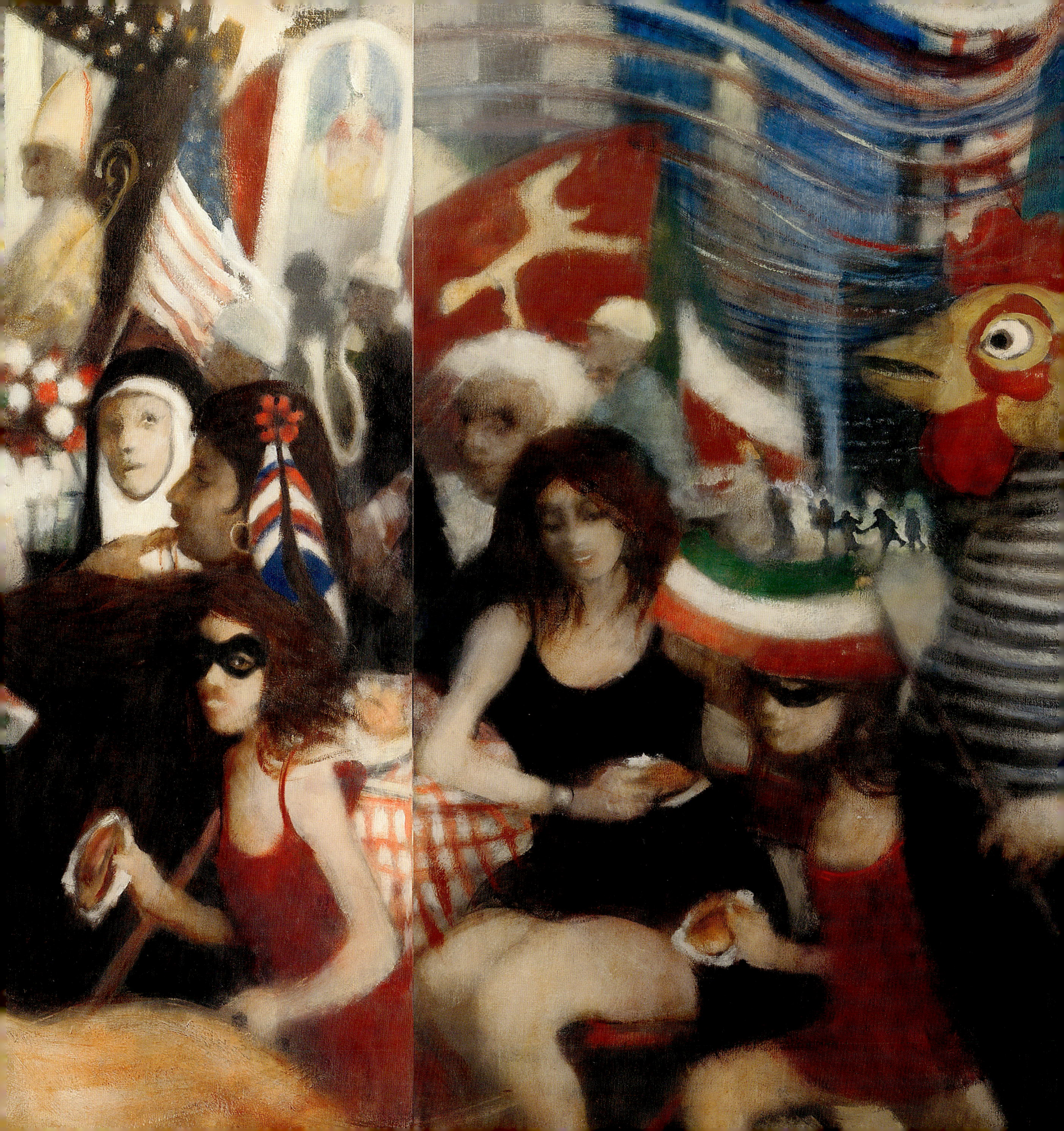

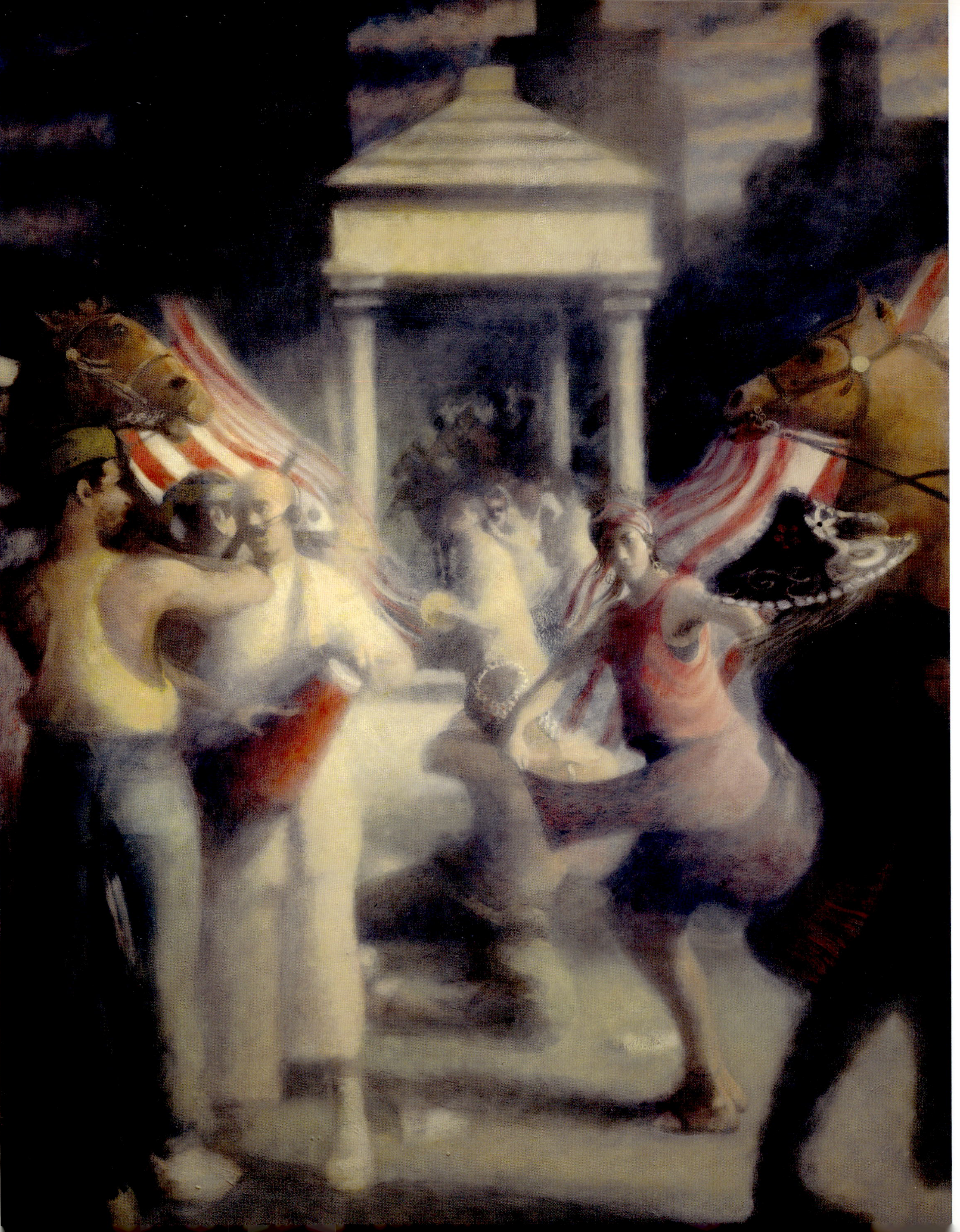

An Englishman in New York
by Sting

I'm not sure how many Englishmen and women live and work in New York City, although I do know that we are legion and yet, despite our numbers, largely invisible as a distinct group. In public life we tend to be discreet for the most part, and preferably singular in our habits and customs. We would never, for example, be caught revelling in some noisy annual parade down Fifth Avenue proclaiming our patriotic allegiance to Albion or what's left of our constitutional monarchy; and thankfully there is no official day given over to our patron saint (it's St George, by the way) nor any extravagant waving of Union Jacks or the drunken rendering of dubious loyalist anthems into the early hours to upset our former colonial subjects and currently generous hosts. While centuries have passed since the American War of Independence, we believe that any vulgar trumpeting of our continued presence here would neither be welcomed nor applauded.

And yet we can quietly salvage some gratification in the fact that we live in what is still New England, and the names of the boroughs of the metropolitan area sound comfortably familiar to us, and when we raise our eyes above the downtown traffic in Greenwich Village, we see what is clearly still a Georgian English enclave of fine proportion and grace. We have history here. We are part of the city's fabric, a muted tone woven unobtrusively into its warp and woof.

Bill Jacklin, an Englishman in New York for most of his working life, combines in his art an intimate knowledge of the city's visual drama with the detached eye of the outsider.

I'm reminded of Bill's epic canvas of the Tompkins Square riot. (See pages 62–63. Disclosure: I own this painting.) The police are drawn up behind an impenetrable wall of shields like a Roman cohort about to charge into battle. One of the officers mounted on a horse breaks through the ranks towards an arbitrary and motley collection of hippies and the homeless. An unequal and violent struggle is about to take place, a moment frozen in the stillness before defiance gives way to terror and panic. I have spent many hours perusing this painting: its epic theme, its fascinating figurative details, its slabs of abstraction layered into a compelling and dramatic narrative, and there to the left of the action, easy to miss under a gaily striped awning, is a tiny portrait of the artist himself, the observer, the discreet foreign correspondent in a war zone, almost hidden behind dark glasses. Bill has painted himself into the drama. It is a subtle cameo worthy of Hitchcock (another discreet Englishman).

The Dance, Tompkins Square
1990
Oil on canvas
243.8×182.9 cm.
96×72 in.

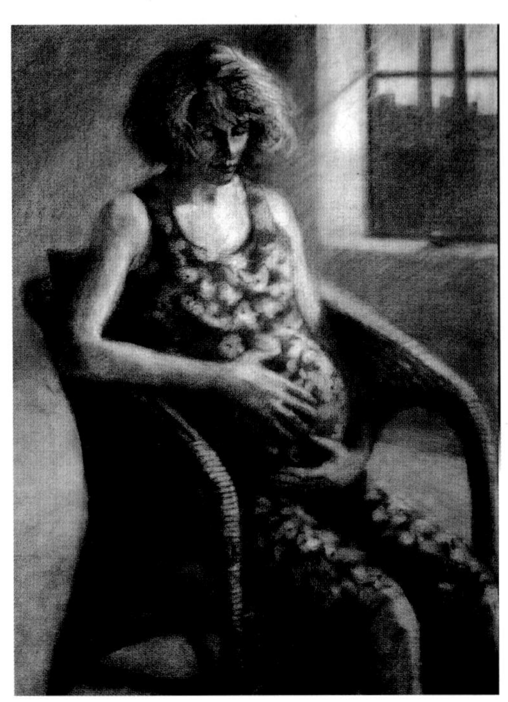

**Mother and Child
(Trudie Styler)**
Charcoal on paper
105.4×75.6 cm.
41.5×29.75 in.

(opposite)
**Sun, Sleet And Snow
Over 5th Avenue**
1997
Oil on canvas
198.1×152.4 cm.
78×60 in.

It was the great Dr Johnson who observed that, "When two Englishmen meet their first talk is of the weather." It should be no surprise then that the vagaries and variety of our island weather should have impressed itself upon the sensibilities of our iconic artists. Turner and Constable spring to mind, but Mr Jacklin too is a great observer and renderer of the air in all of its moods and vapours. Another of his paintings which I own, indeed one of my favourites, is of a rainstorm on Fifth Avenue. St Patrick's Cathedral glowers murkily in the background, shoppers and shadows hurrying across the street under umbrellas, a Stars and Stripes bravely fluttering in the wind, and a torrential rain falling from a lowering sky. This is a painting by a man whose natural habitat has inured him to foul weather, the Turneresque drama of the brush strokes creating a palpable atmosphere, both violent and numinous.

I believe that there is a subtle spirit of melancholy that pervades English letters, English music and also English art. It may partially be a function of our weather, as mentioned, or it may be our long history, our mystical island sensibility. Melancholy is hard to define but it lies somewhere on the emotional spectrum between sadness and longing. I detect this English characteristic in Bill's work. Even his most vibrant subjects are imbued with a contemplative stillness. I have a drawing of Bill's, a portrait of my wife Trudie, heavily pregnant with our fourth child. There is quiet grace in the portrait, but also a sense of the burden of pregnancy. Behind her in the window are a pair of smokestacks pouring filth and pollution into the sky, reminiscent of William Blake's "dark Satanic mills", a silent threat to the new life-in-waiting, a compelling and melancholic vision, a vision of the new world stripped of its optimism and its innocence by the eyes of an older world of experience.

Bill Jacklin's paintings of New York reveal his singular vision, with an émigré's unique point of view unaffected by fashionable mores or styles, navigating an exile's quixotic course through largely uncharted seas, an Englishman in New York – and to paraphrase the lyrics of the song:

"Always himself, no matter what they say!"

January 2015

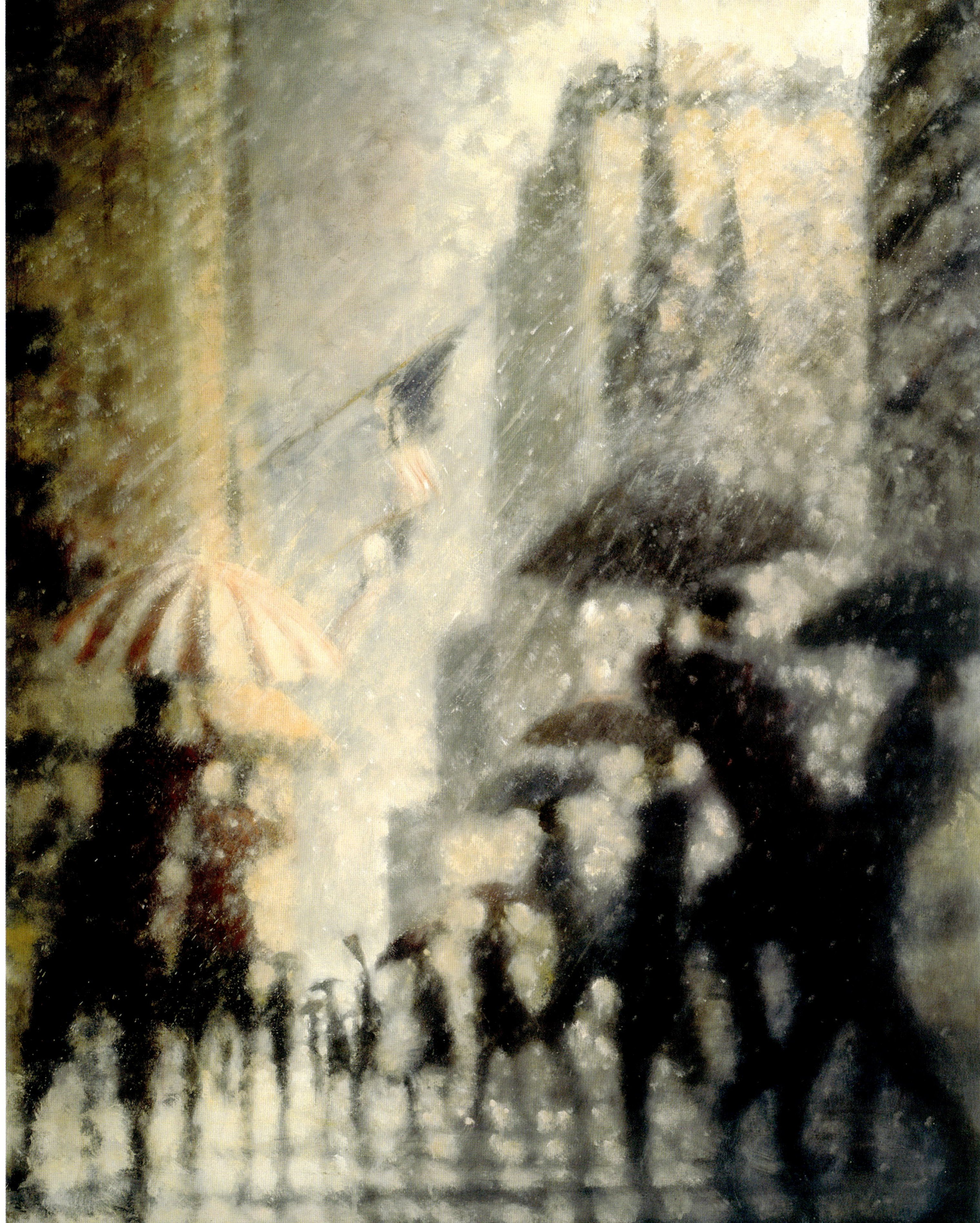

In Conversation: Bill Jacklin and Michael Peppiatt
New York / London 2011–12

MP   Bill Jacklin and I have talked so often over the past thirty years, usually during long congenial evenings in London or New York, that we were both convinced we had already done an interview together. When we realised that we'd never recorded any of our conversations, we decided to try to get something on tape. In the end we snatched a moment to meet for drinks while I was in New York in November 2011. The interview could not have got off to a worse start. It was raining hard and I arrived late, having lost my briefcase and having retraced my sodden steps in a vain effort to recover it. Jacklin listened to my tale of woe with polite equanimity, then told me of the number of wallets, credit cards and mobile phones he had managed to lose at critical moments in recent months. He had treated his last mobile phone with infinite care, he added, checking for it at night on his bedside table – only to wake up to find he had carefully settled it into a glass of water. Jacklin's stories, like his paintings, teeter regularly on the edge of chaos when they don't actually plunge headlong into it. Suddenly, in this vista of accidents waiting to happen, the briefcase incident receded. I began to relax and, without any plan or questions in mind, I turned the voice recorder on.

MP   **You told me once that there's always an incident behind what you paint.**

BJ   There's always something that triggers a painting off, although the way I paint it comes afterwards. There has to be a force or something there in the beginning.

MP   **An experience of some sort.**

BJ   An experience that excites me. So to go back, as I was telling you, I was sitting in a bar with a friend in 1985, about a week after I'd arrived in New York. And there was a crash and a bang and it was obvious that someone had shot somebody outside the restaurant that I was sitting in. I was sitting at the bar and a bullet came across and ricocheted and hit down at the end of the bar and there was a silence and then I heard a voice say, "Oh my God, he's coming in." Whoever it was then hit the deck, so there was another silence and then everyone appeared to hit the deck. And what I got, as I started to hit the deck, was the impression that the wine bottles and the glasses moved this way and everything was on diagonals. So I fell to the floor from my stool at the bar. And then there was another silence, and suddenly everyone sort of collectively decided they better get the hell out of there. So everyone started running out towards the kitchens at the back. And it was mayhem in so far as there was one moment of silence and the next moment it was chaos. The result was that I don't think the man ever did actually come in. But there was someone who was shot in the eye and he was taken to hospital and the police came and we were all kind of huddled in the kitchen, then everyone started to leave, and being the only Englishman there, I was the only one actually saying, 'Well, can I pay my bill?' Then I realised that this was a different place and that the cashier was looking at me like I was just crazy and I'd just said the craziest thing. And that was my first impression of Manhattan.

MP　**And is the memory of the various things that have happened to you in New York still coming through in the paintings you're doing now? Are they recollections or reflections of events?**

BJ　Well, yes, I think everything is a reflection of itself. I think it's all about how you receive things. Maybe we want to recapture the dramas that we've had. You know, I was thinking as I was walking over to talk to you this evening that I was born in 1943 when the Doodlebugs were dropping on London, and I was trying to work out what it is that gives you the sense of actually being alive, and I think certainly in those early years I had a heightened sense of being alive through those bombs, that were like an external force. I think you're a product of your time, and I was a war baby. As a result, certainly in artistic terms, I was brought up with a whole kind of existential group of people that had a particular attitude to how they perceived the world. And I guess I became part of that. But I was sufficiently younger not to be philosophically in tune with a pessimistic way of

15

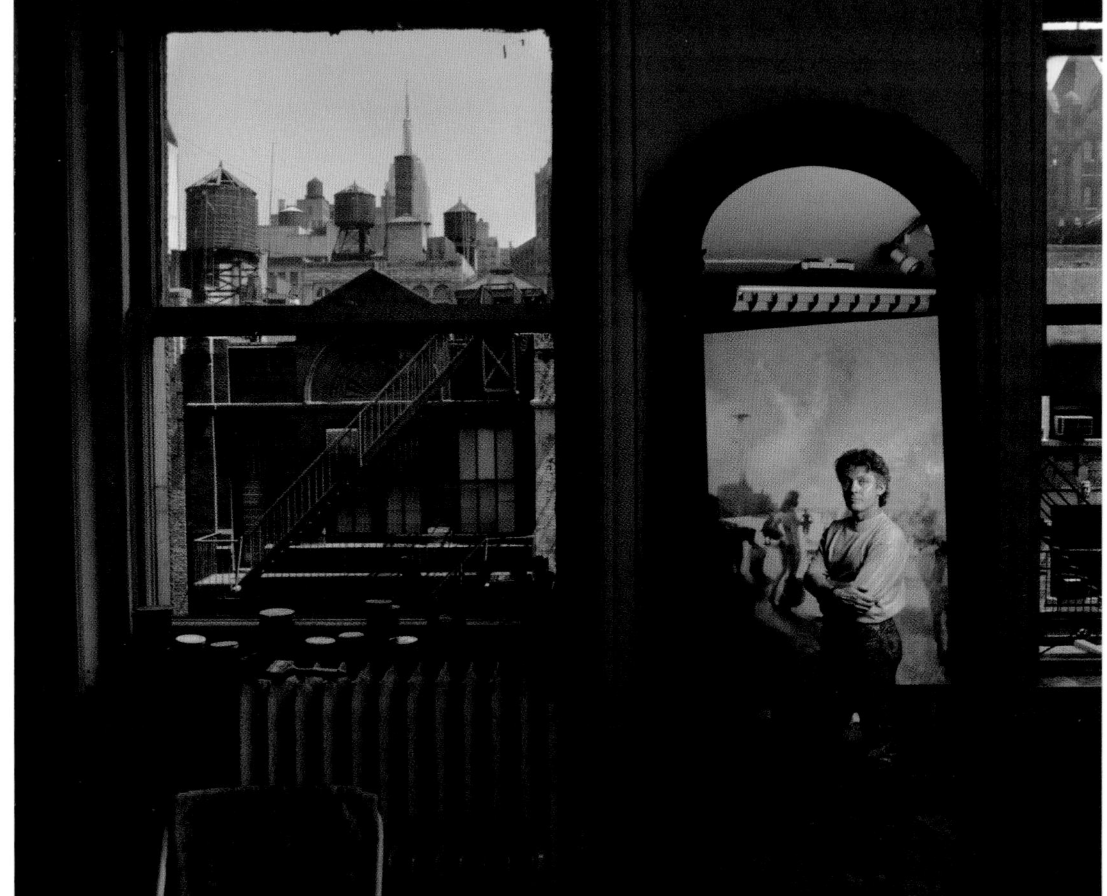

Bill Jacklin
studio view
Photograph by
Abe Frajndlich

viewing the world. I basically viewed the world as post-war, and I'm still caught up by the idea of drama and the drama of life.

MP   **That we can be extinguished from one second to another?**

BJ   Well, the idea that you go very quickly from a structure to a sort of chaotic situation. My early artistic career had a kind of parallel of non-figurative equivalence, of drawing structural things that were systematic and held in abeyance what I perceived to be chaos, a chaotic situation. I thought that if you put together all these ramifications you could hold chaos.

MP   **But are the more recent paintings about chaos, because some of them are apparently celebratory scenes, with people enjoying themselves at the beach or in restaurants?**

BJ   That's what I aspire to but there's always a kind of dark shadow moving over and the sense of people wanting to escape. I don't have any a priori principles or beliefs. I don't have a position. I have a kind of anxiety, if you like. But I have an aspiration beyond that anxiety.

MP   **Which is what?**

BJ   Well, it comes from being a post-war baby. I mean, like I was part of that Sixties

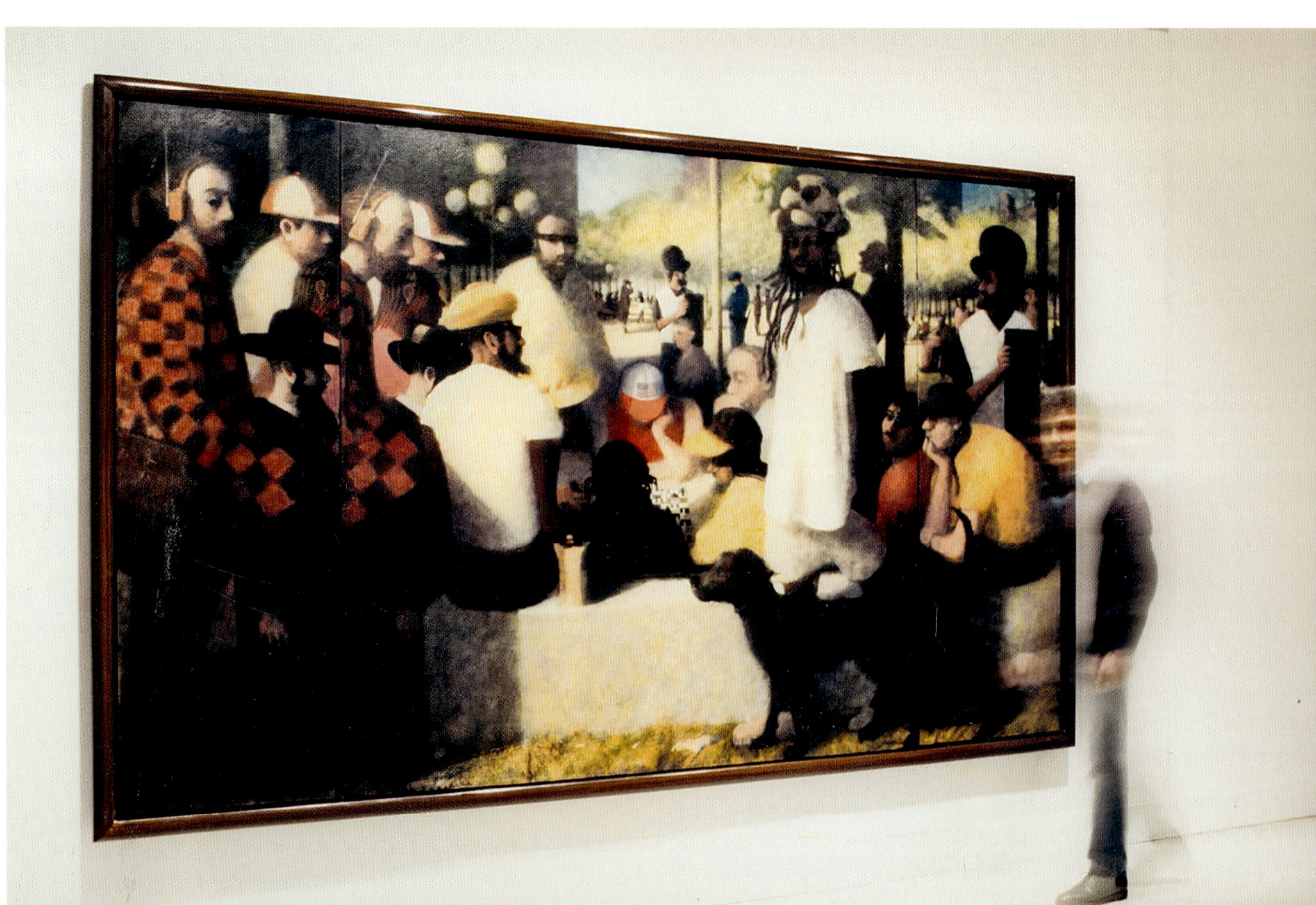

Bill Jacklin with
"The Chess Players"
Photograph by
Abe Frajndlich

moment in the way you rejected a certain position about how everything was dire, everything was black and the black cloud hovered over everybody and every day you could wake up and have…

MP   **So are you saying your paintings are either about a fragile stability, a fragile order, or about chaos to a large extent? Is it order on the edge of chaos, or is chaos always lurking under the surface?**

BJ   Well, yes, I think chaos always is lurking, I think we're all aware of that. And we're well aware of what's going on in the world right now. I've always been interested in what's going on around me and for quite a while now I've felt much more like a reporter of my time than someone who's involved in artistic pursuits. I'm not part of an artistic culture. I'm way beyond that, I'm too old for it. Like at the moment I've been down at Zuccotti Park to paint, I go down there to paint like a reporter.

MP   **To look at the people in protest against Wall Street…**

BJ   And I want to be involved in what's going on right now. I don't have a philosophy about it. I just have an instinctive position.

MP   **Did you know you were going to start painting those kinds of scenes, or did you just go and look and then suddenly you thought, this is something I'd like to get down on canvas?**

BJ   I think it's to affirm a sense of life. As I said, I don't have a particular ideological position but I do believe in being at the centre of energy. I mean, my paintings are above all about energy. I'm a closet abstractionist and I've always been that way. I find ways of swirling things out of focus, so they become something else. Maybe in another lifetime I'd have made a movie. I don't have an adherence to style. I don't have a stylistic position within the art world because that for me is a kind of death sentence.

MP   **But you actually came out of abstraction?**

BJ   I came in and out of abstraction. My early work was very much a reflection of what I was looking at. After that as I got more involved in the art world and had some degree of success, I got more involved in systems of painting which ultimately I determined were less interesting.

MP   **You mean in the 1970s, when the art world was very given to theory?**

BJ   Yes, and I thought that was fine in its way but that it was better for me to kind of walk away from it.

MP   **And come back to life?**

BJ   Come back to waking up every morning and having a sense of energy, a kind of "How do I see the world?" I think in the end every artist is based on that very simple principle. You wake up in the morning and you say, how do I see the world, how do

I feel, and what do I want to say? And even if it's in a contradiction of what you did yesterday, there's a life to it. And that seems to me to be the most wonderful thing to be able to do.

MP   **But this isn't a political consciousness, is it? It's a consciousness of what you see around you, what strikes you and what you want to try and record.**

BJ   It's an affirmation of life. You know, for quite a few years I taught. Most artists didn't have any money in those days and they taught in order to kind of sustain what they did, and you saw young students going into the library to try and find a language that would allow them to feel that they were on the road to being an artist. And they were often starting with manifestation. They weren't starting with impressions.

MP   **By manifestation you mean?**

BJ   What to do about it, what to paint. And in my view it always was, I always felt, what am I receiving as an artist? What food am I getting, what am I getting from this street light that I'm looking at, what am I getting from the people I'm talking to? Impressions that you can say something about. You start from stage one, you don't start from stage two. You never say, "How am I talking?" You say, "And what am I talking about...?"

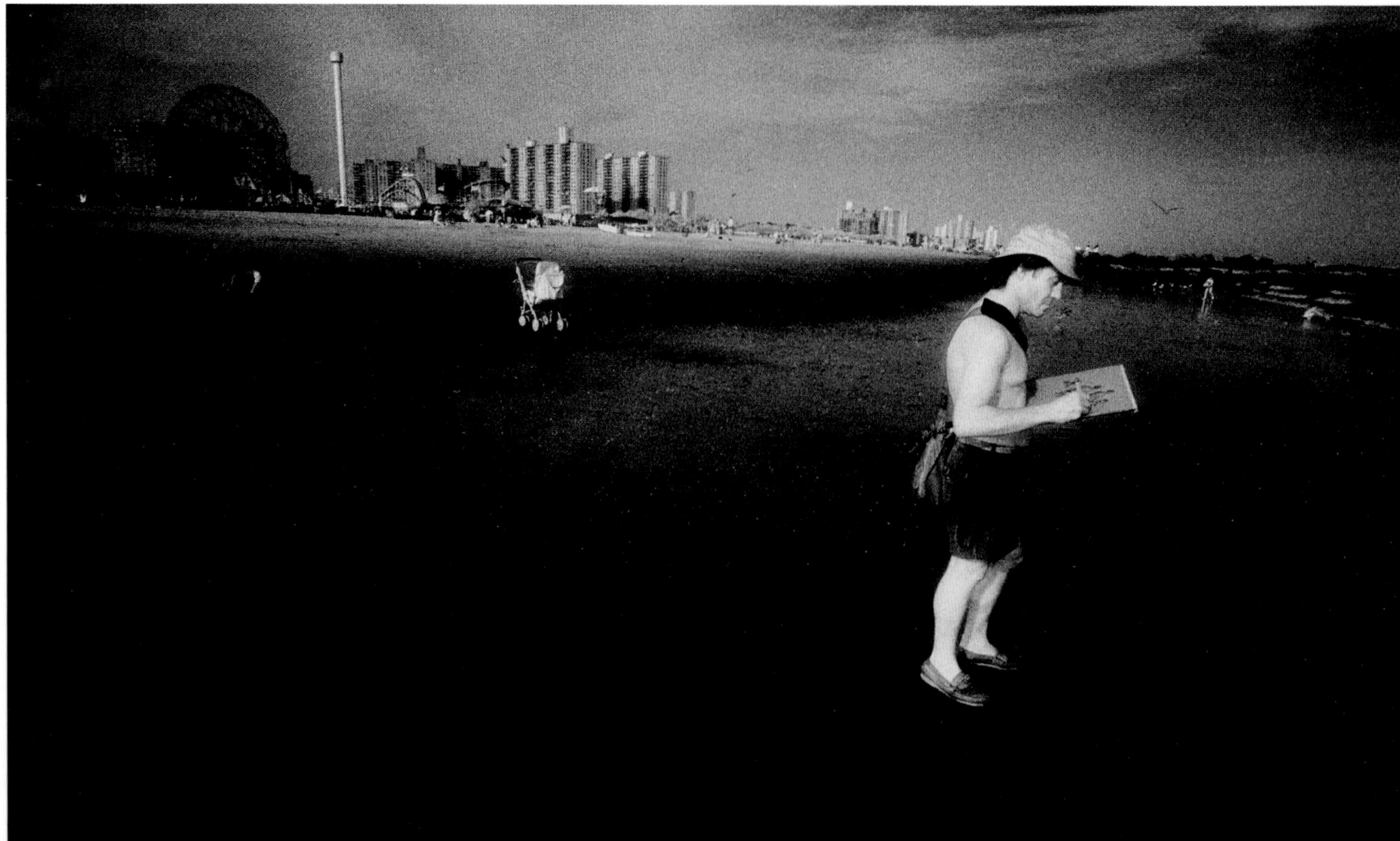

Coney Island
Photograph by
Abe Frajndlich

MP   **The subject.**

BJ   The subject, and that seems to be even more important now because as the art world becomes more and more about money and it becomes stultified and becomes all about business, the real question is how do you cut through that and say: "What am I looking at, how am I receiving this?" And that's not just artistic, that's life.

MP   **From these impressions that you receive, whether it's the incident in the bar, where a bullet comes whistling through, or a feast that you've seen and appreciated in a restaurant in Little Italy – do you think very closely how am I going to relay this on the canvas? Do you start doing drawings or compositions? Do you say, oh I should get that fat waiter in or the dog snapping around at the end of the table? Or do you just go in and reinvent as you go along?**

BJ   Well, I think it's about a sense of place. I think a lot of artists, a lot of painters, speak about space and the relationship that you have with it. And I think a lot of the best work is all about that relationship. It's not about the image. The image is important, but it's the relationship you have with something, it's the relationship you have with anybody, at any moment. Like when I'm speaking to you: I have a sense of being with you and there is that moment of space between us. If you look at a wonderful Rembrandt self-portrait, what you're actually aware of is the space between you and him. That's what the emotional content of your relationship is and that is the relationship, not just the image. So in anything, if I'm really serious, I'm aware of being in a place at a certain time and it becomes a memory for me ultimately, that has a resonance for me. And it's real. It wasn't concocted. And if it was concocted and if I'm critical enough, then I'll say, "That wasn't so good, it was a concoction." But if it was real, I know it.

MP   **Do you have a very clear idea about what you want to paint, or at least an overall impression, before you start a canvas? Or is it very spontaneous?**

BJ   Usually in terms of the process of how I work, because of the life in the particular areas I'm working in, I have a kind of figurative base. I know for example that if I'm working on a group of people in Times Square everything will move and change, often quite dramatically. So much of my work is about movement, you know, that I don't hold to a rigid structure at all.

MP   **But does this come from a drawing to begin with or do you go straight into the canvas?**

BJ   I use whatever I can. I'll work from drawings, and I'll work from a sense of being in a place. For me it's very important that I was there.

MP   **But not from photos?**

BJ Well, I'll take whatever I can. But there was an intense period when I went scouting around on different locations in the city like 42nd Street, which was a lot rougher then, and Sheep Meadow, that amazing green arena in Central Park. A lot of the time I went round with Abe Frajndlich, a photographer friend of mine. I drew, he took photos, and I think we were both influenced by the way the other made images of the exact same thing we were both looking at.

MP **Sure. But you might have taken the photos yourself?**

BJ I might have, or I might not. If I fail in the image that I make it's because I didn't make it my own. And that's all.

MP **And do you know when you've made it your own?**

BJ I serve myself into it, so that it's coloured by my feelings because it's a subjective process that we're involved in here. I don't pretend to think it goes beyond that.

MP **Do you judge one of your paintings according to how successful you were in imparting your own feelings to it?**

BJ I'm always totally in conflict about that. I'm confident enough to know that I'm engaged in the dialogue. I'm not confident enough to believe that what I saw was real and every day I wake up and feel that there is another opportunity to see the world. At the end of the day, Michael, I just want to say that as I get older I'm hitting a certain point. I want to be able to say to myself that I kind of saw something and I had the presence of mind to record it in a way that has a resonance. So when I paint, if I'm talking in formal terms, I've always said to myself, well the painting is a residue of what happened. I don't just put it down, because it seems to me everything is always shifting and changing and moving, and if I try consciously to find a way for painting something, it won't work. I don't know in advance how a picture is going to come out. That's why I still believe in painting. I still believe it has a relevance because the very simple old-fashioned process of hand to canvas allows an immediacy, you know, it's not technically rigid.

MP **It's straight down the nerve ends.**

BJ There is still a kind of touch, a feel, by which I can say something. I think the less interesting work for me is where someone's identity is attached totally to their stylistic content.

MP **Yes, because it becomes empty.**

BJ I think the most interesting artists are the people who have a handwriting and their stylistic content maybe can shift and change accordingly. Once it goes into that place, and every artist knows that, where you try to hold on to something that's already been done or seen in some way, it always has its downside. You have to cut through that. So it's not easy.

MP **So how would you describe your average day in the studio?**

BJ You know, Michael, I basically spend my time sitting alone in a room, viewing the world through the reflections on a doorknob – or on water or whatever – reflections of something I've seen or experienced, but at one remove.

MP **You want the distance or a different angle on a moment that you've lived through?**

BJ I think of the artist as a voyeur, the person who's watching. There's the observer and the observed, right? You're watching the world go by, and you're watching your own life go by. Time is ticking.

MP **So you're snatching a moment?**

BJ You're waking up to the moment. Because I think a lot of the time you go through your life when you're not aware of the moment. You're caught up in things and not very aware. Then this very particular moment comes along, and a very particular feeling – of being removed. Some people might call it loneliness.

MP **Is that what Joyce called an epiphany – an unusual awareness of existence? And is that when you think you've got a picture, an image, when you have this moment of heightened reality?**

BJ The image is another stage. What you do about it is another whole issue. You might or might not make something of that feeling. You know, in New York, you're always out on location, the whole city is a location. I paint about an energy mass, it gets figurized in various ways, if you like, but it's actually about a flowing, pulsating energy. That's what Manhattan is – it shifts and changes, people love it or hate it, but it's always pulsating.

MP **This is what attracted you to New York in the first place, isn't it?**

BJ Yes, I found my subject. It was a conduit for me to experience all those things that excite me. When I first arrived, every street corner I went round I found something. New York, for want of a better word, is my muse. Suddenly all these images were given to me that I could transform. And what really transfoms them for me – I should have mentioned it earlier – is light. Light, or the absence of it, holds everything together. I look at certain scenes, certain situations, and I see either light or darkness and that to a large extent decides how I paint. Light is spirituality and emotion. Light for me is everything.

MP **Yes, that comes across very strongly in your pictures. And it's often as though one doesn't know how long the light will last before darkness descends... To change focus for a moment, who are the artists you look at with most pleasure? I believe Seurat is one.**

BJ   Did I tell you the story of buying a little Seurat when I was quite young? Well, I had a show in the West End and there was a gallery in Davies Street and I went in and I saw a little Seurat drawing. I didn't know it was a Seurat drawing at the time and I didn't have any substantial money, but I had £1200 to spend and there were certain contemporary artists that I could buy, but only a graphic. And I went into this little gallery in Davies Street run by a man called Christian Neffe, and there was an artist called Josef Herman who had bought a little Seurat drawing and I admired it. There were Bonnards there and Vuillards, and I always had an affinity to that kind of attachment to urban life they had towards the end of the last century. I've sometimes felt I was out of my own time in a funny kind of way. Anyway, the drawing had been bought, but about a month later Christian called me and said, that drawing of Seurat is available again if you'd like it. I said I don't have that kind of money, I've only got £1200.

MP   So what did he say?

BJ   Well, he said you can have it for £1200, so I bought it and I've had it ever since. It's always been a kind of little spiritual supplement.

MP   What's the scene?

BJ   It's a man sitting on a little donkey, an art school donkey. It's not one of his big expensive charcoals; it's just a very minimal little pencil drawing. But it was the idea that there was someone viewing urban life in another century that drew me to it.

MP   You are an urban person, you like big cities and you like going around and watching people carry on and...

BJ   Yes, I'm basically a street kid. And I'm an observer, a voyeur, as I said. And the relationship between the observer and the observed is a very interesting one. You know, it's always in flux. I mean why I like Manhattan is because it's contradictory, it's not what it seems, nothing is what it seems. You know there is always a moment where things will happen, that you're taken unawares, you have your wallet stolen or you lose your briefcase and you're always on one foot. What interests me is that sense of waking up in the morning and being alive and feeling that you can go out and see something and from that perspective I really am an old-fashioned artist. I have a sketchbook and I sit in a corner and I draw things and I make notations of things that I've seen. And they are notations and they are dots and splushes and blibs and blobs and they are actually the subjective equivalent of something seen. It's not a record.

MP   It's your notes.

BJ   It's a subjective equivalent.

MP   But to finish, so it would be Seurat, Vuillard, Bonnard and...?

BJ   And then I wrote my thesis as a student at the Royal College of Art on Rauschenberg and Jasper Johns. So if you like you make a sandwich and you make a BLT, it's really what you show, it's like the top of it can be the bacon or the lettuce or whatever, and although a lot of people will only see what's on top, the sandwich is composed of …

MP   **Different layers?**

BJ   That's right. You could say Seurat was a very important influence on my life but so was Rauschenberg and so was Jasper Johns. When I was student I did a philosophy class at the Royal College and Iris Murdoch was my tutor for three years. So I had all that English sandwich compressed into me as well.

MP   **I hadn't thought of you as a sandwich before, but I'll look anew to see what level I'm at.**

BJ   I think we're all a bit of a sandwich really.

MP   **In one of the interviews I did with a painter friend called Miguel Condé, I tried to pin him down about something and, you know, he clearly wasn't going to be pinned down and he wriggled out by saying: 'I'm just a salad of comings and goings.'**

BJ   There you are. I think we all are.

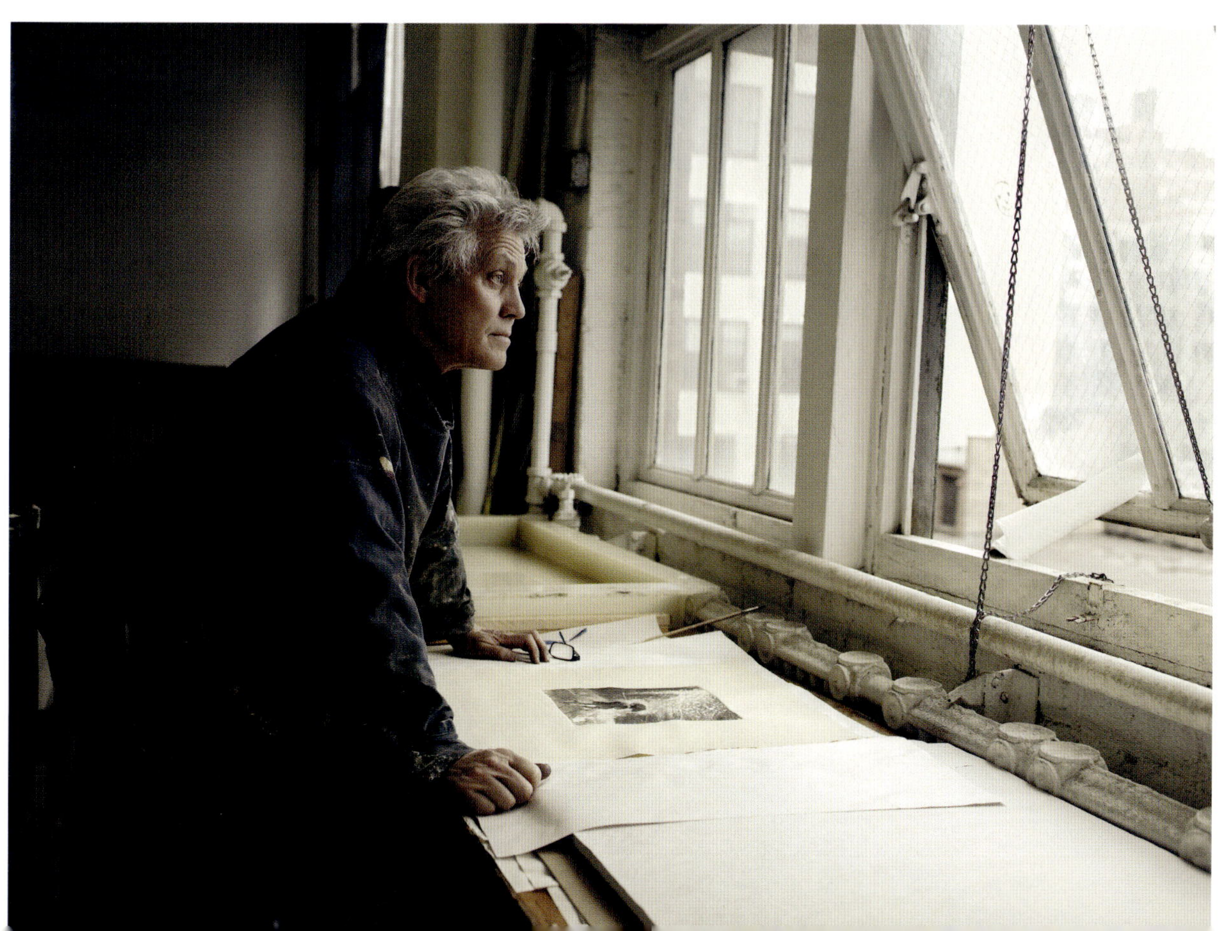

Bill Jacklin in
New York studio
Photograph by
Jason Bell

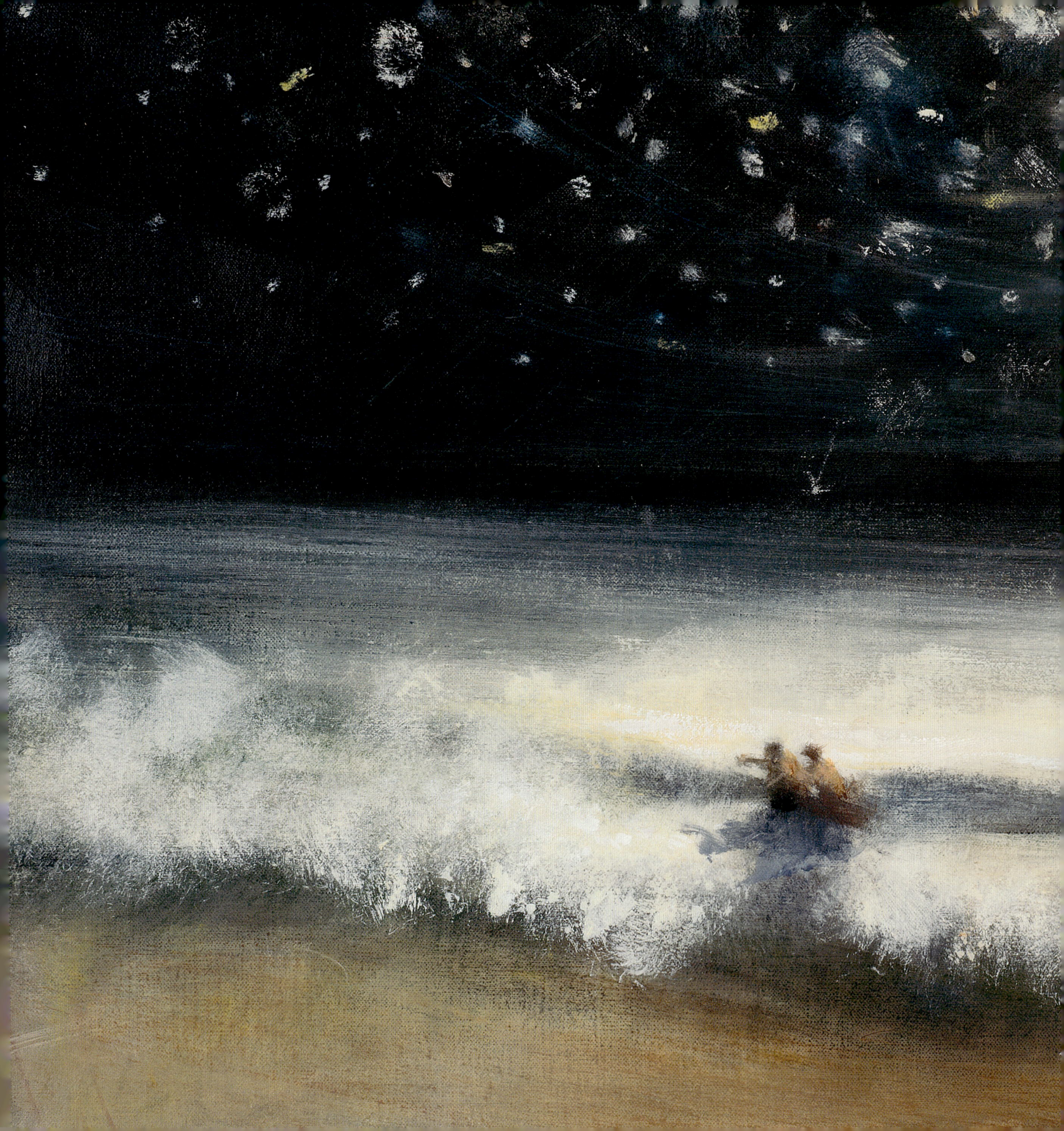

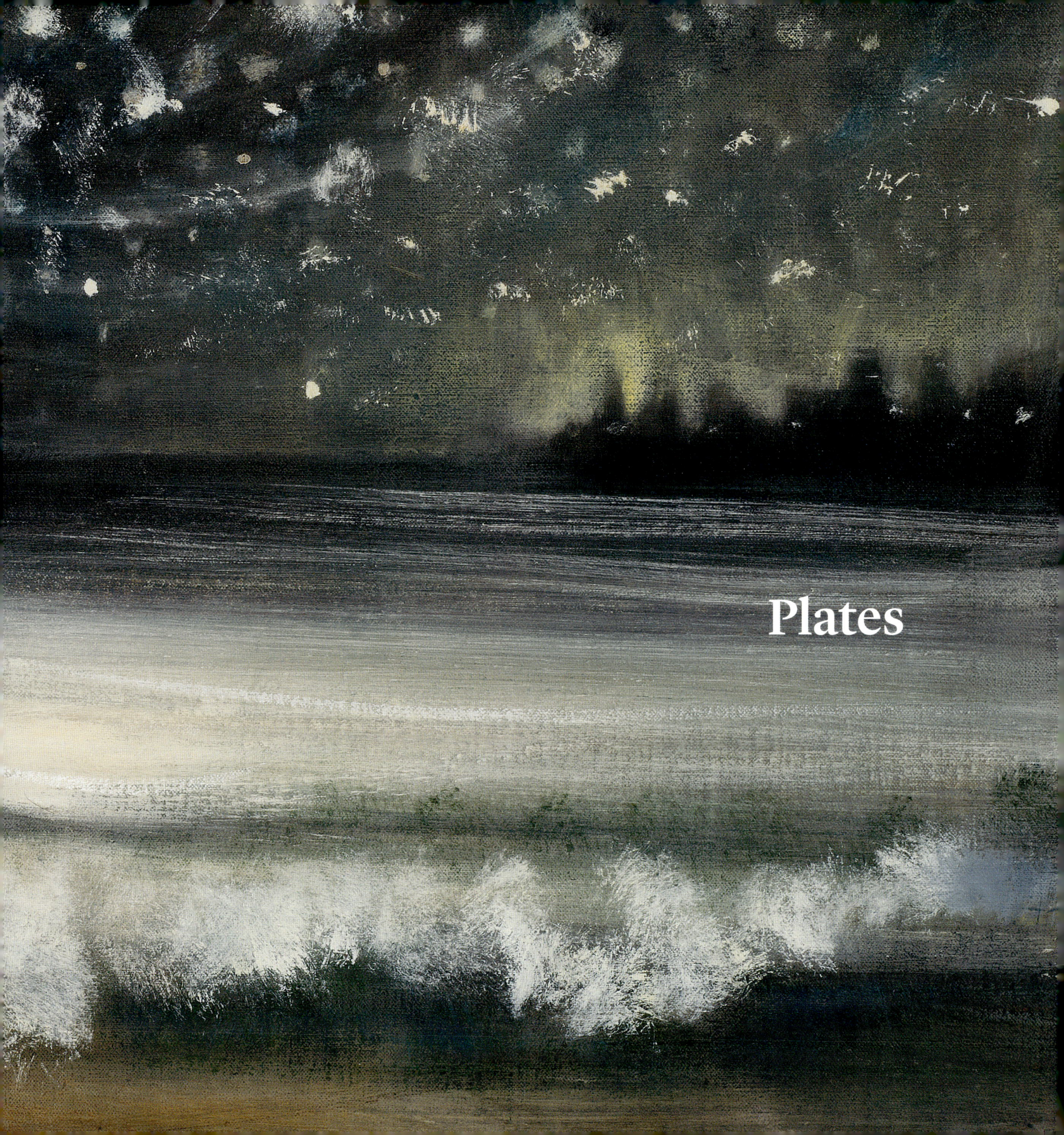
Plates

(pages 24–25)
The Edge Of The City By The Seashore
2013
Oil on canvas
61×76.2 cm.
24×30 in.

The March, Sixth Avenue
1986
Oil on canvas
198.1×152.4 cm.
78×60 in.

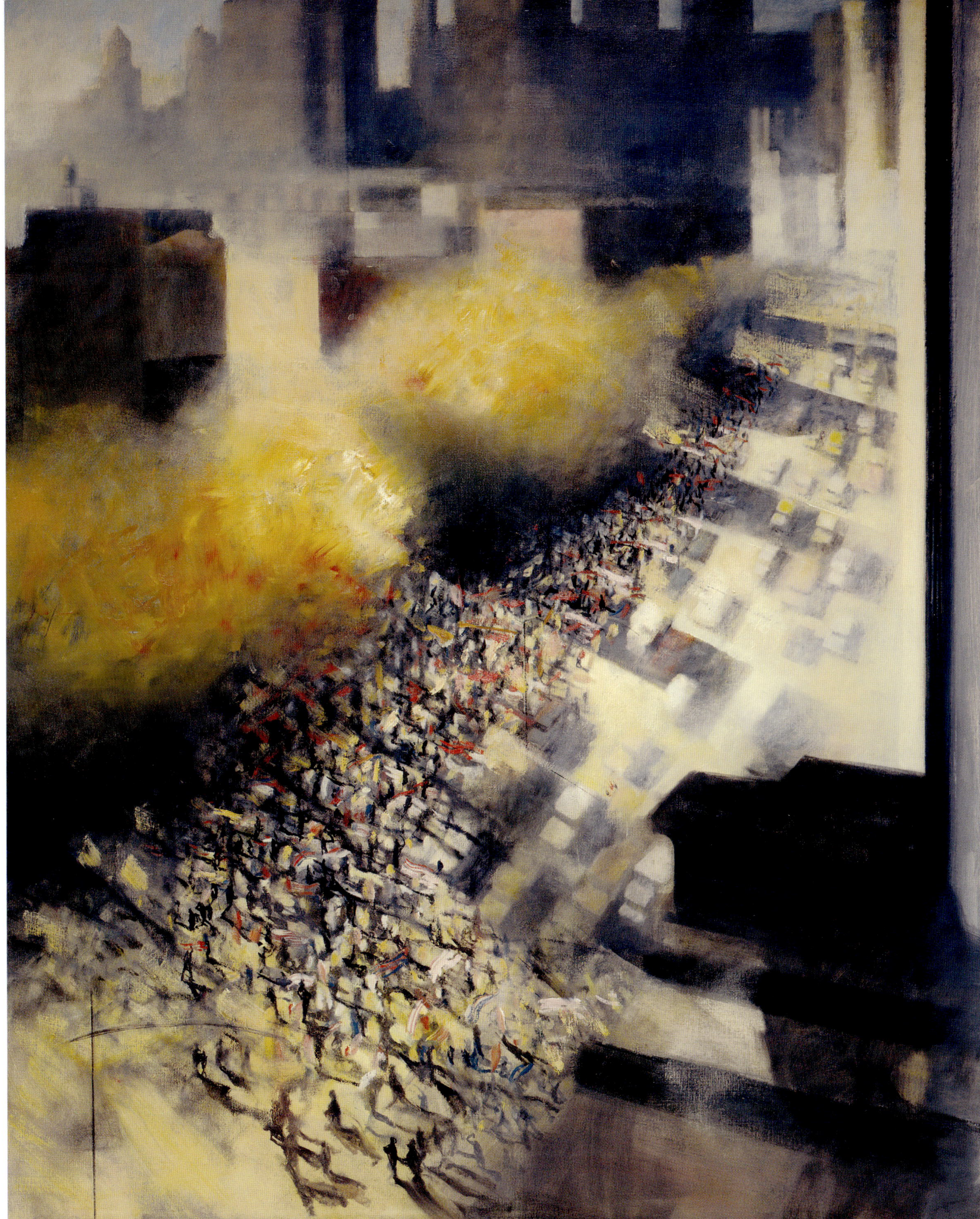

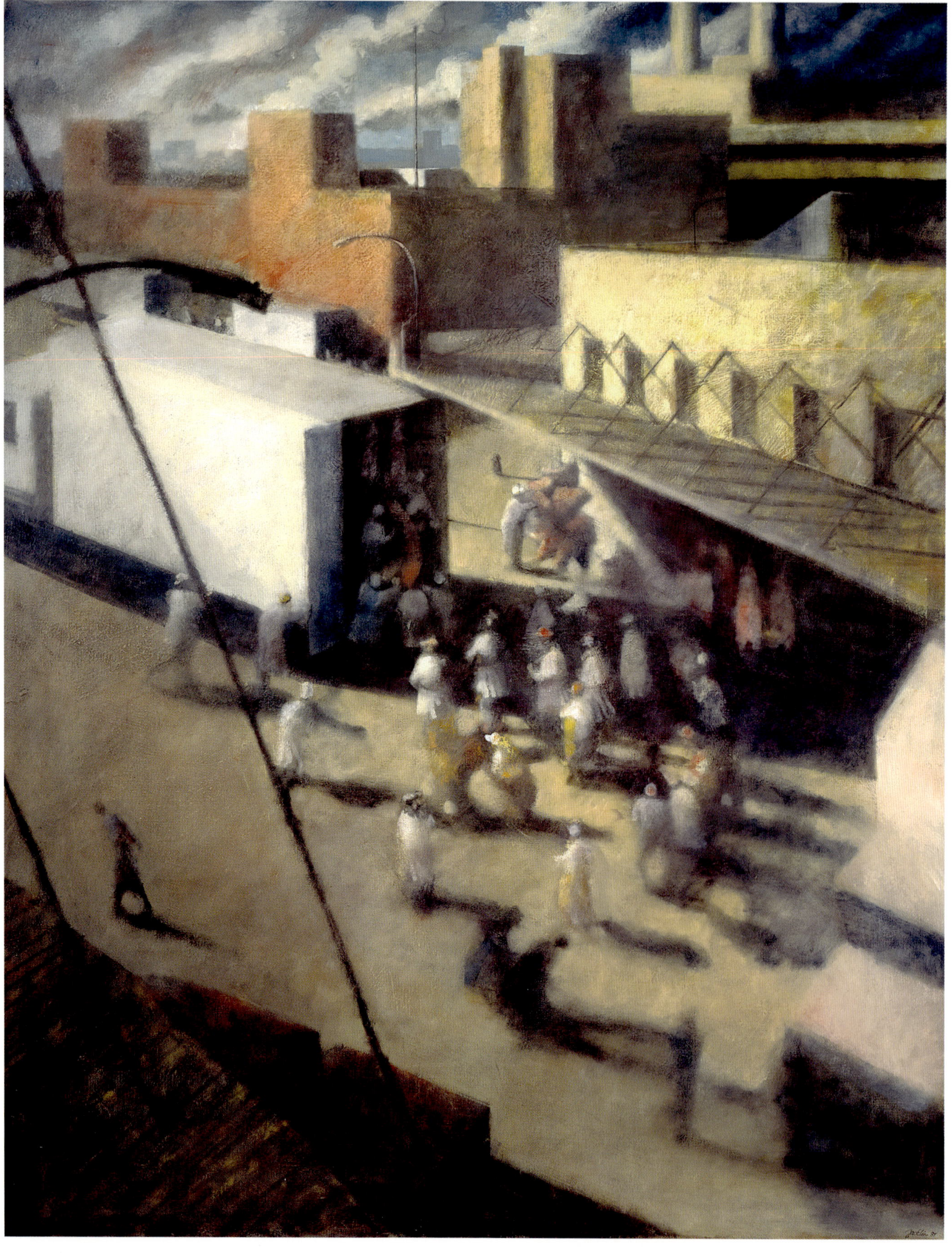

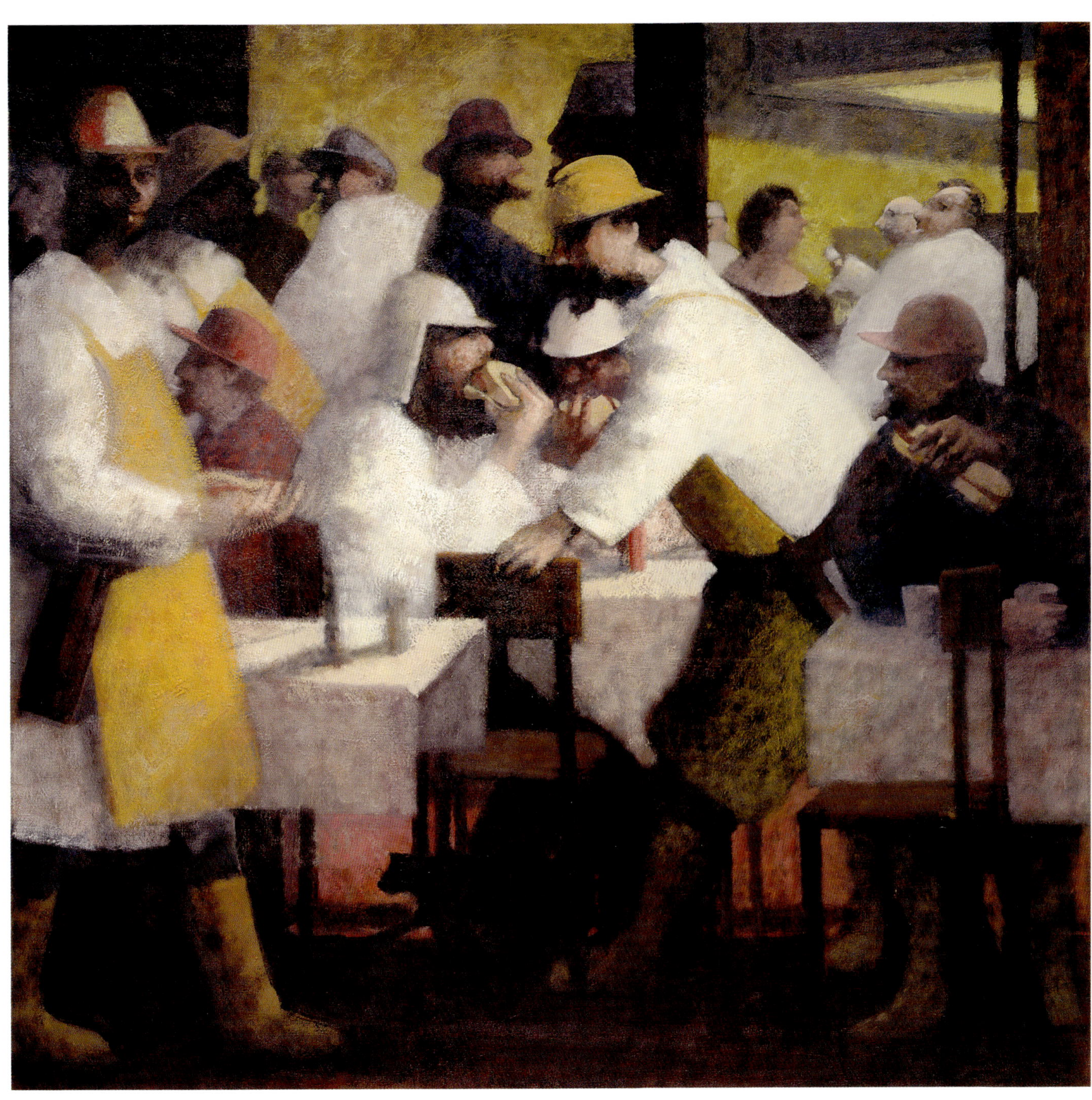

Meatpackers II
1986
Oil on canvas
198.1×152.4 cm.
78×60 in.

The Sandwich Eaters
1986
Oil on canvas
198.1×198.1 cm.
78×78 in.

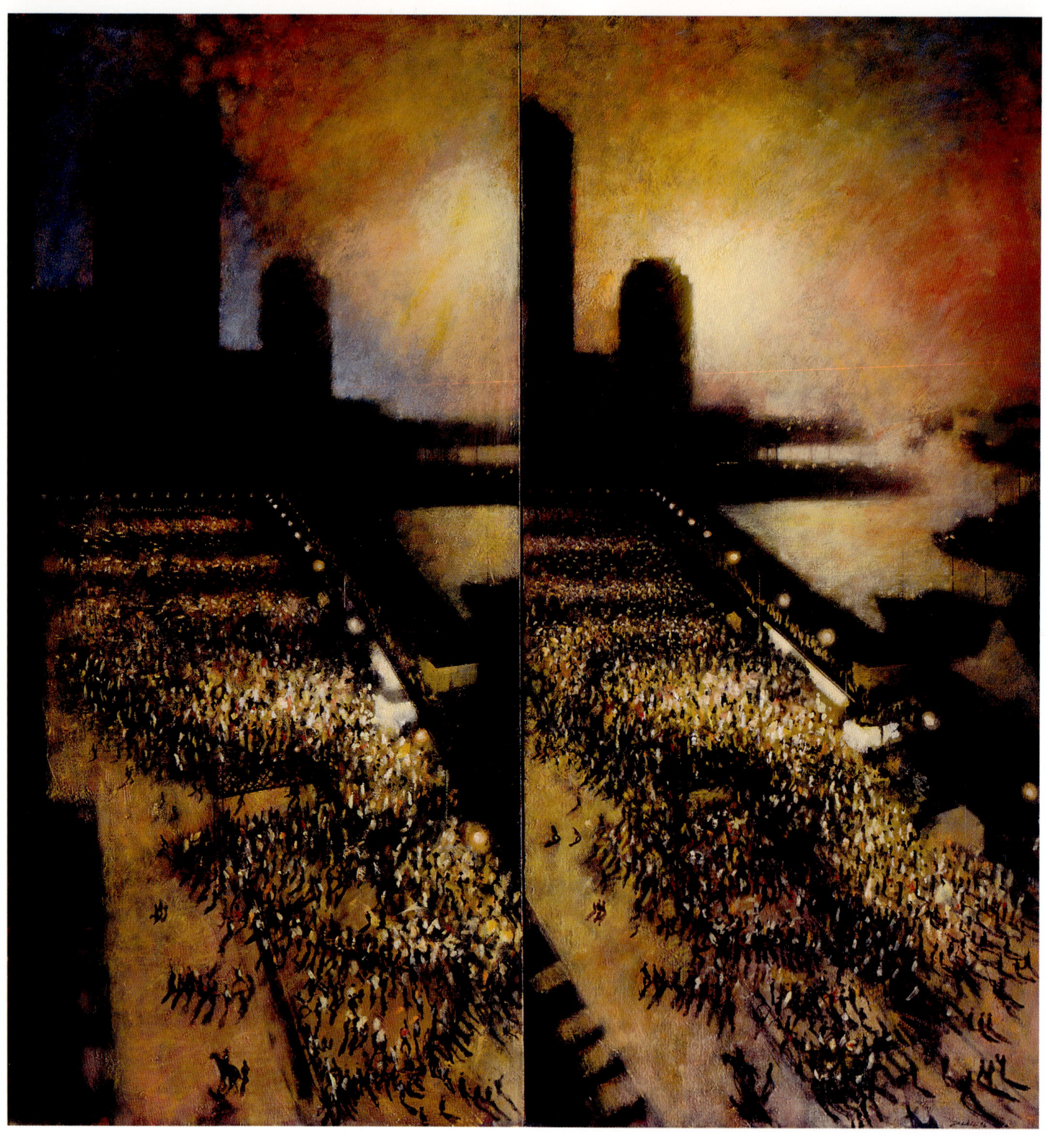

The Fourth Of July

1986

Diptych; oil on canvas

198.8×184.1 cm.

78.25×72.5 in.

The Promenade, Fifth Avenue

1986

Oil on canvas

244.5×183.5 cm.

96.25×72.25 in.

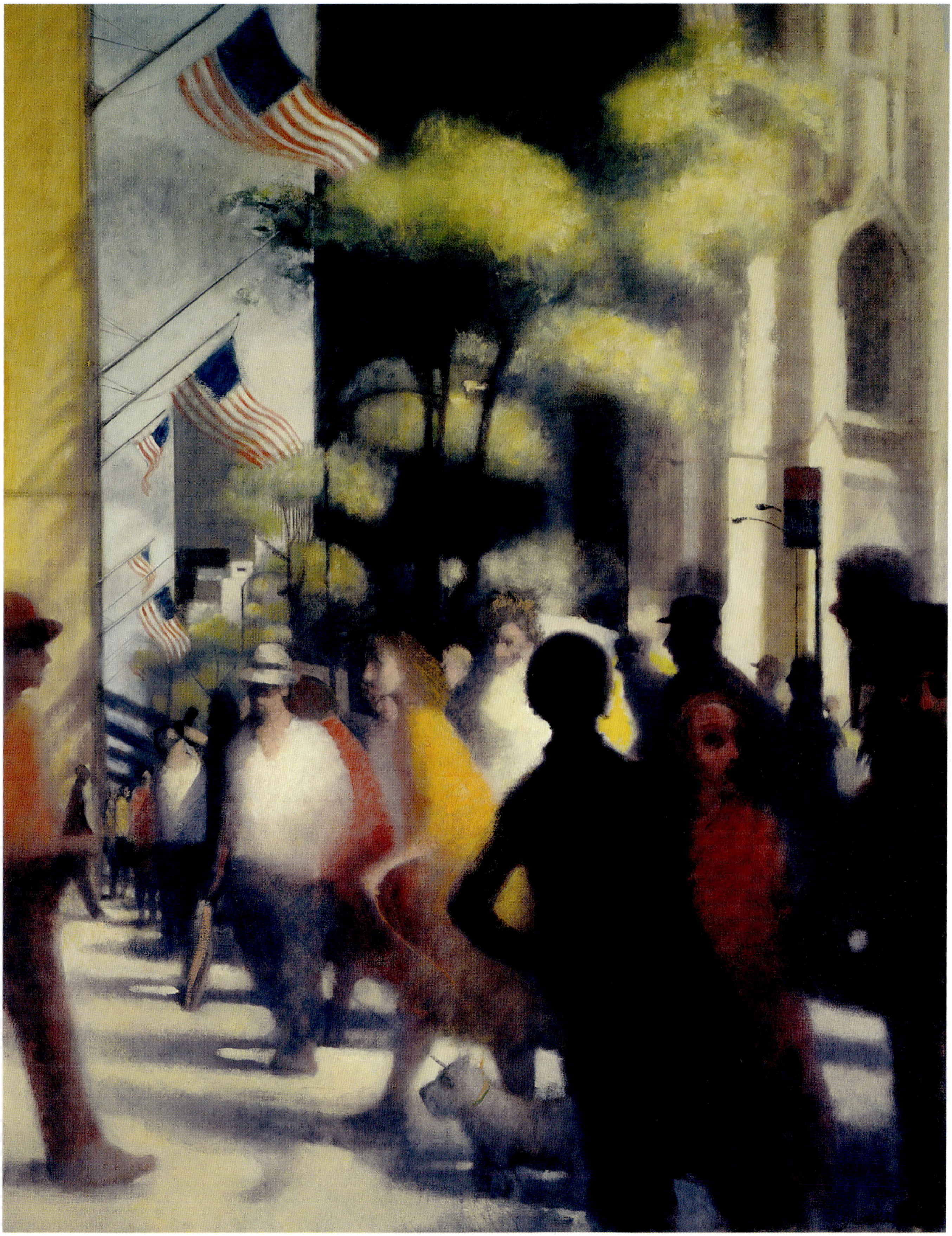

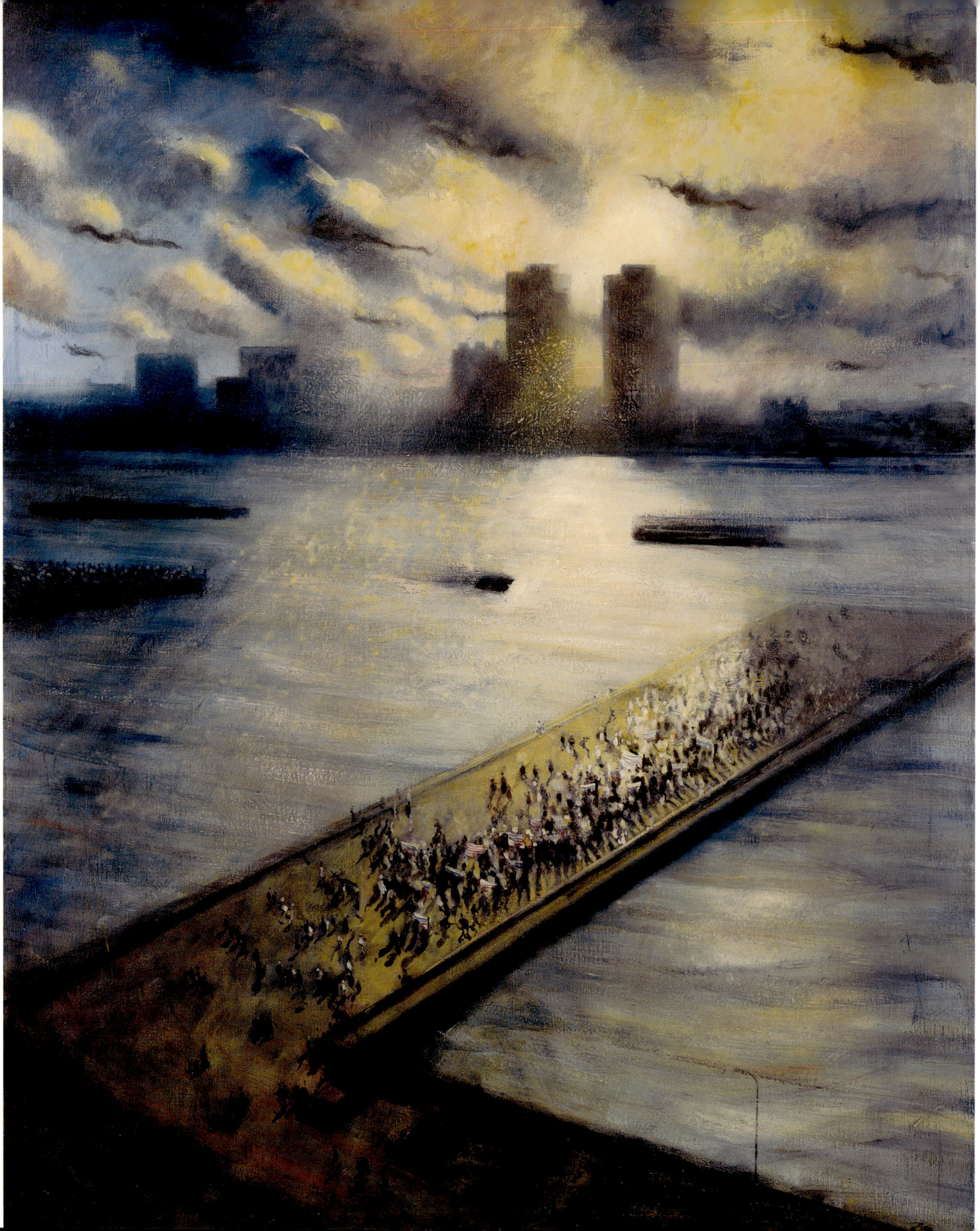

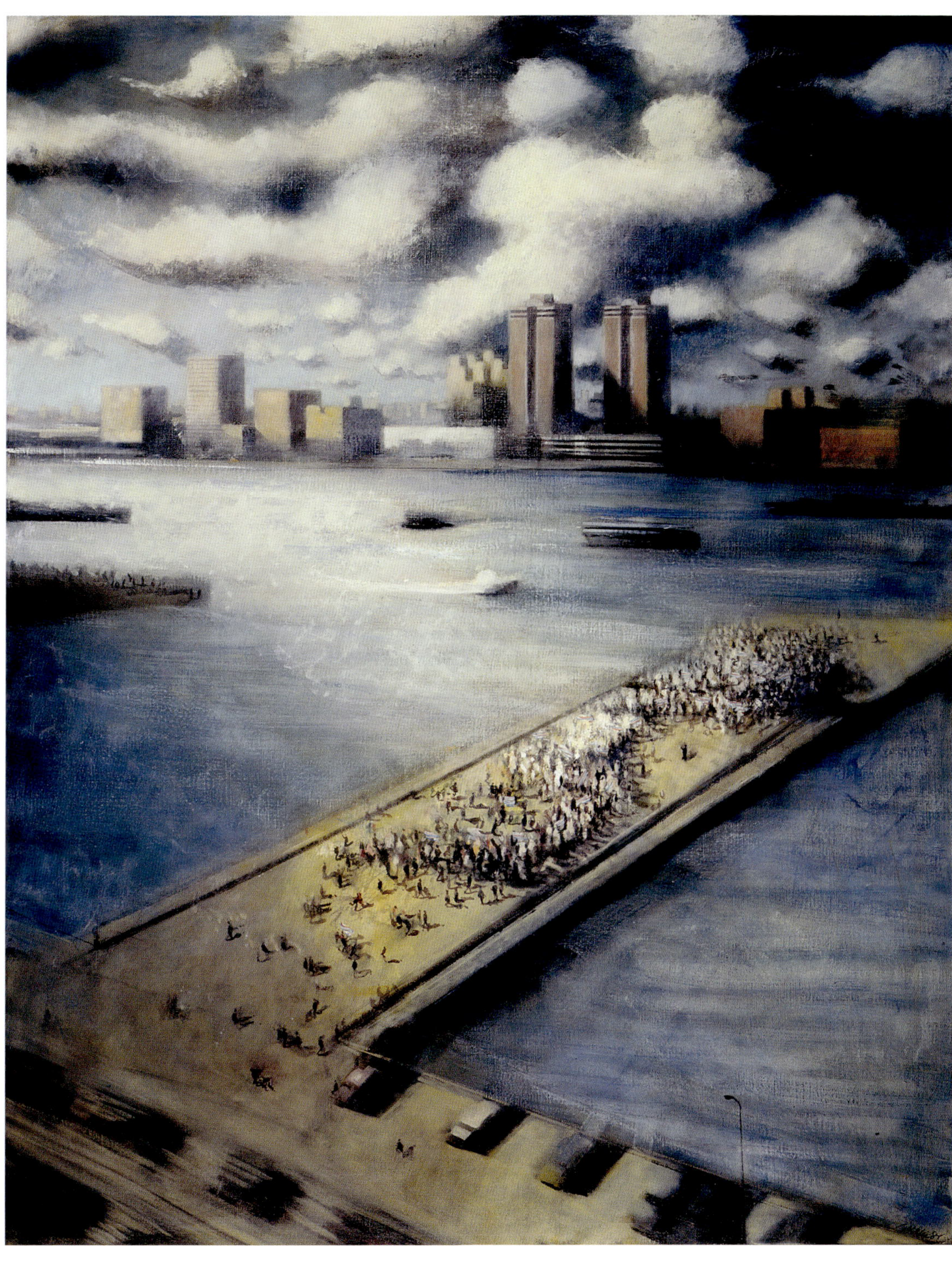

The Piers At Dusk
1987
Oil on canvas
198.1×152.4 cm.
78×60 in.

Mid-Day On The Hudson
1987
Oil on canvas
198.1×152.4 cm.
78×60 in.

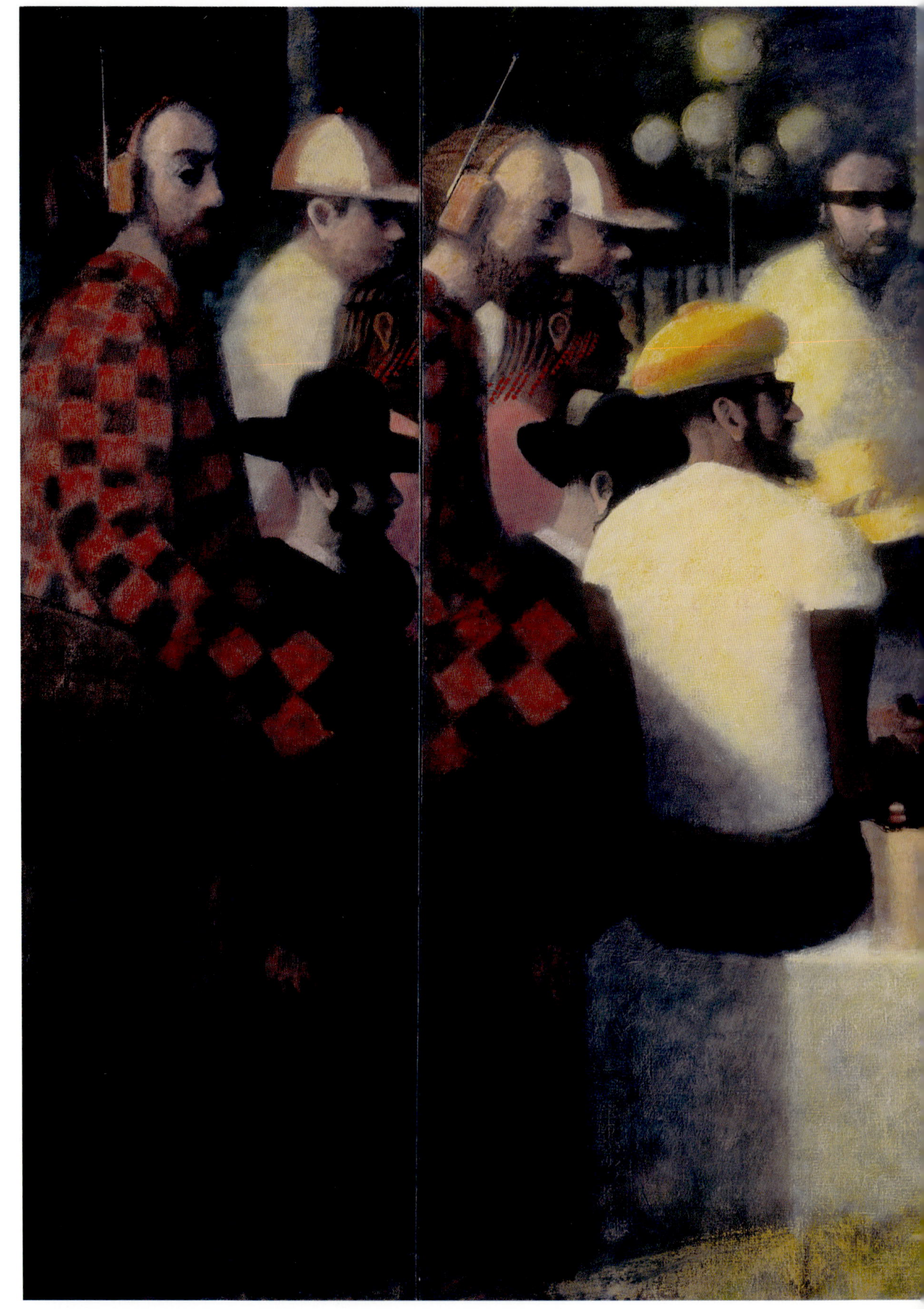

The Chess Players
1986
Triptych; oil on canvas
233.7 × 355.6 cm.
92 × 140 in.

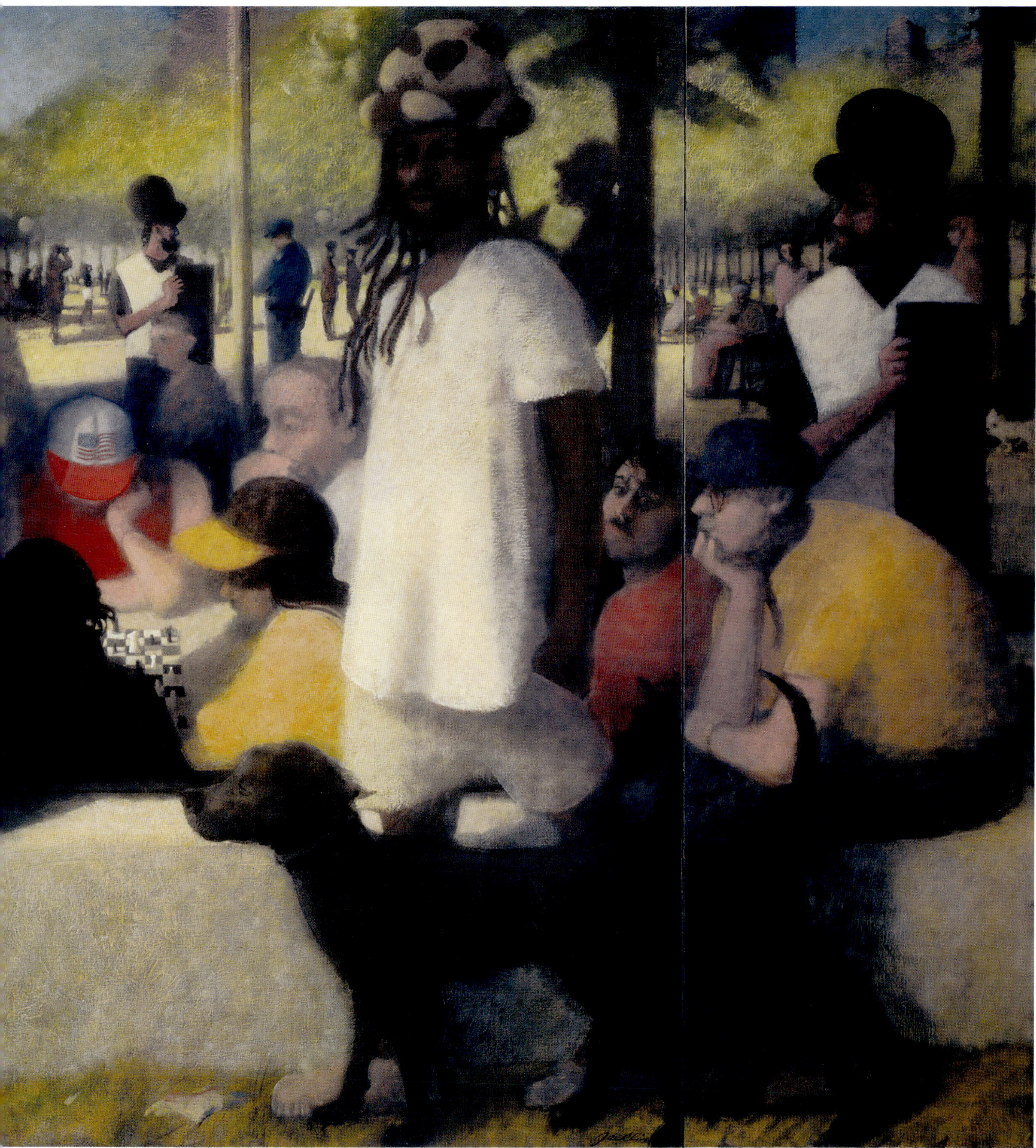

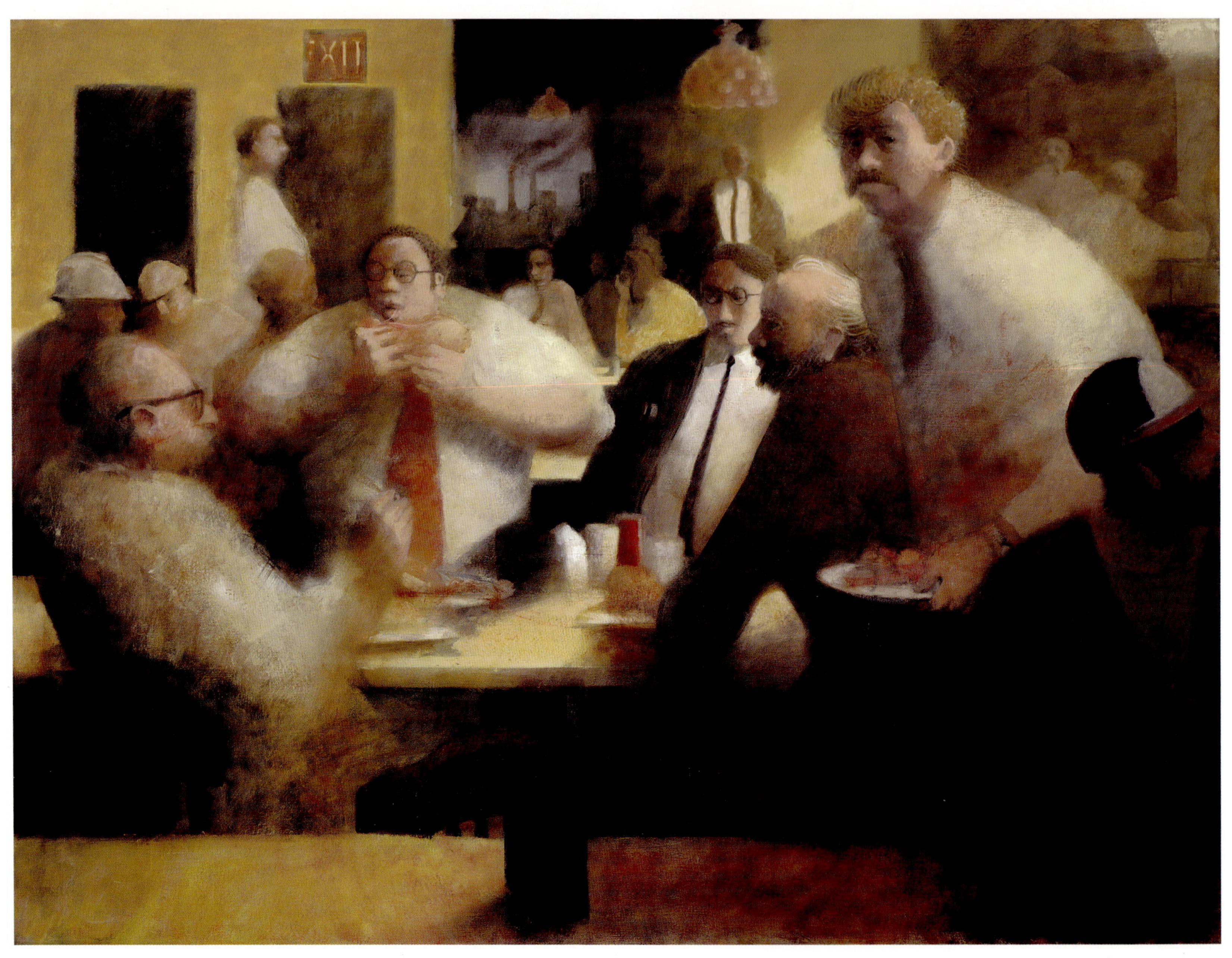

The Salesman's Lunch

1988

Oil on canvas

152.4×198.1 cm.

60×78 in.

Howley's

1986

Oil on canvas

152.4×152.4 cm.

60×60 in.

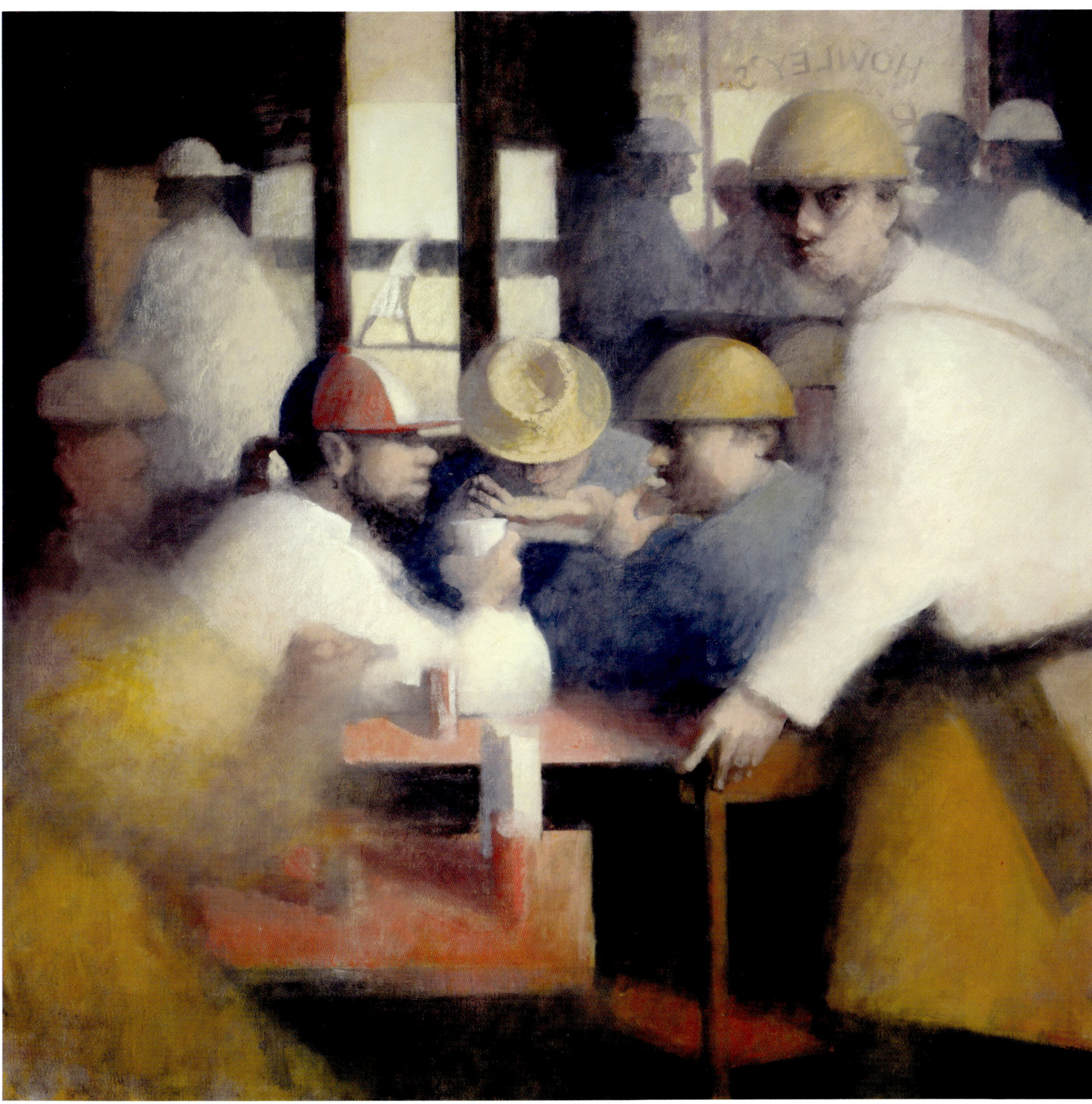

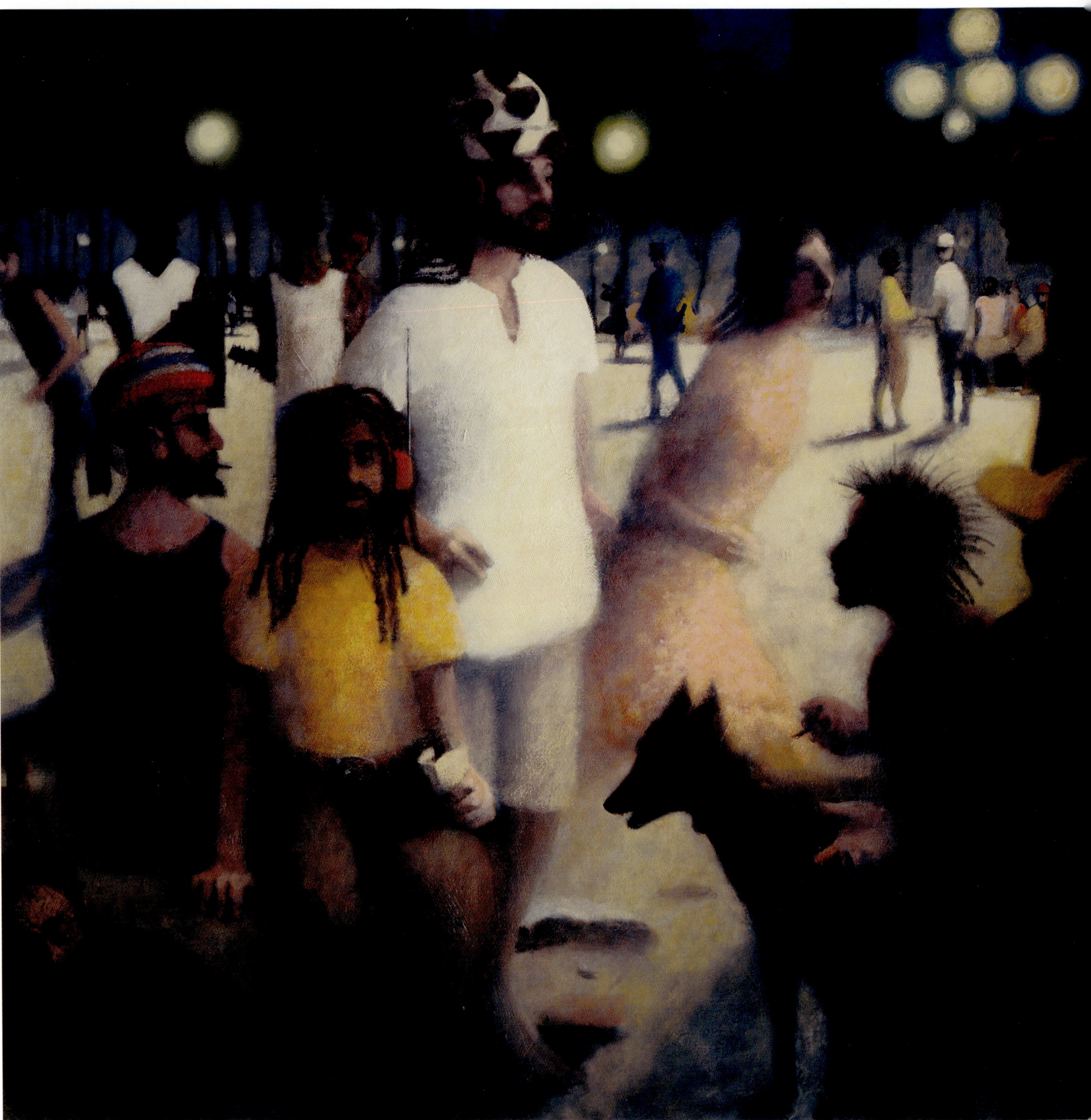

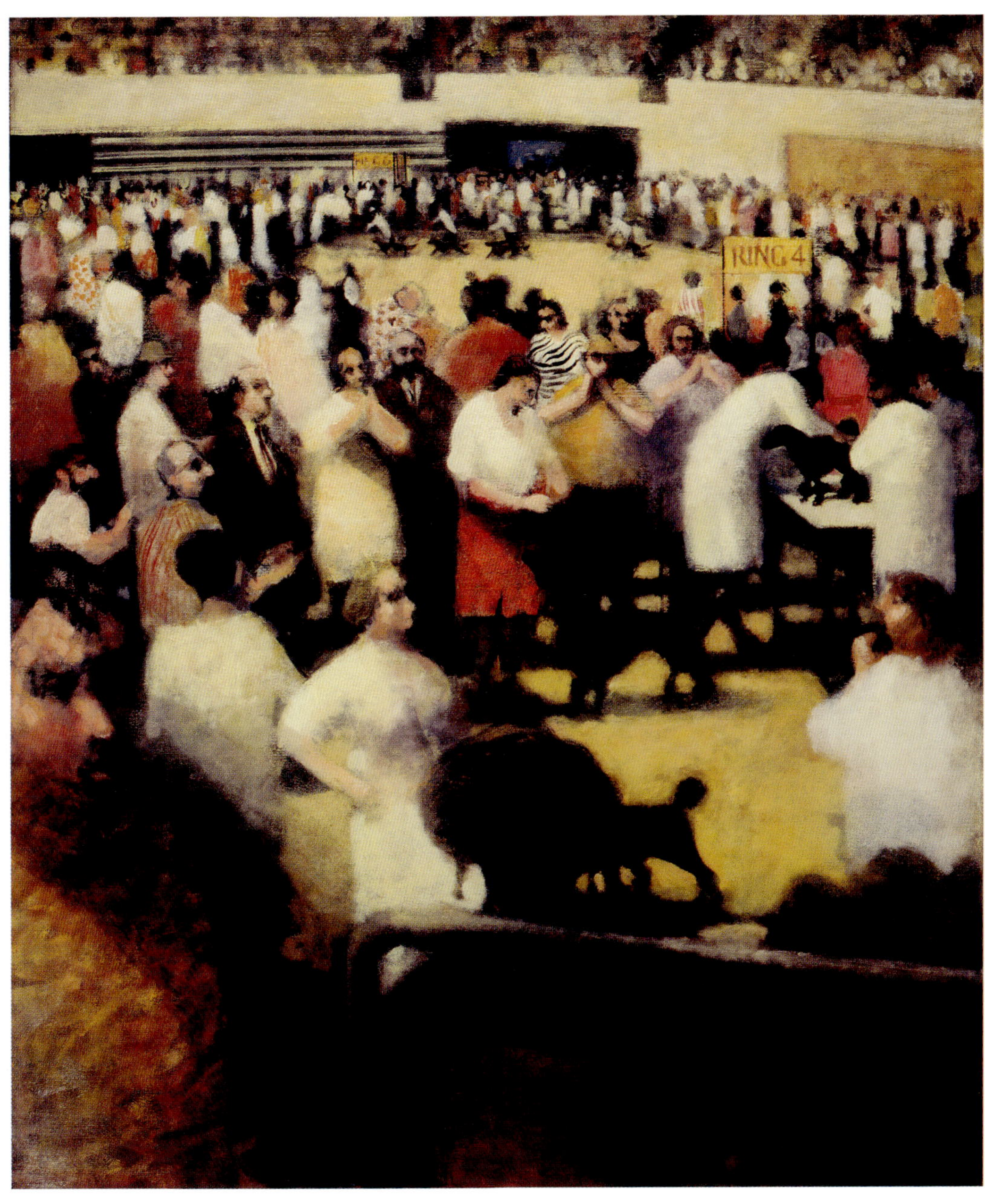

Washington Square At Night

1986

Oil on canvas

198.1×198.1 cm.

78×78 in.

Madison Square Garden 11th Annual Dog Show Ring 4

1987

Oil on canvas

91.4×76.2 cm.

36×30 in.

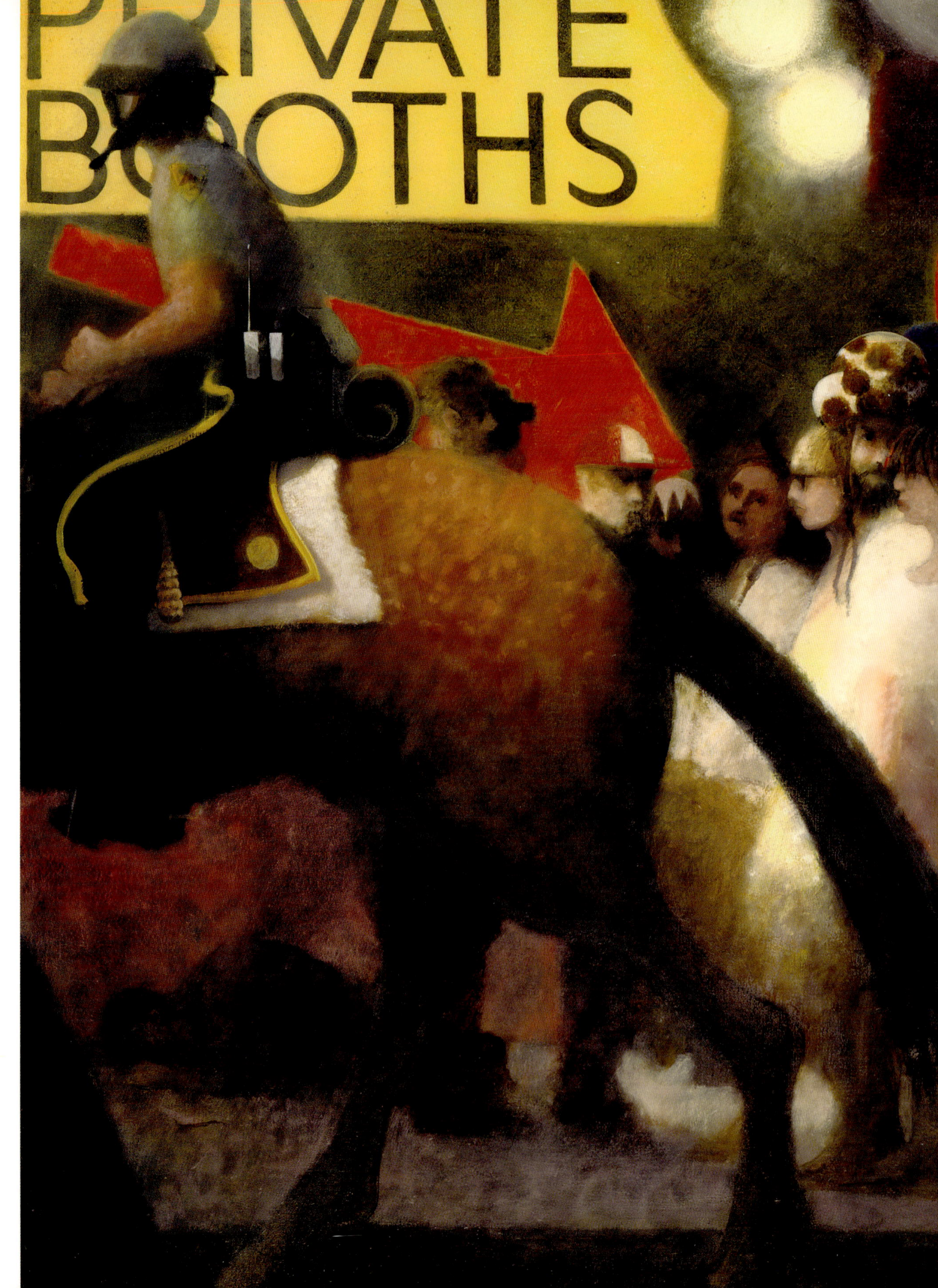

Incident On
42nd Street
1988
Diptych; oil on canvas
198.1×304.8 cm.
78×120 in.

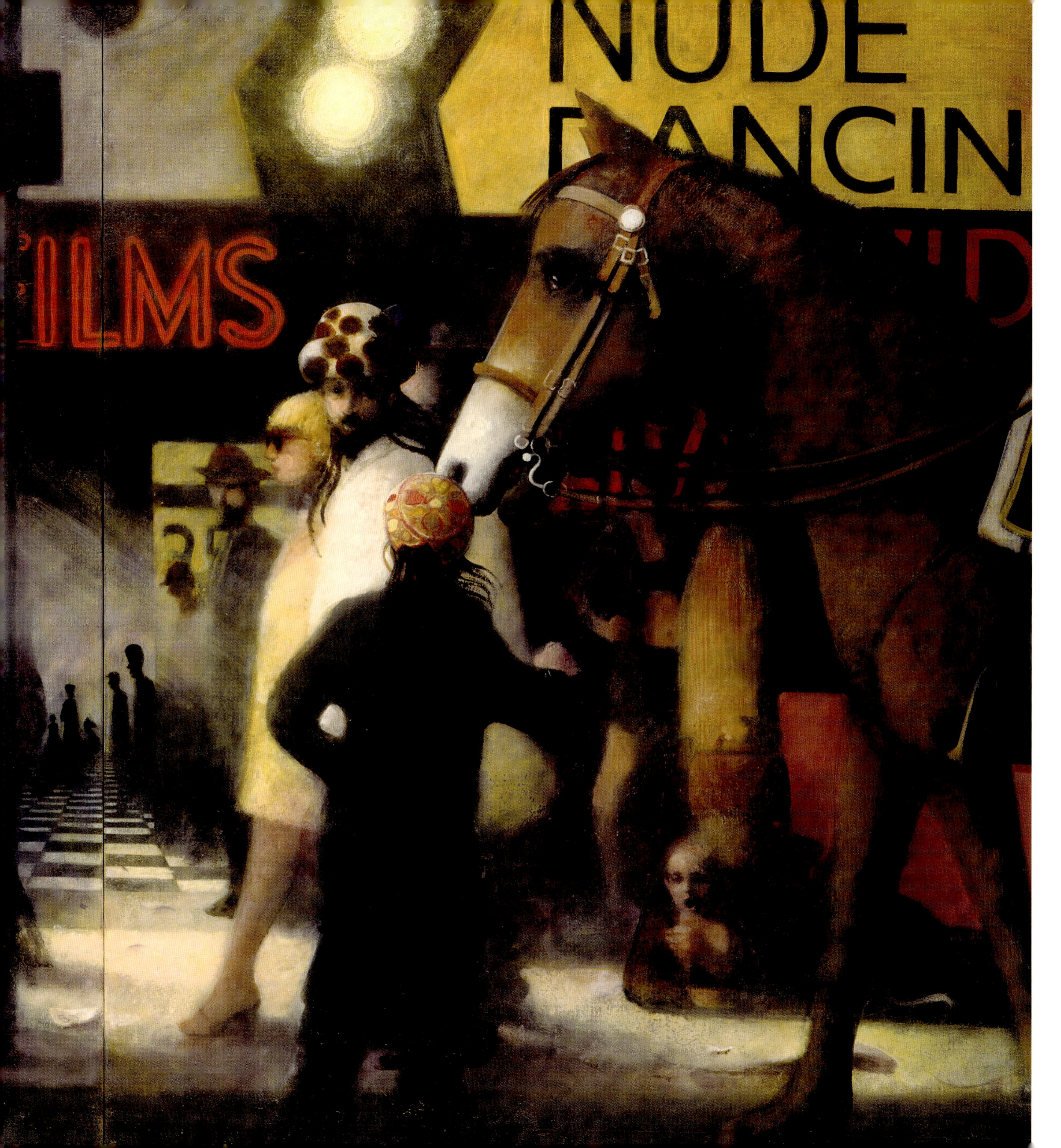

NUDE
DANCIN
FILMS

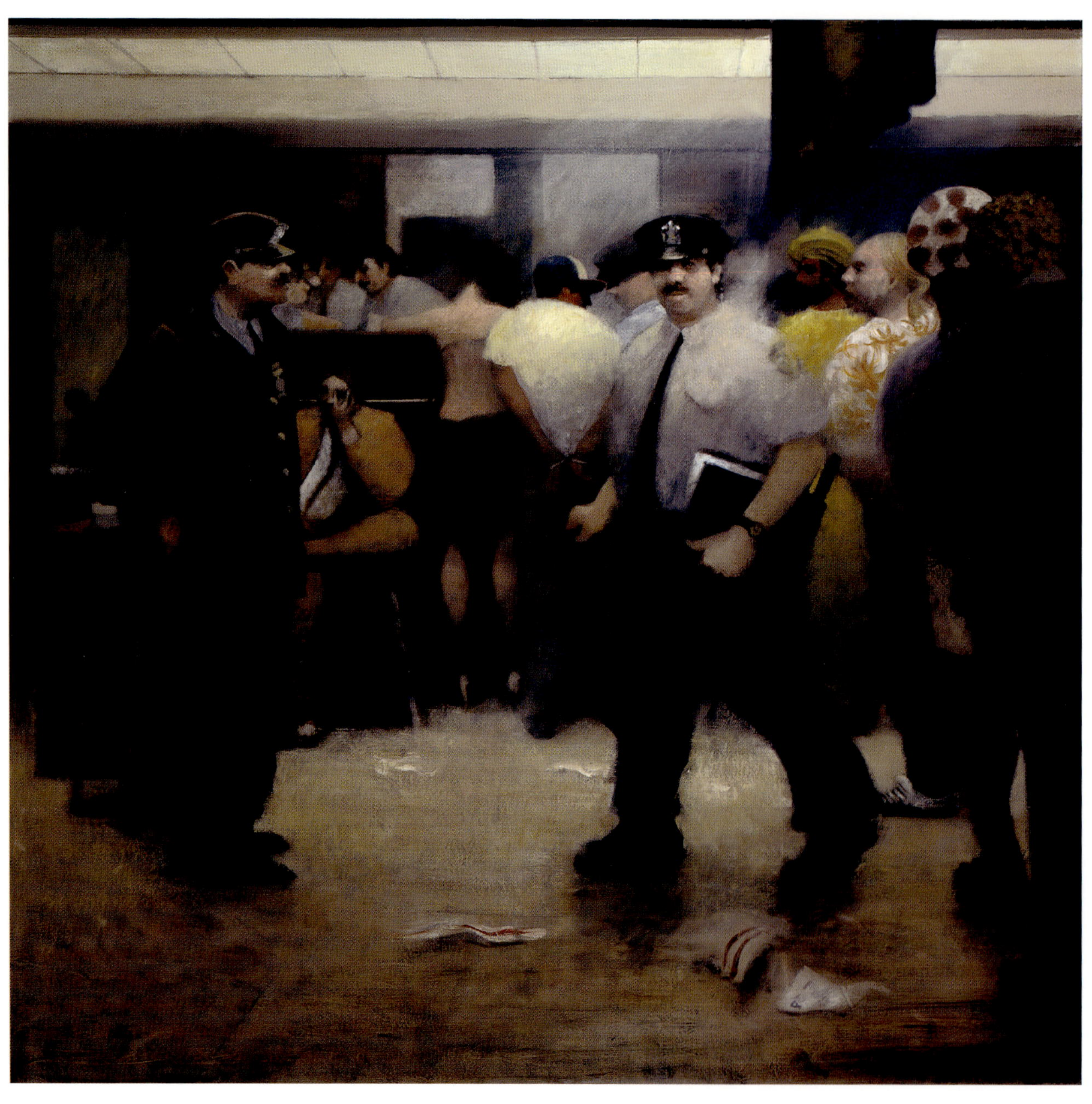

The Desk 35th Precinct

1988
Oil on canvas
198.1×198.1 cm.
78×78 in.

42nd Street

1988
Pastel on paper
105.4×75.6 cm.
41.5×29.75 in.

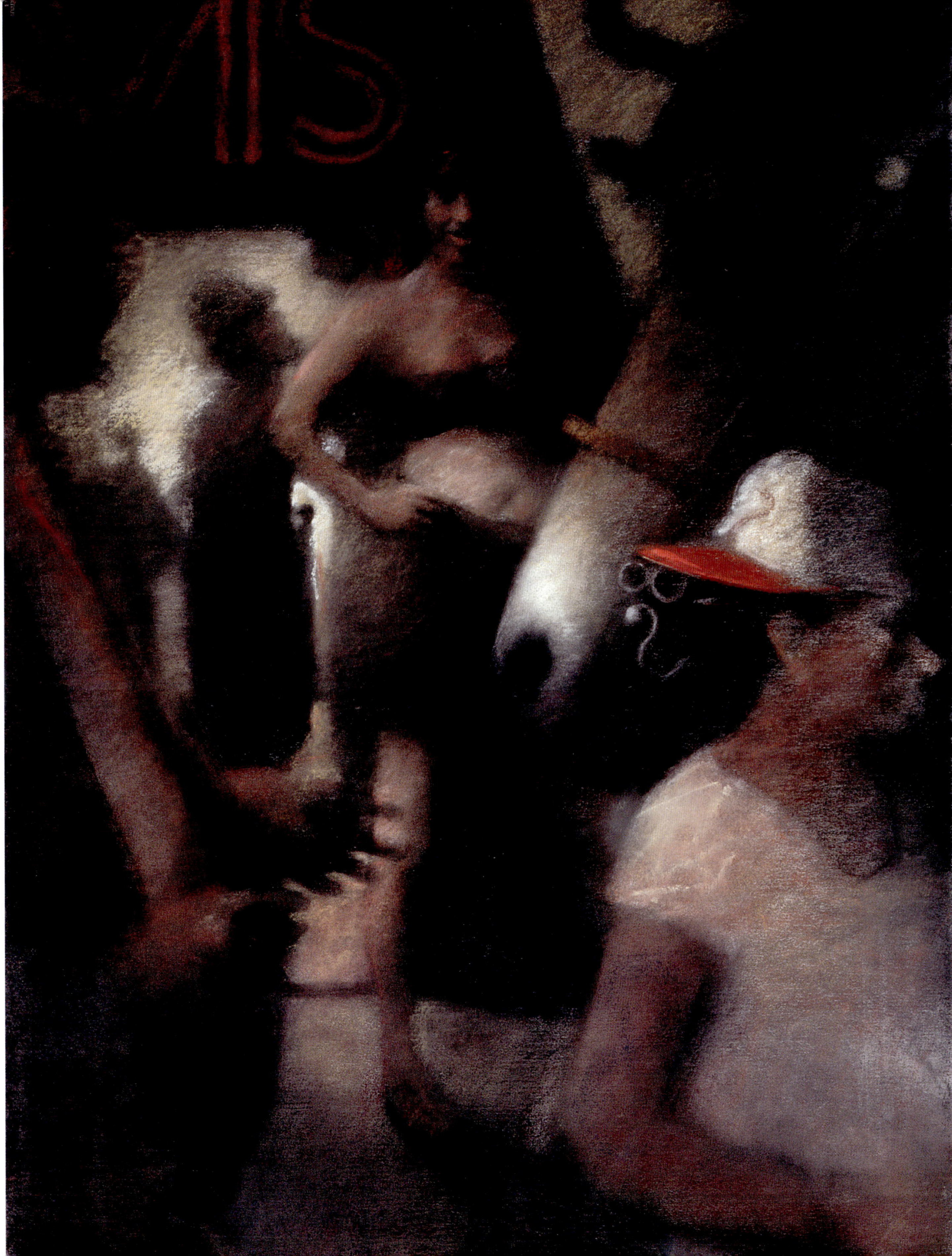

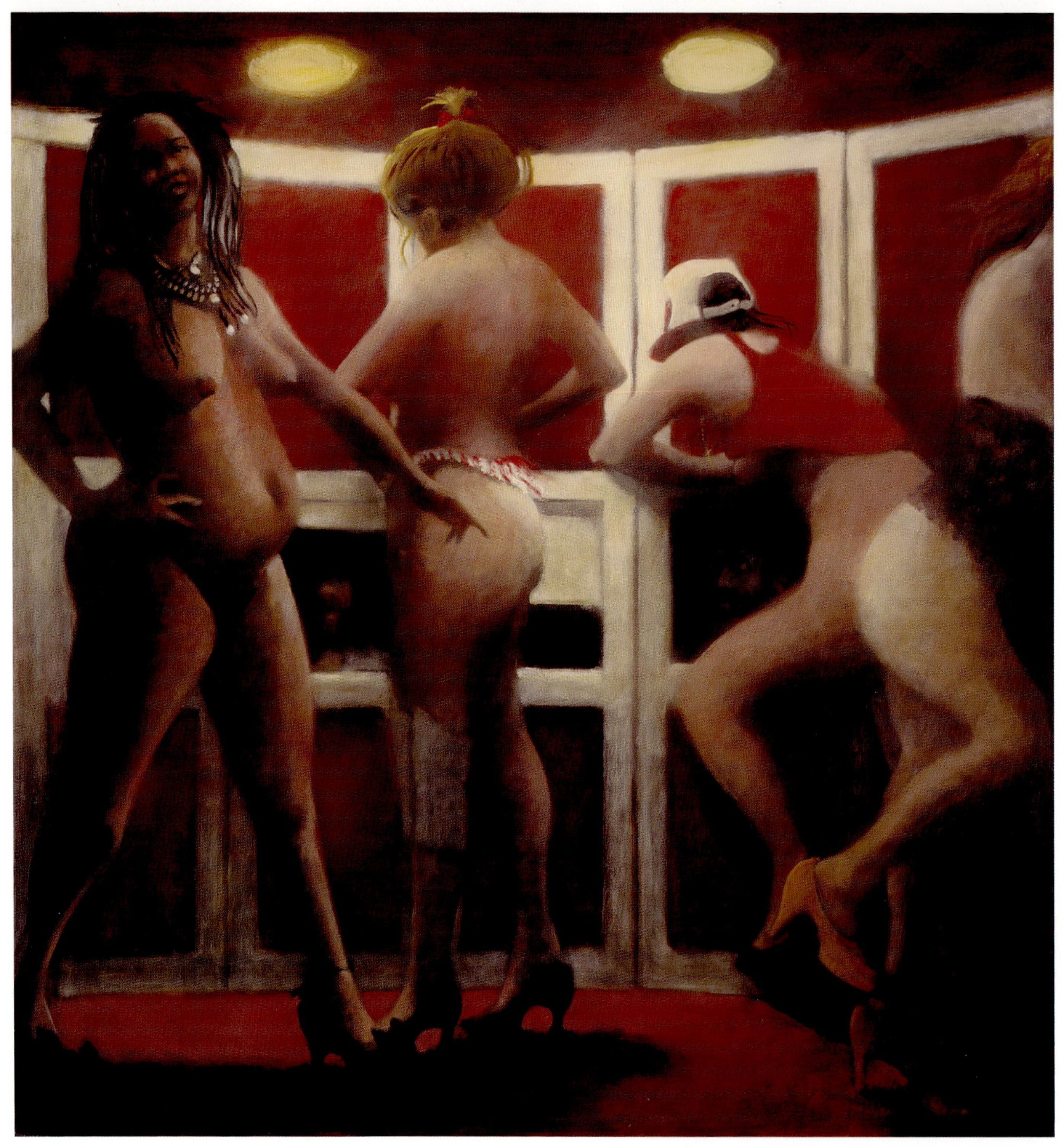

Dancers 42nd Street

1990
Oil on canvas
198.1×182.9 cm.
78×72 in.

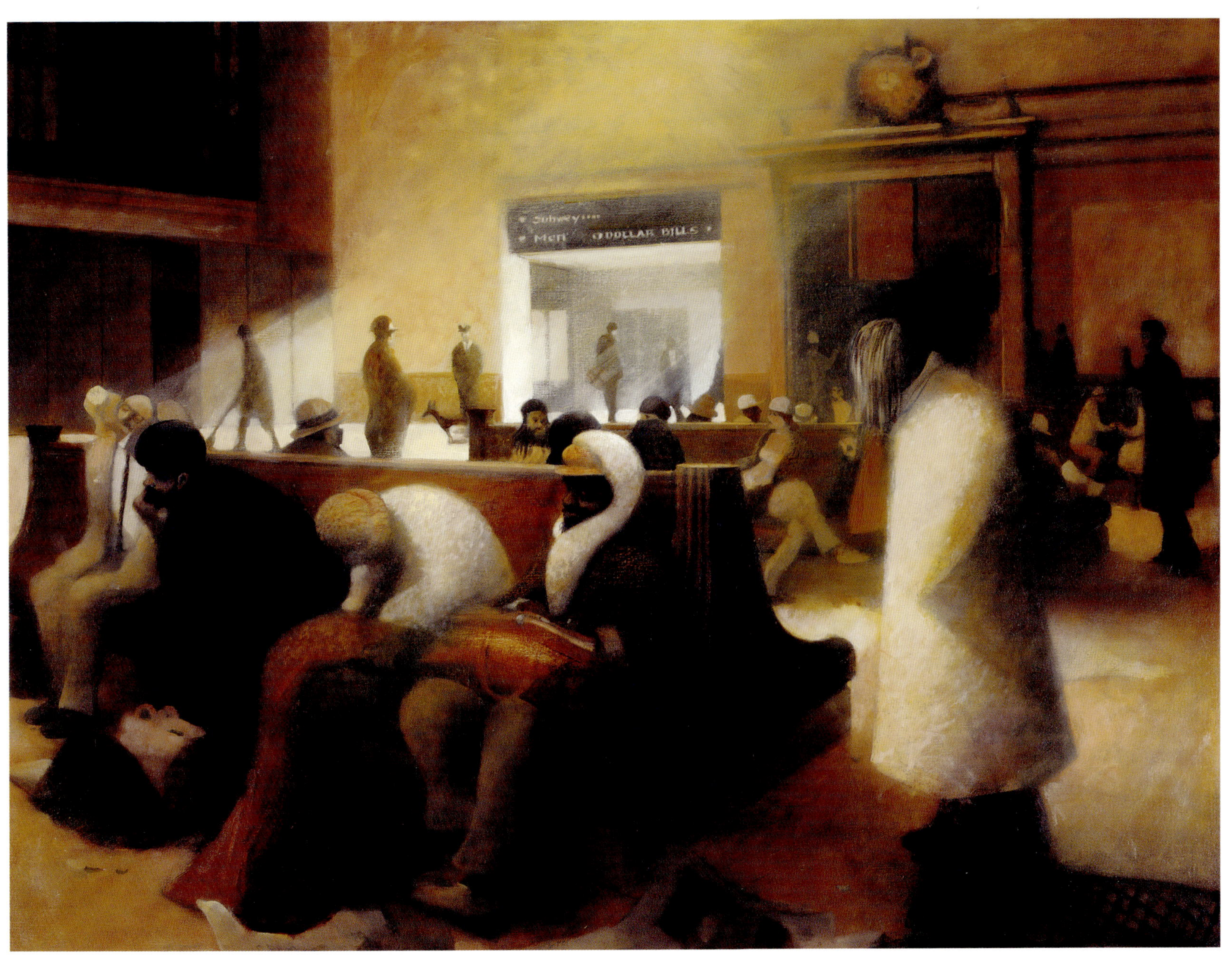

Grand Central Station
1988
Oil on canvas
152.4×198.1 cm.
60×78 in.

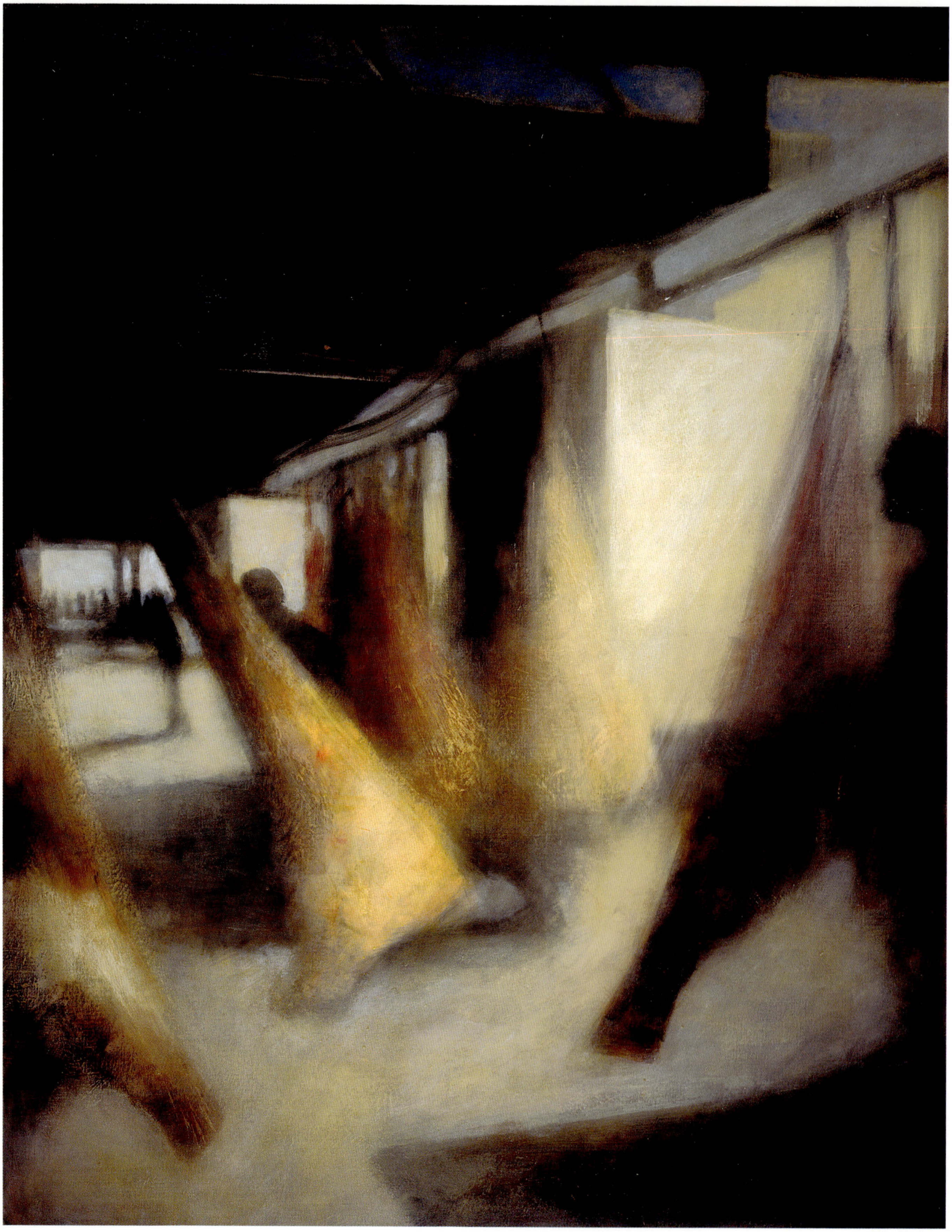

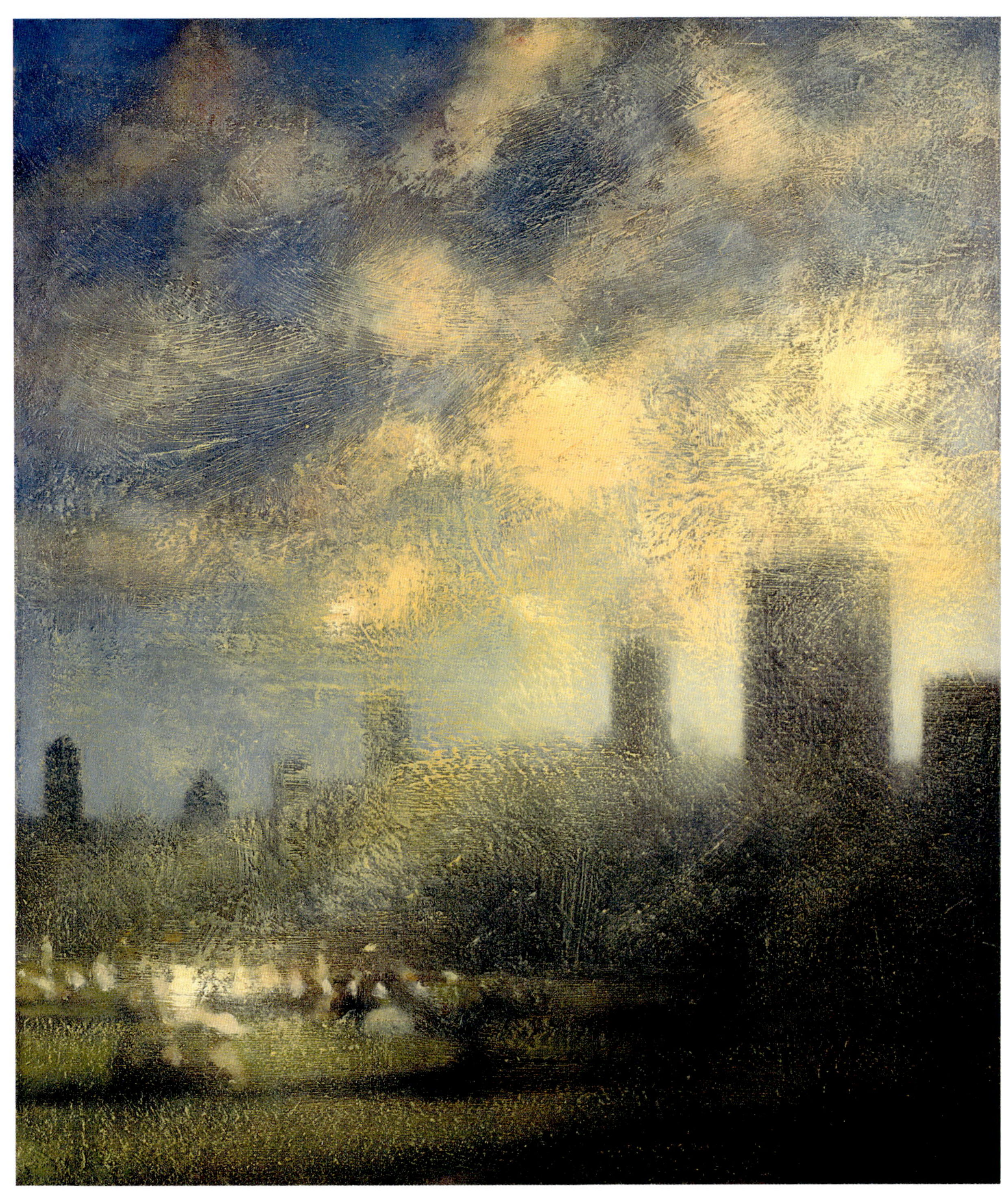

14th Street

1990
Oil on canvas
198.1×152.4 cm.
78×60 in.

Sheep Meadow 8pm

1989–90
Oil on canvas
93.3×78.1 cm.
36.75×30.75 in.

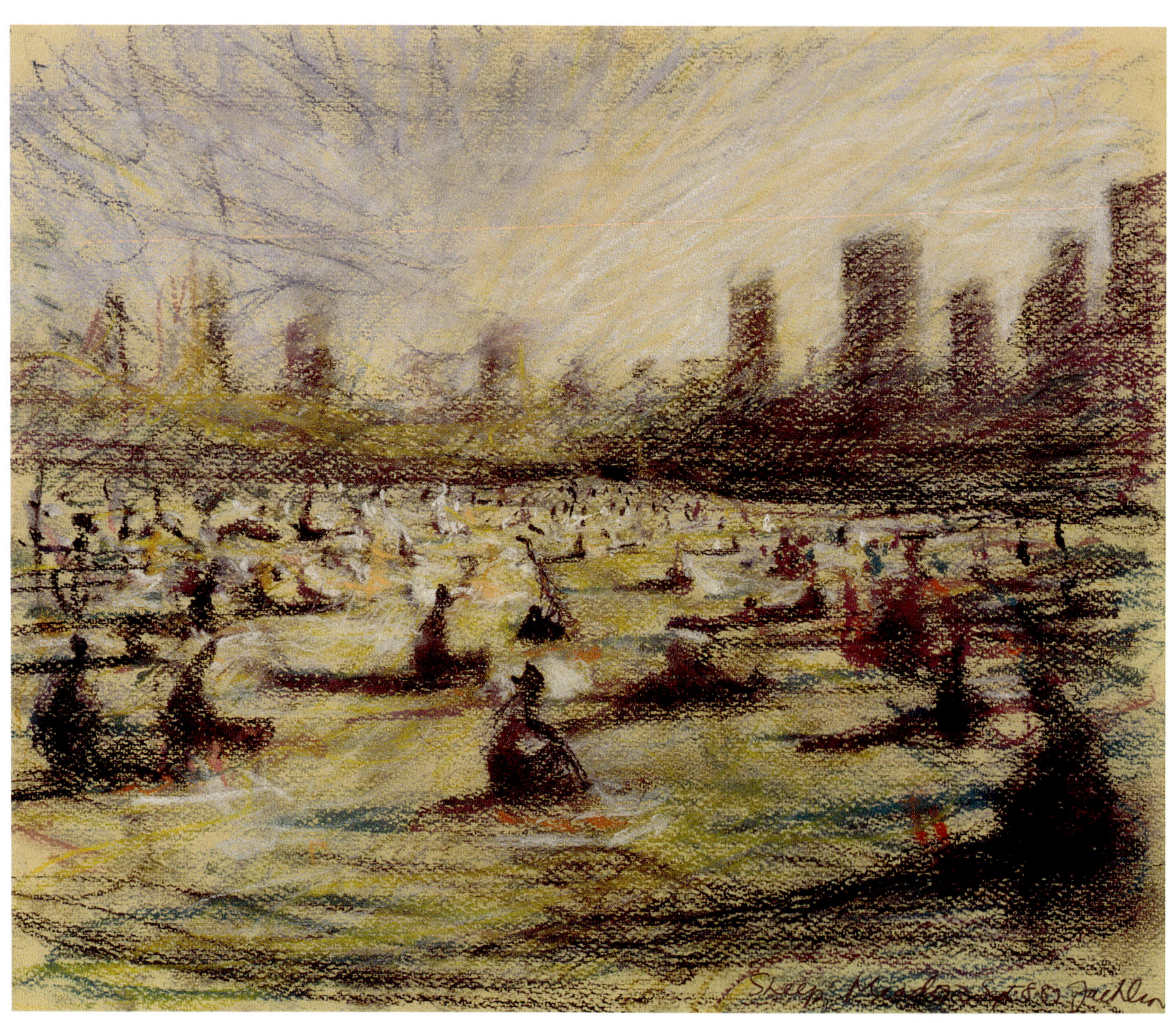

Sheep Meadow, September

1989
Pastel on paper
34.3×39.4 cm.
13.5×15.5 in.

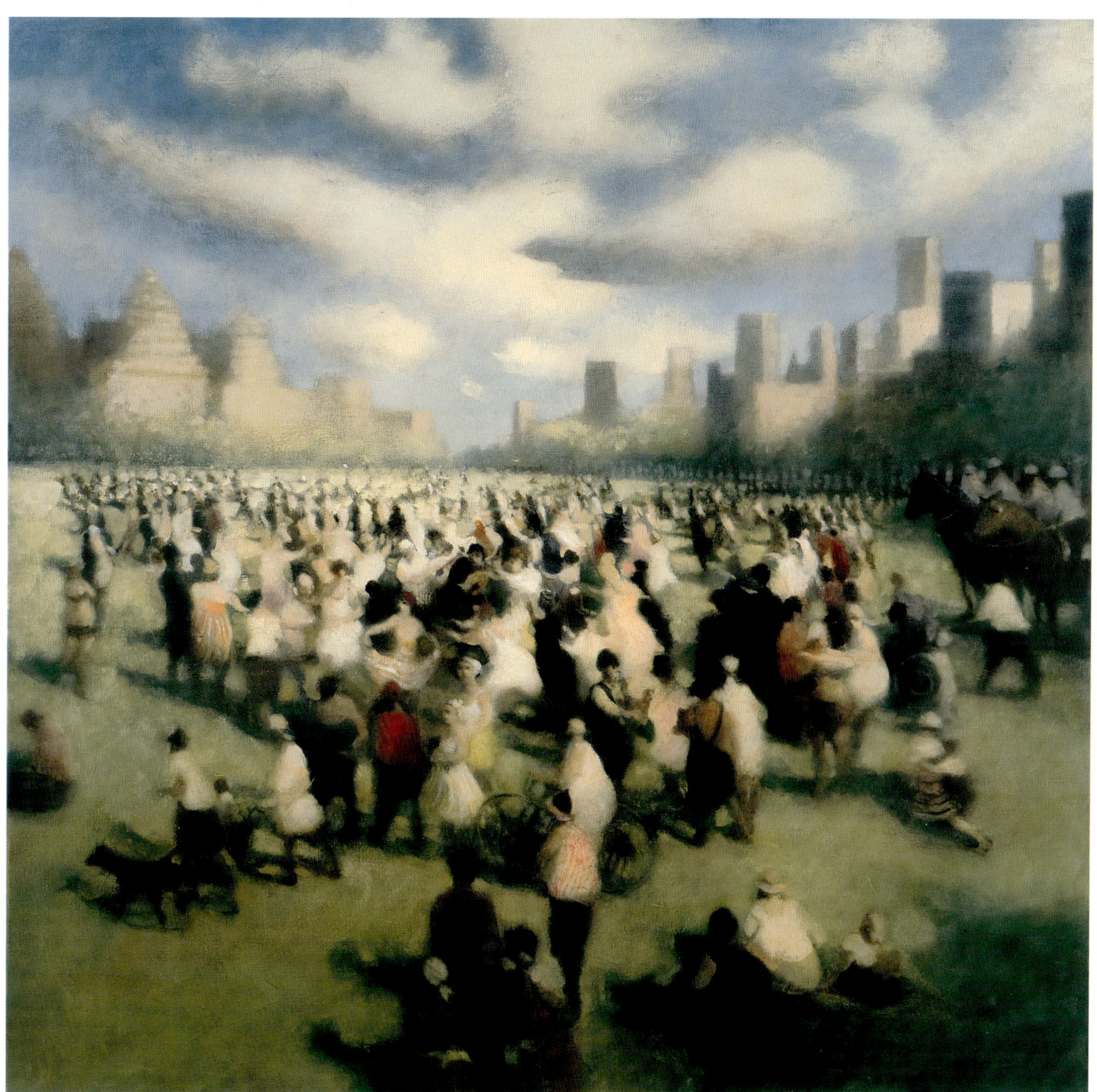

Before The Rains, Great Lawn
1998
Oil on canvas
152.4×152.4 cm.
60×60 in.

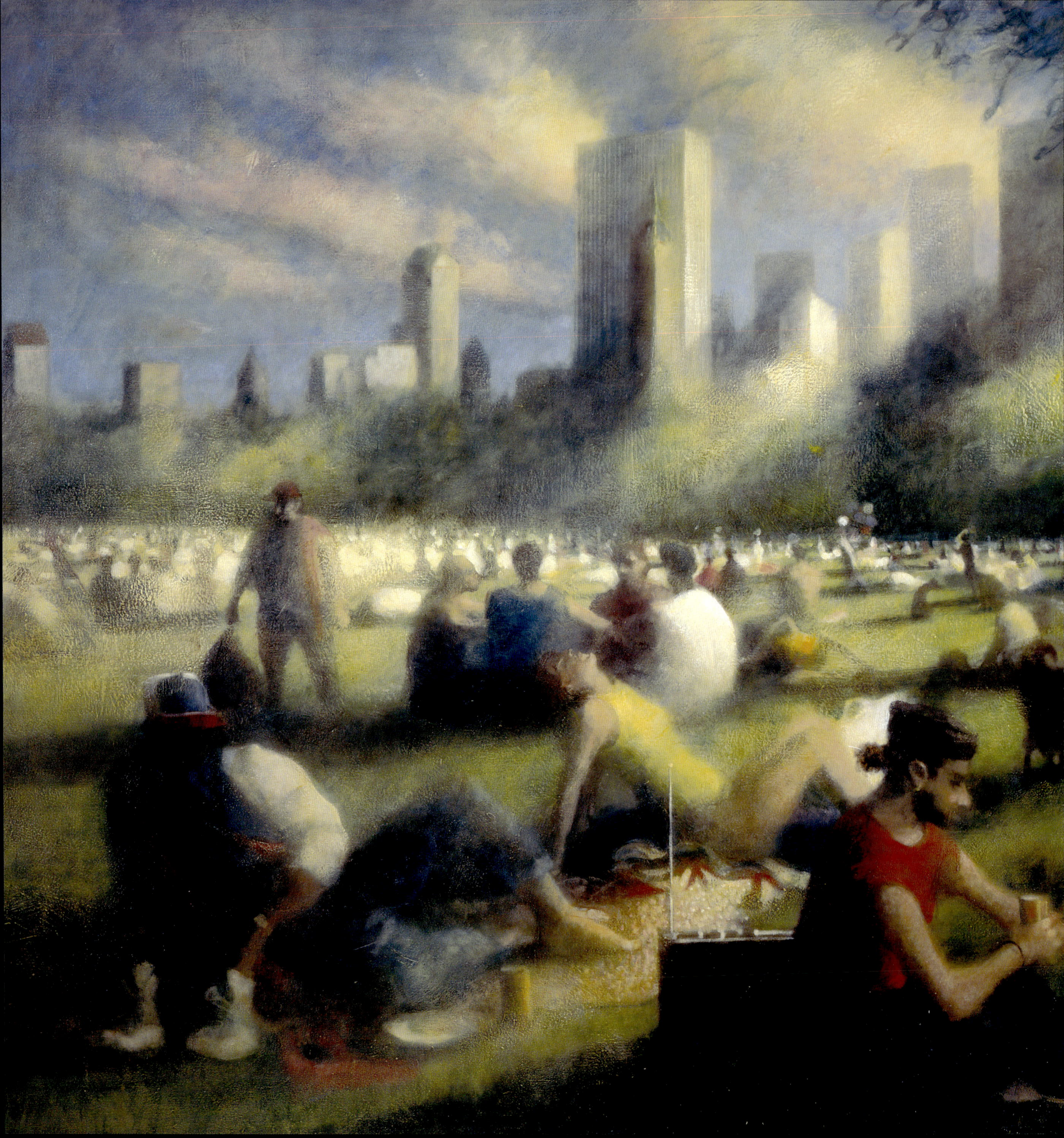

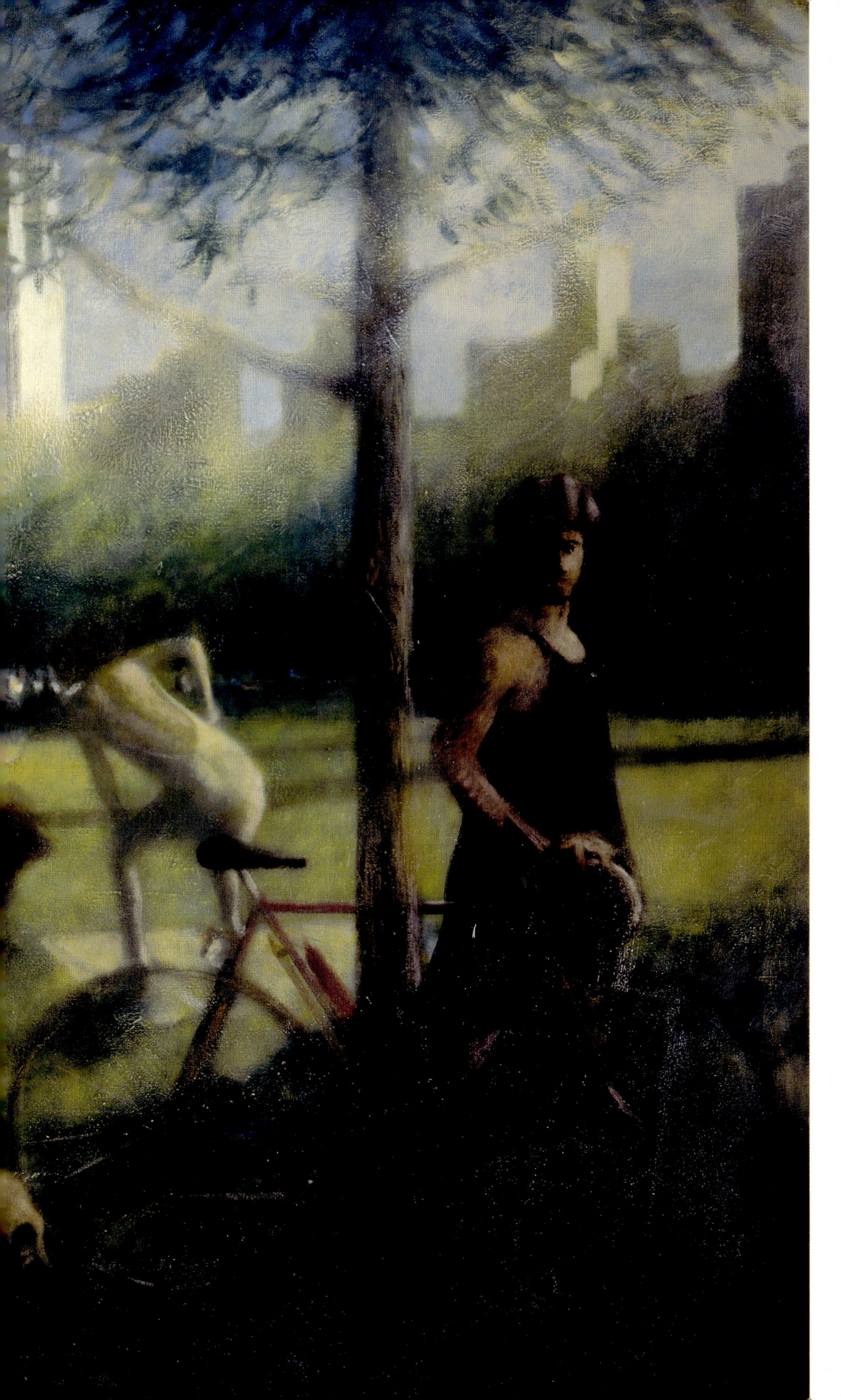

Sheep Meadow III
1990
Oil on canvas
243.8×365.8 cm.
96×144 in.

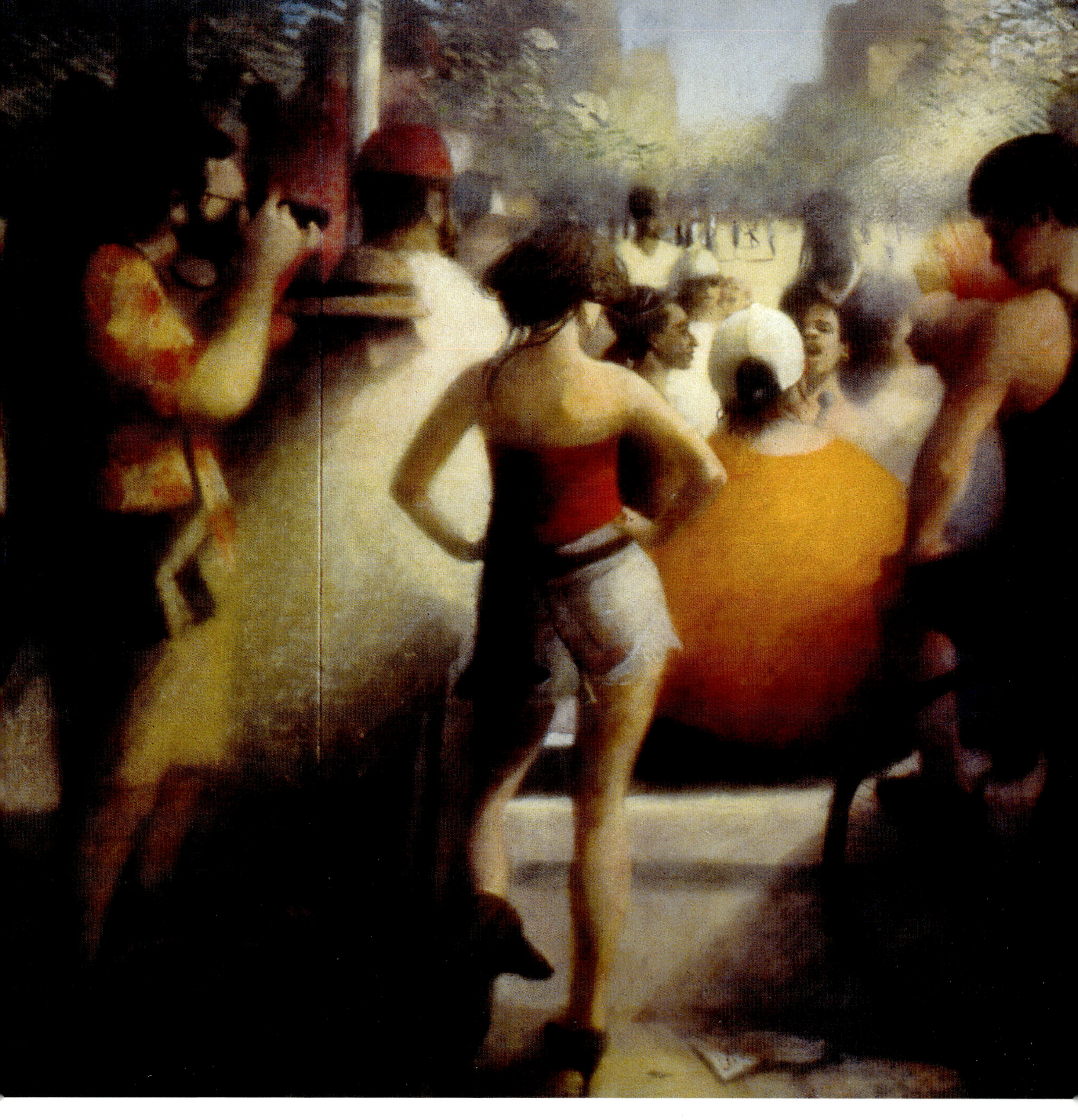

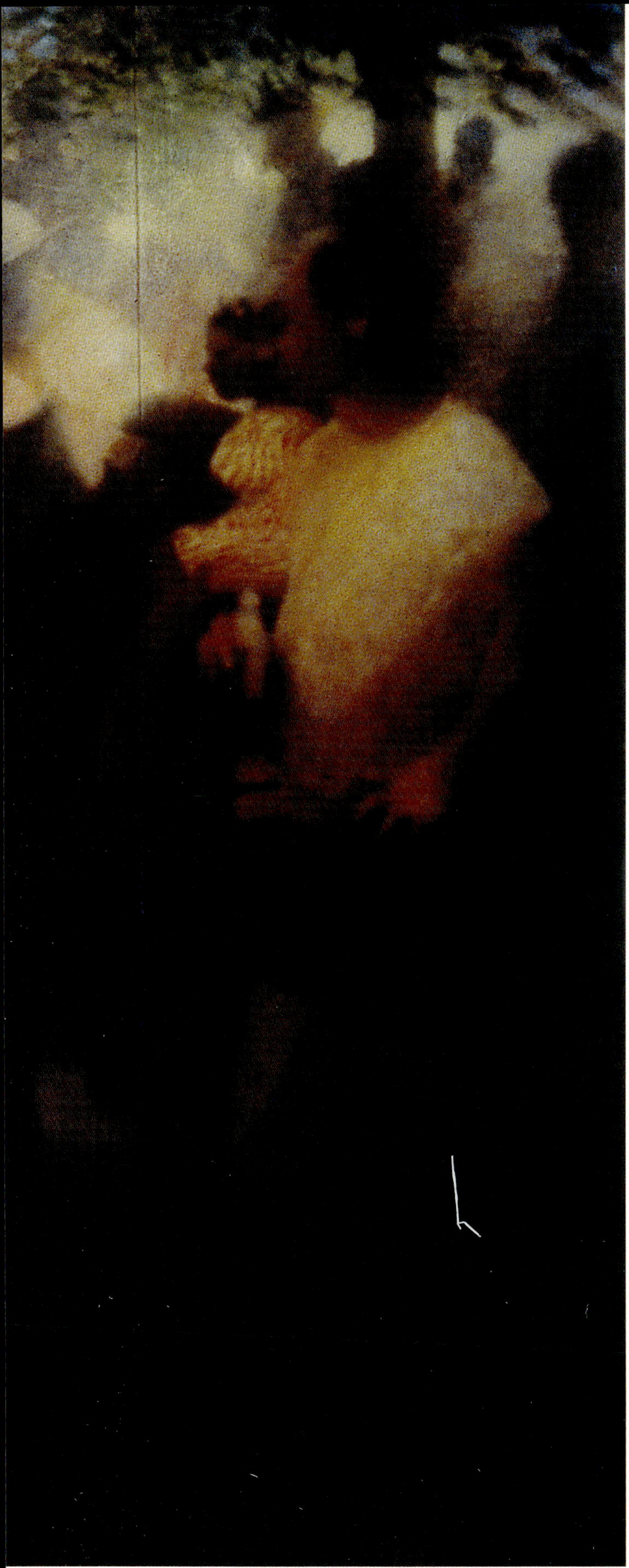

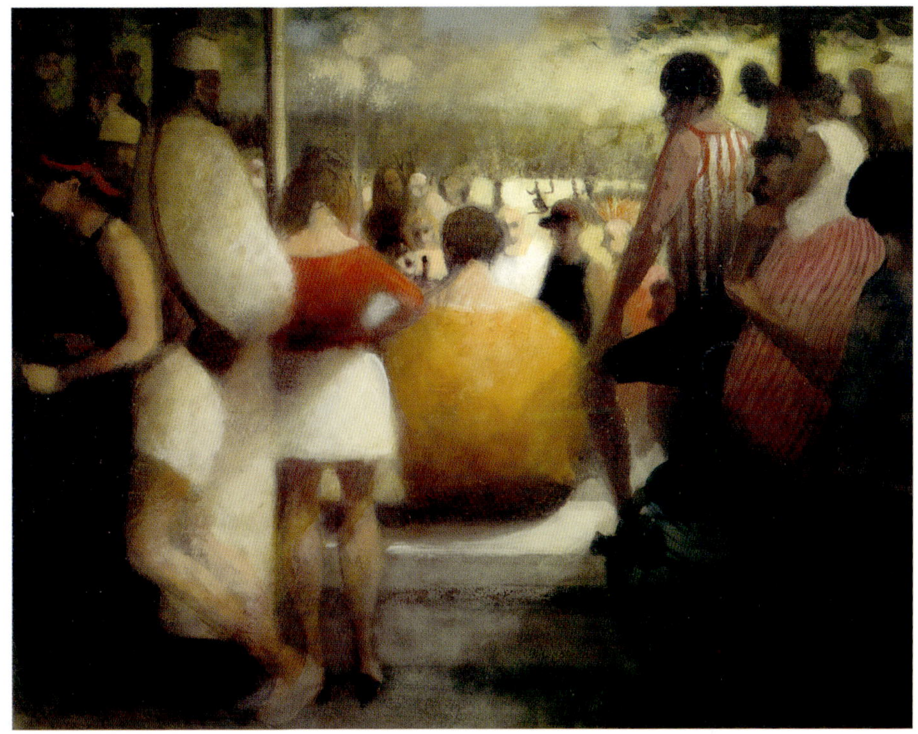

The Onlookers

1989

Triptych; oil on canvas

198.1×274.3 cm.

78×108 in.

Study For Onlookers I

1989

Oil on canvas

40.6×50.8 cm.

16×20 in.

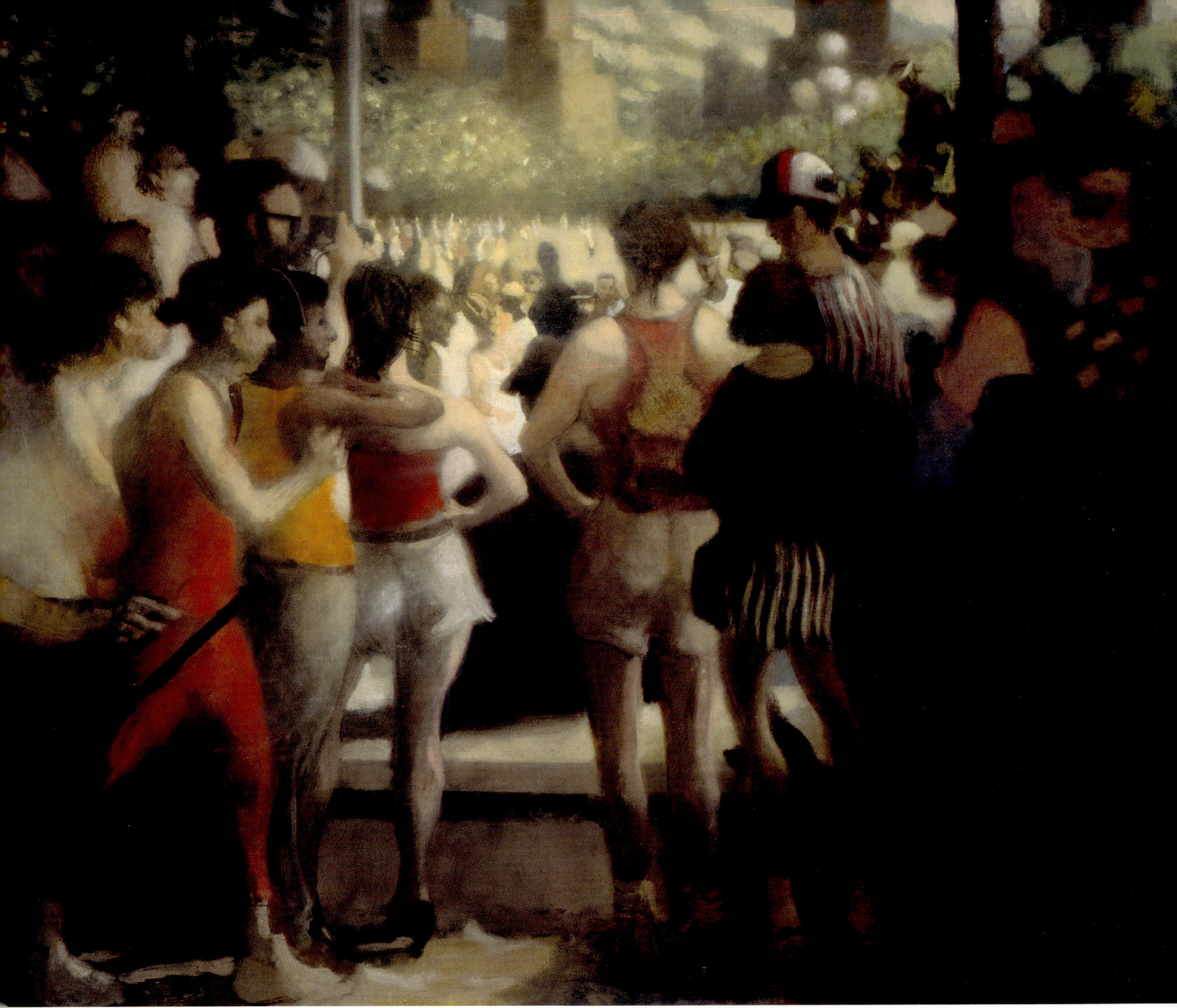

Onlookers II

1990
Oil on canvas
76.2×91.4 cm.
30×36 in.

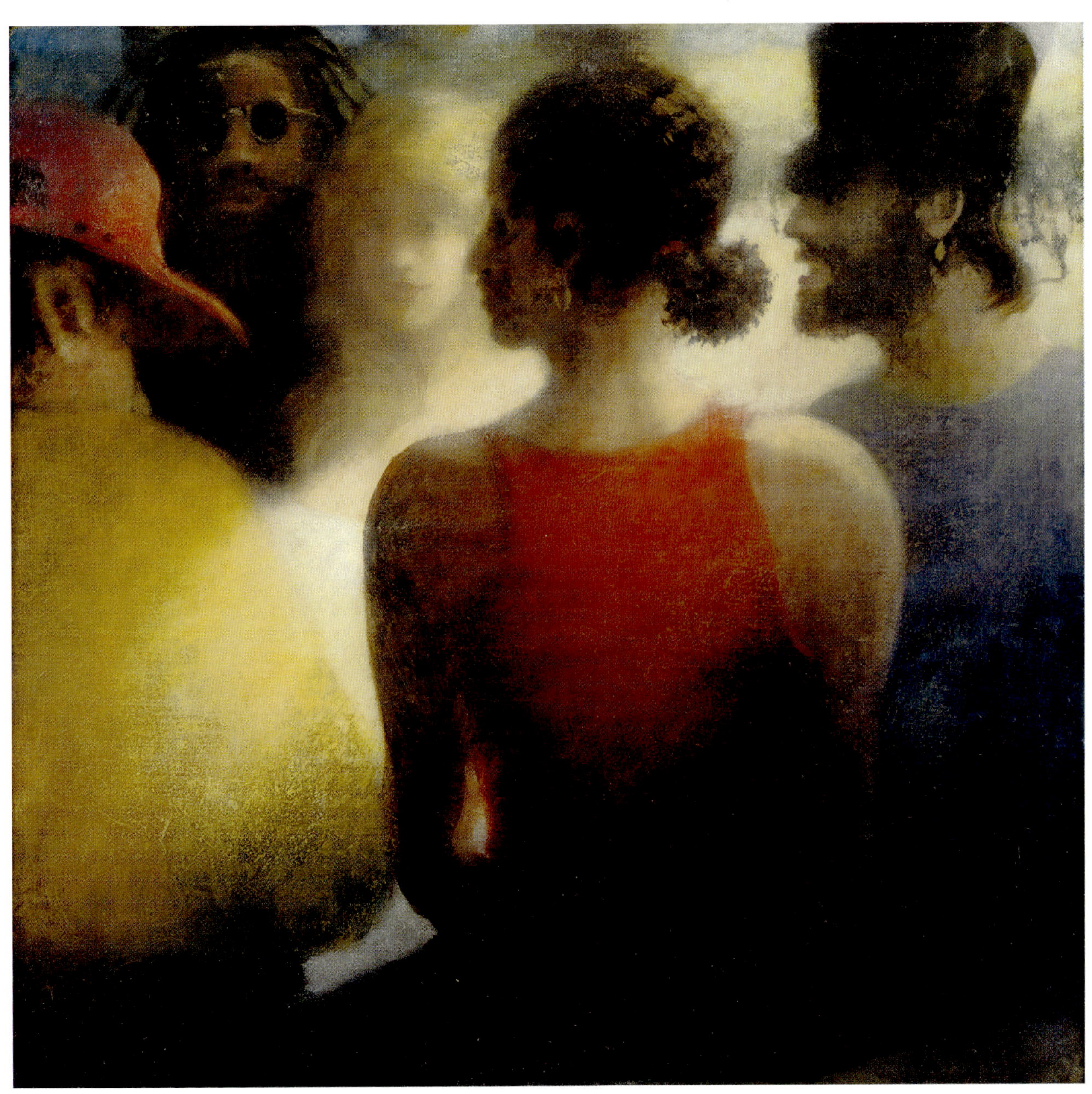

Washington Square
1989
Oil on canvas
40.6×40.6 cm.
16×16 in.

55

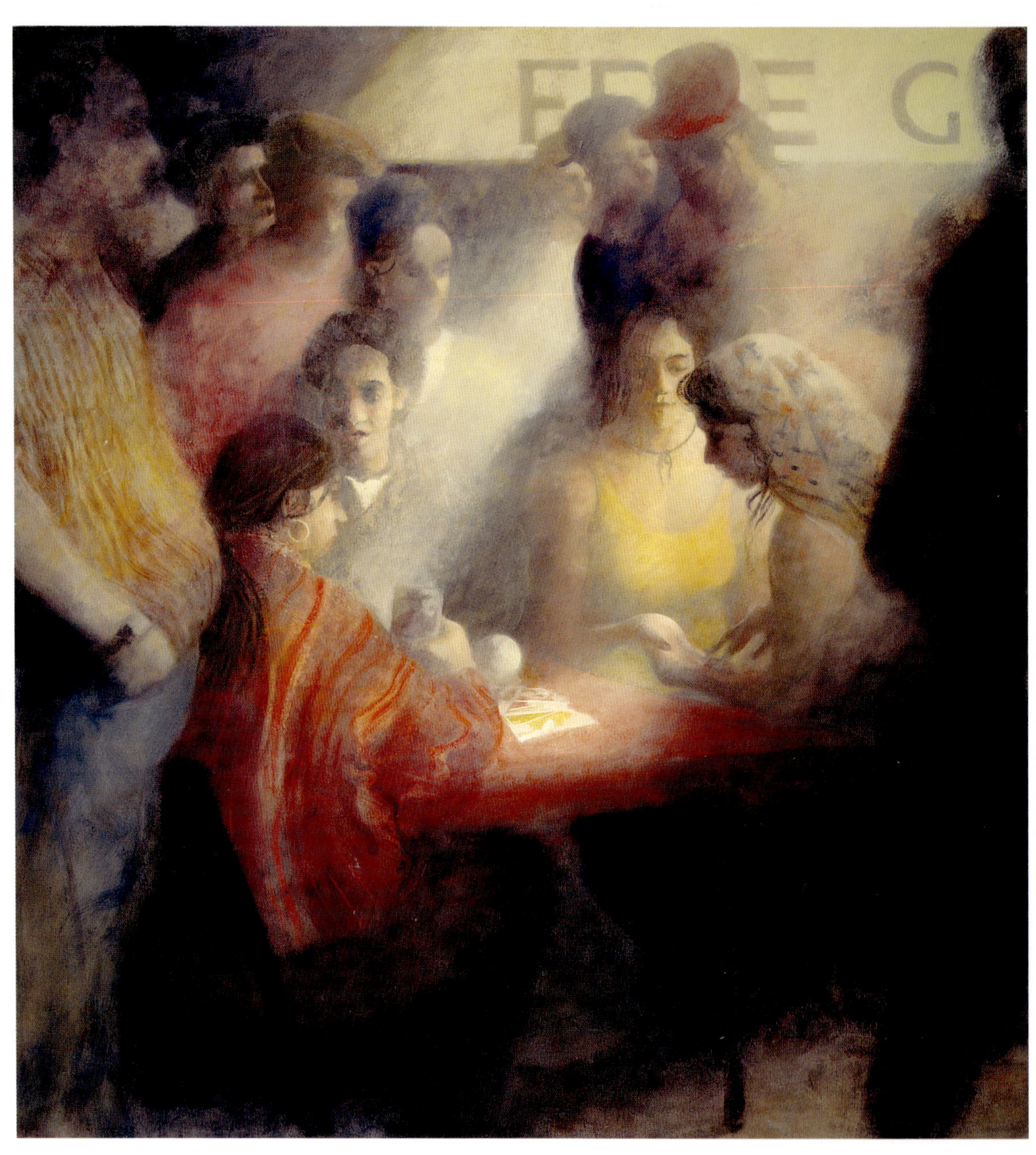

The Palmist I
1986
Oil on canvas
167.6×152.4 cm.
66×60 in.

Dervish Dancers, 63rd Street
1990
Oil on canvas
198.1×182.9 cm.
78×72 in.

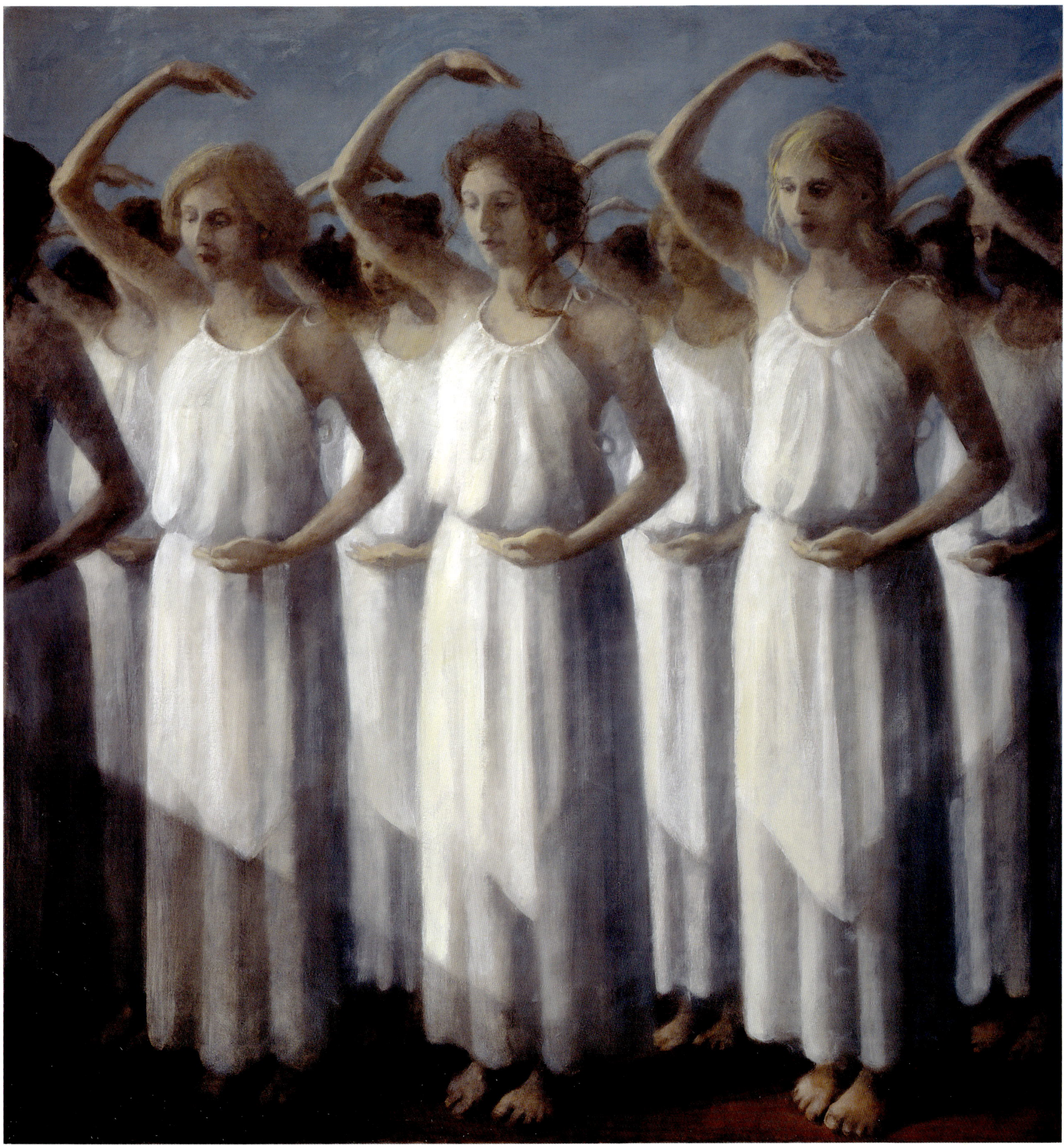

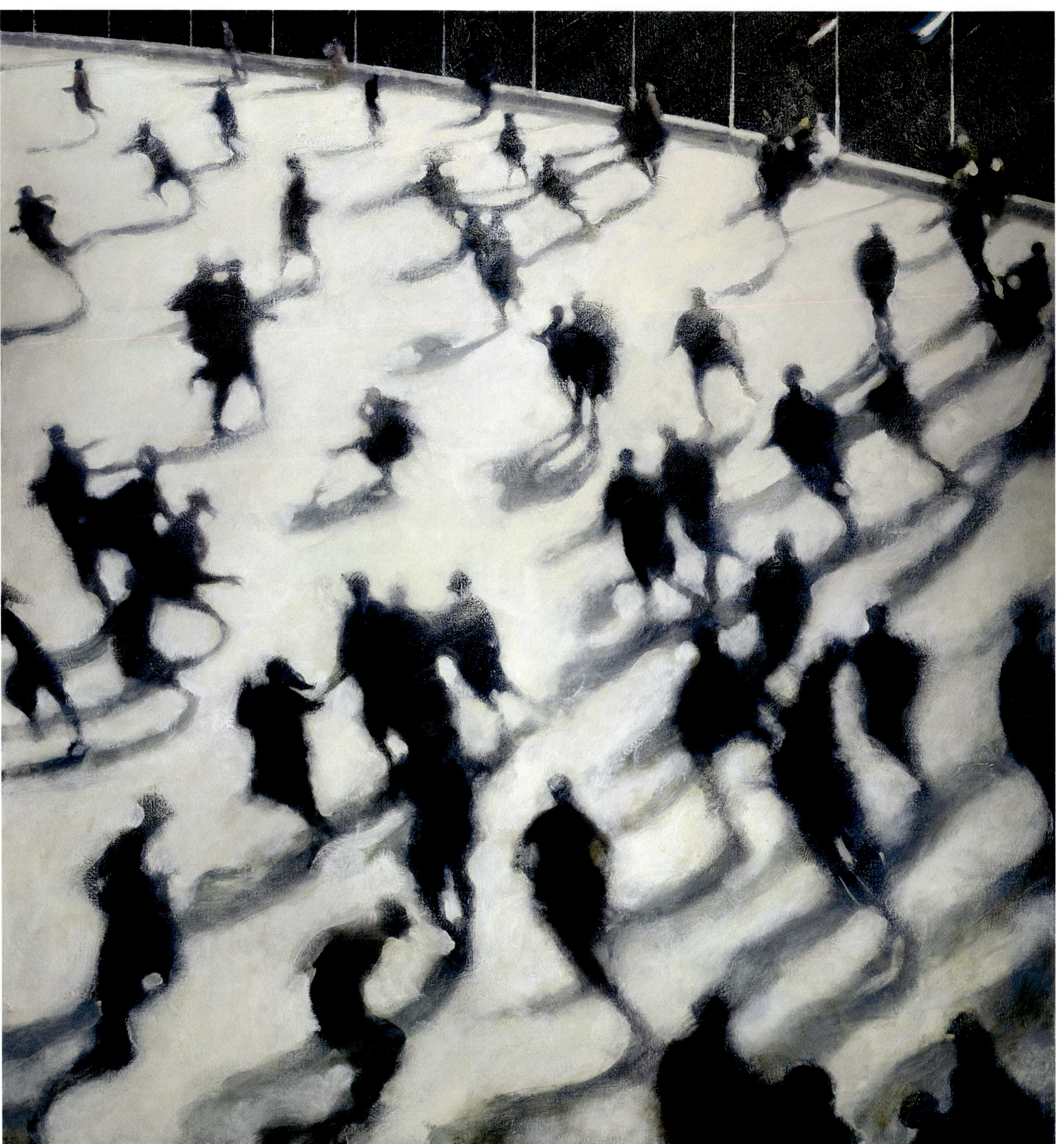

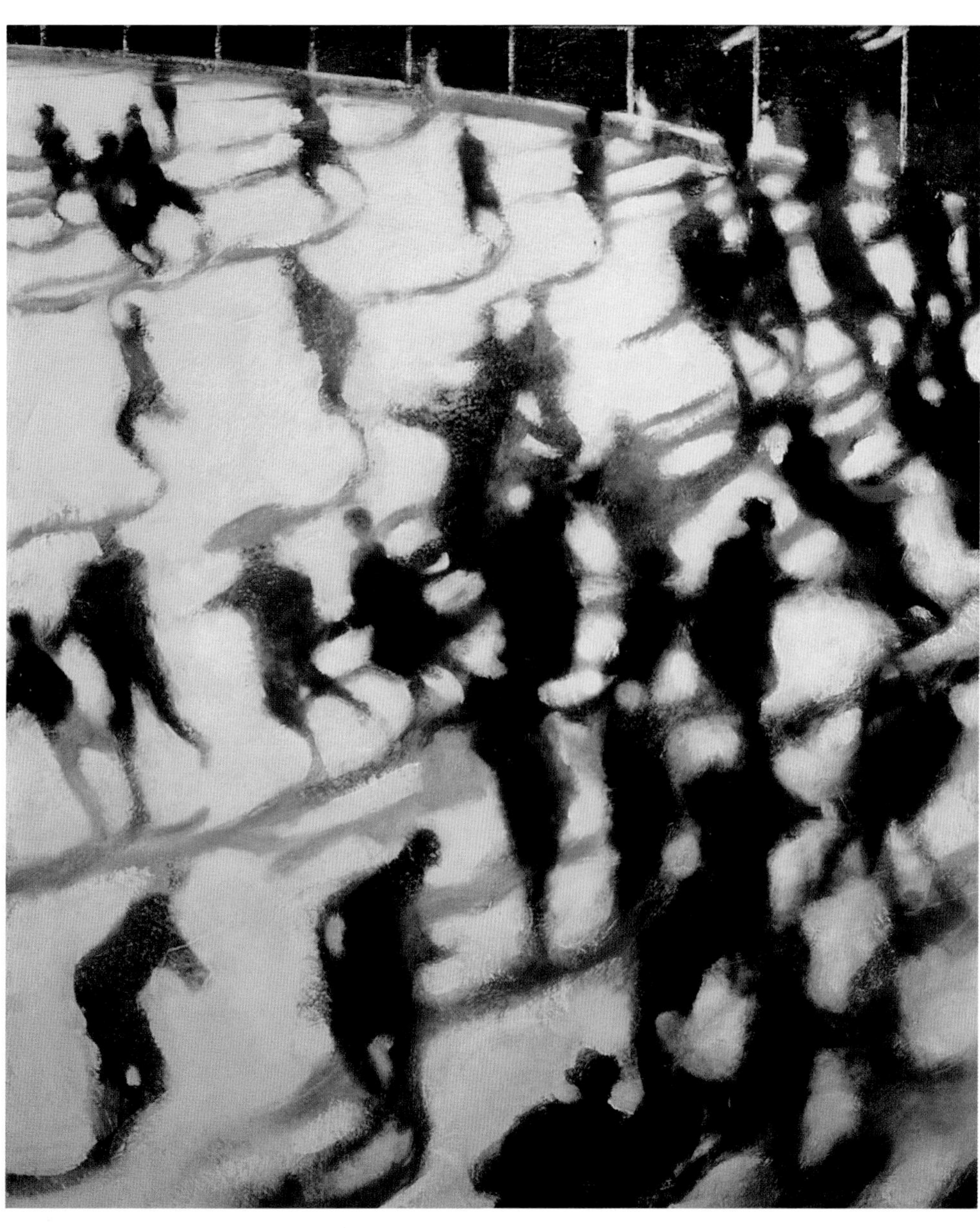

The Rink III
1990
Oil on canvas
198.1×182.8 cm.
78×72 in.

The Rink I
1990
Oil on canvas
91.4×76.2 cm.
36×30 in.

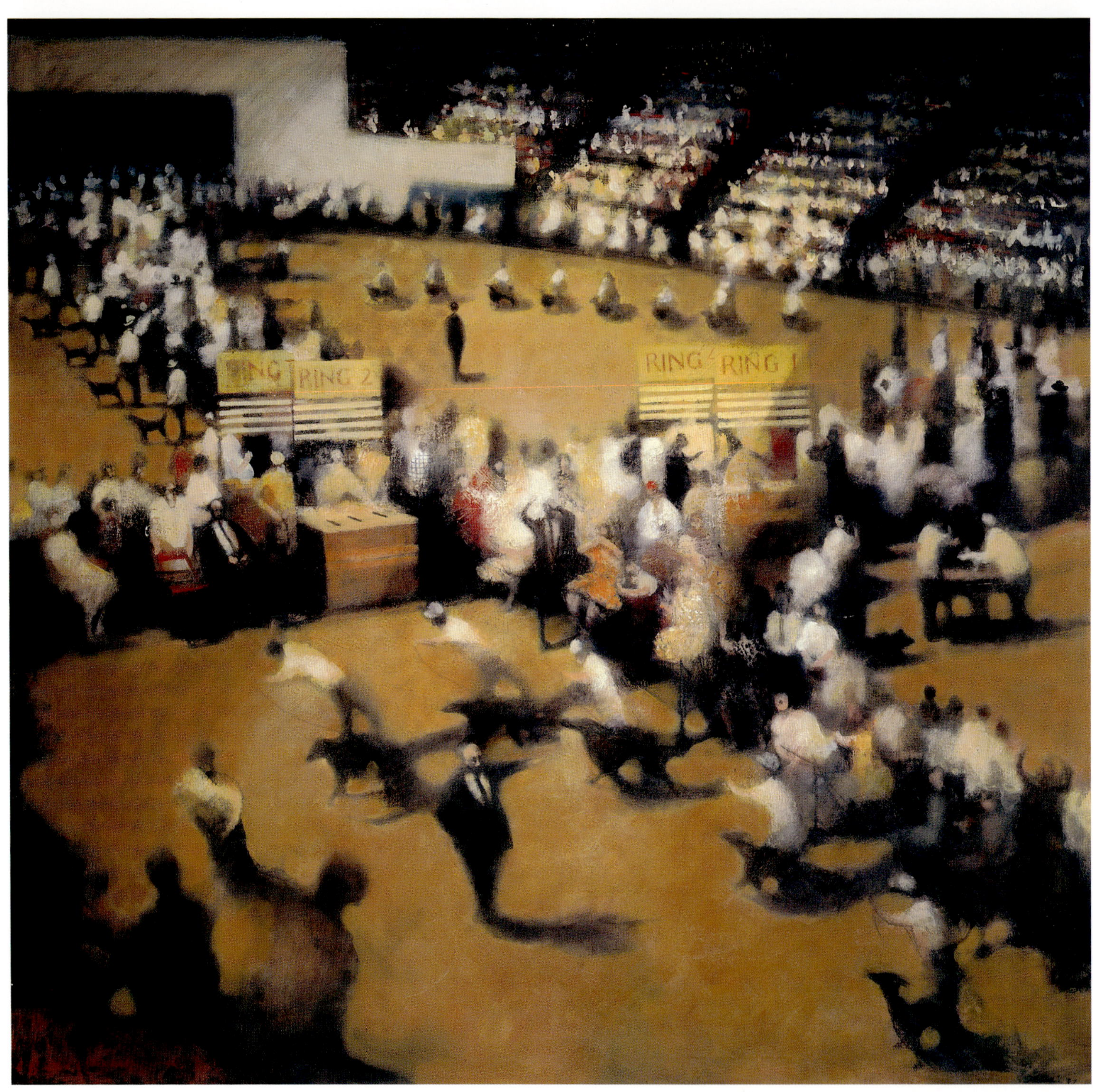

The Finalists I	**The Audience III**
1987	1990
Oil on canvas	Oil on canvas
152.4×152.4 cm.	167.6×152.4 cm.
60×60 in.	66×60 in.

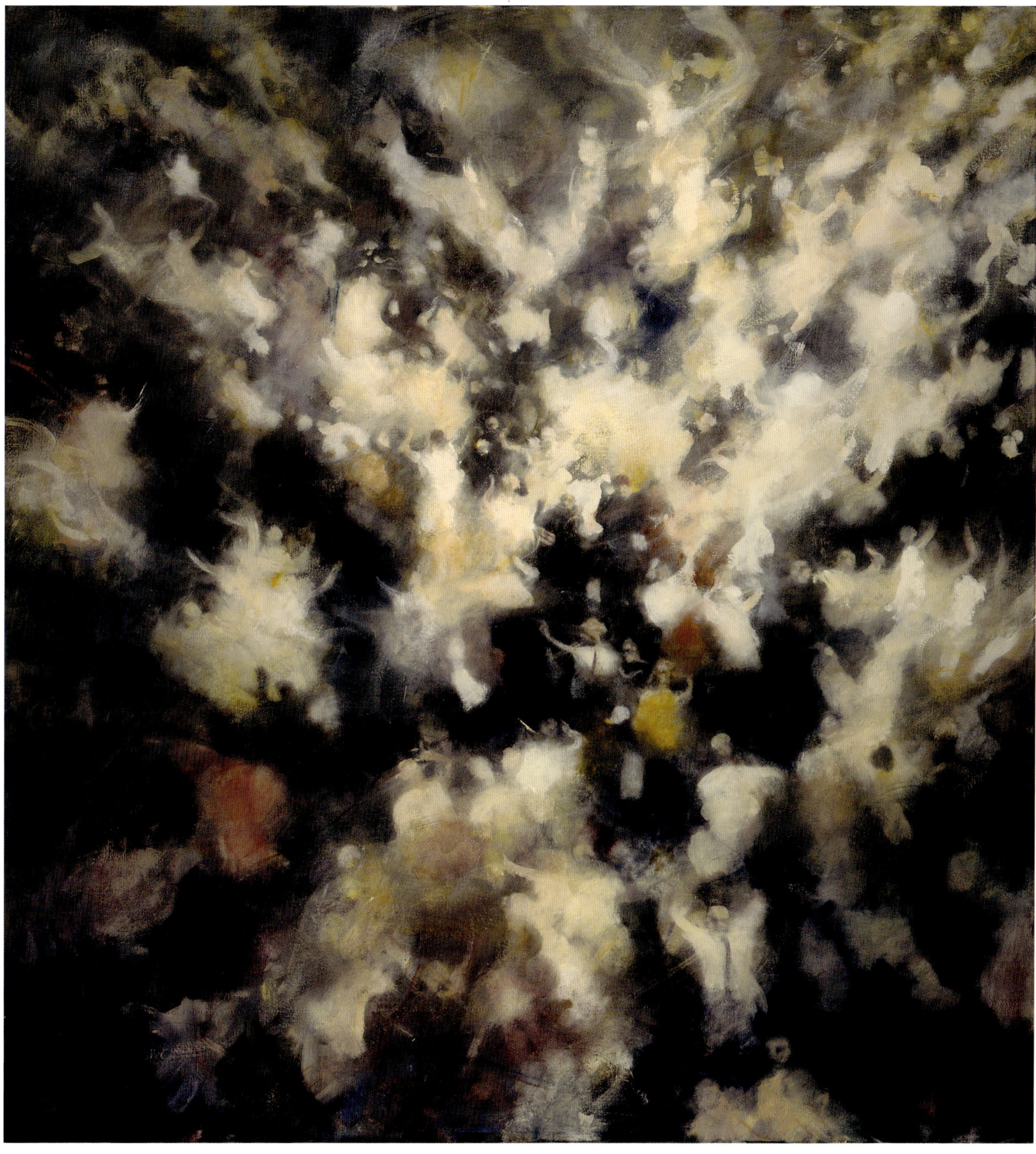

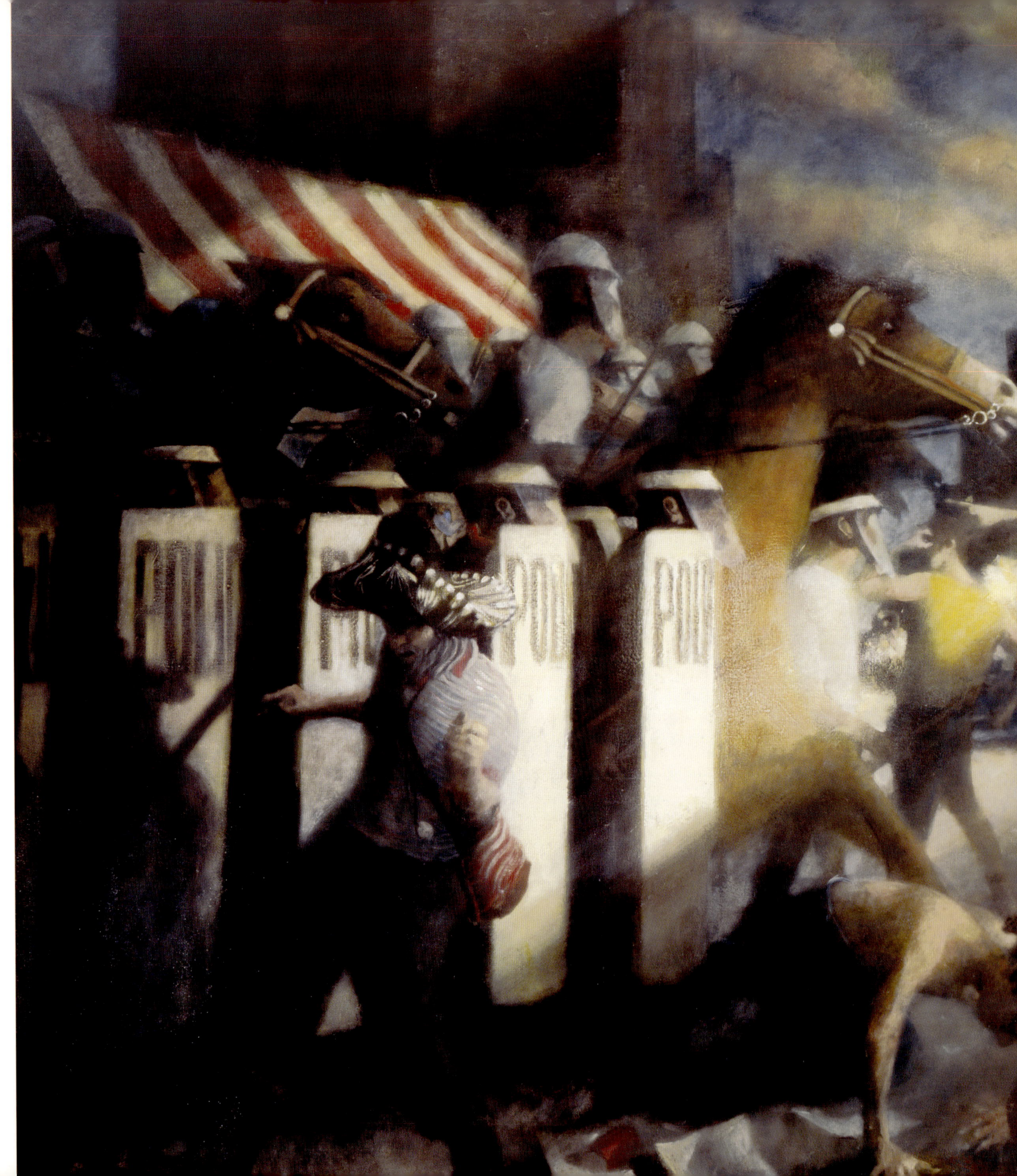

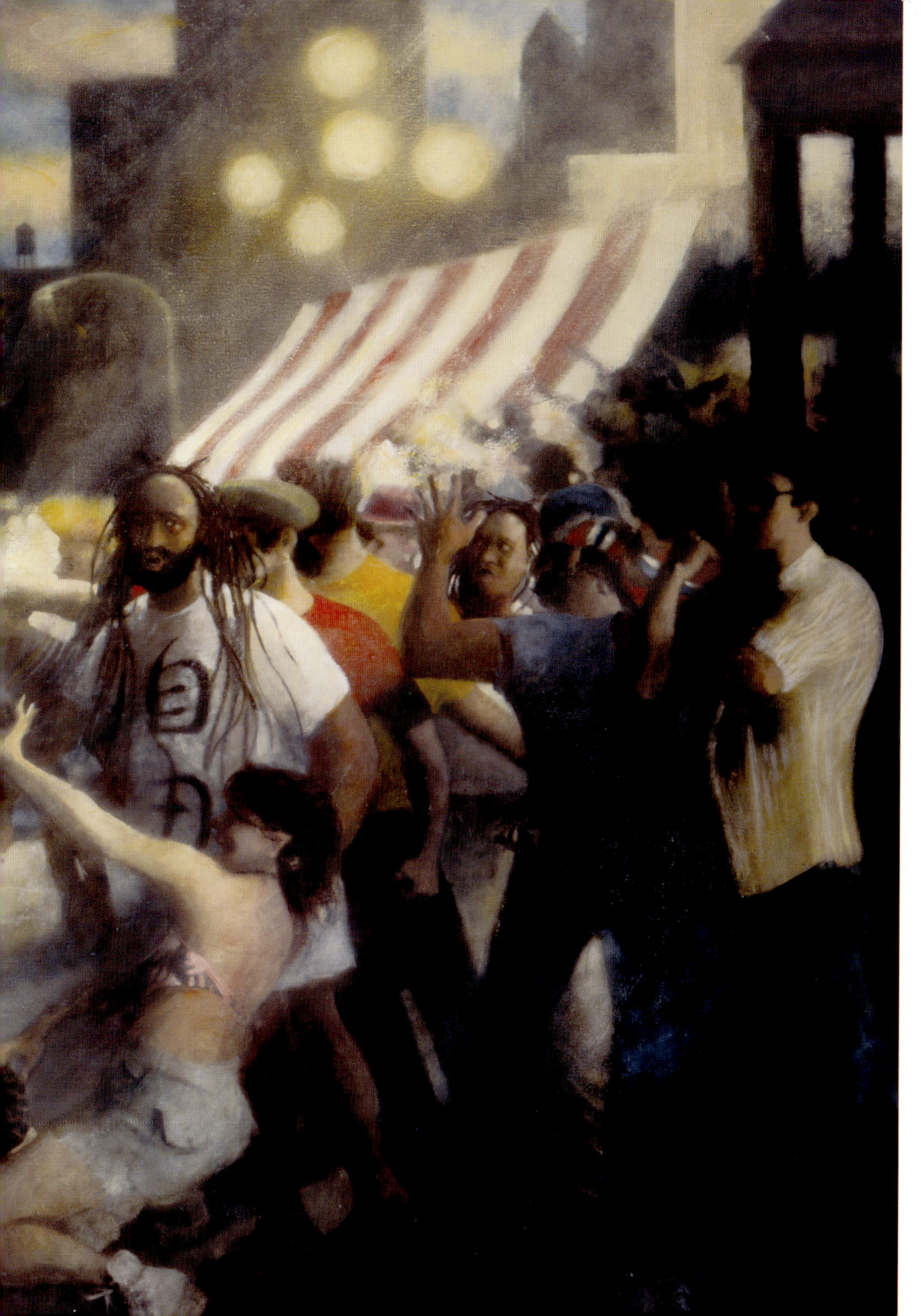

The Battle,
Tompkins Square
1990
Oil on canvas
243.8×365.8 cm.
96×144 in.

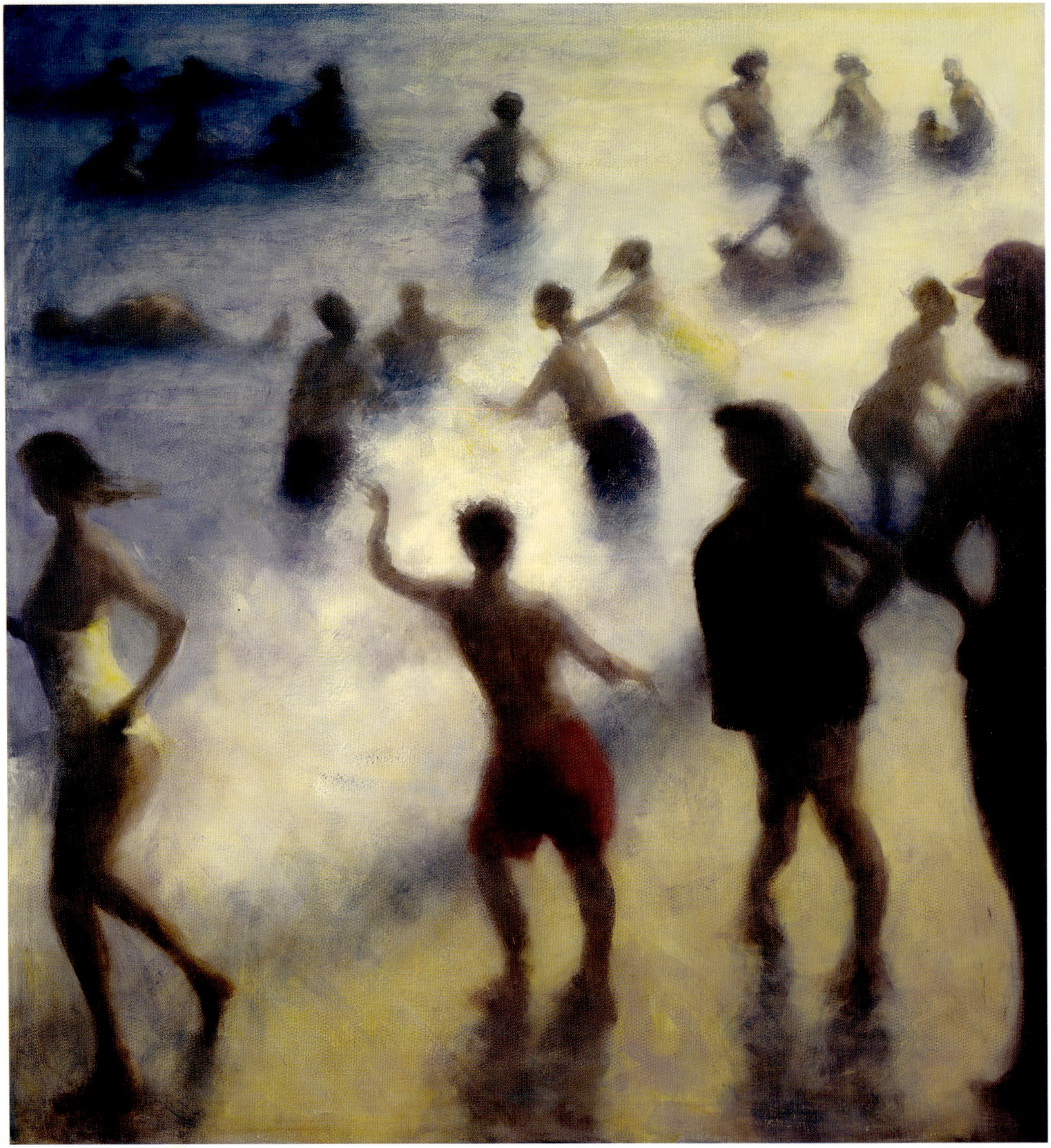

The Bathers IV
1992
Oil on canvas
198.1×182.8 cm.
78×72 in.

St Francis And The Birds, Coney Island
1992–96
Oil on canvas
198.1×152.4 cm.
78×60 in.

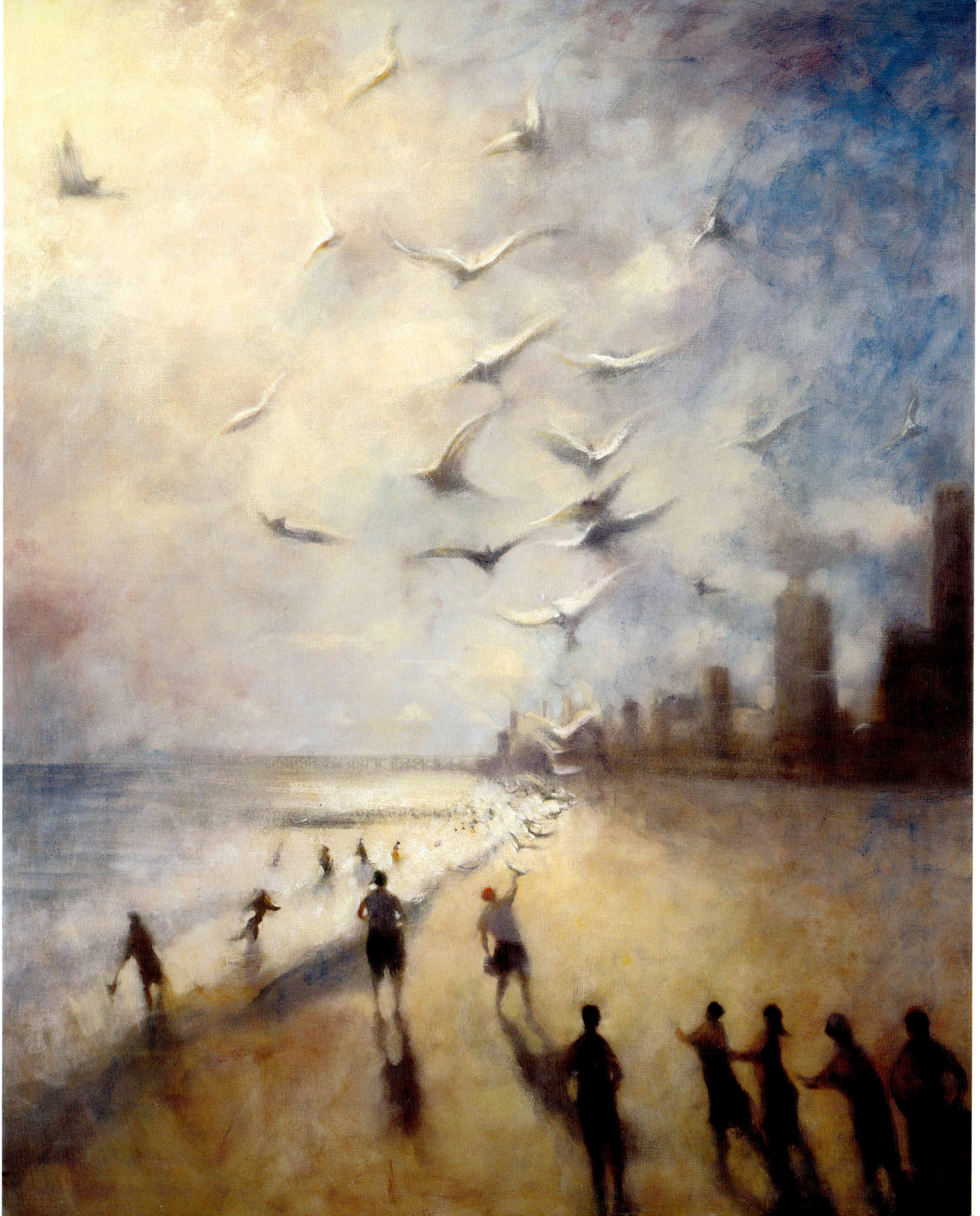

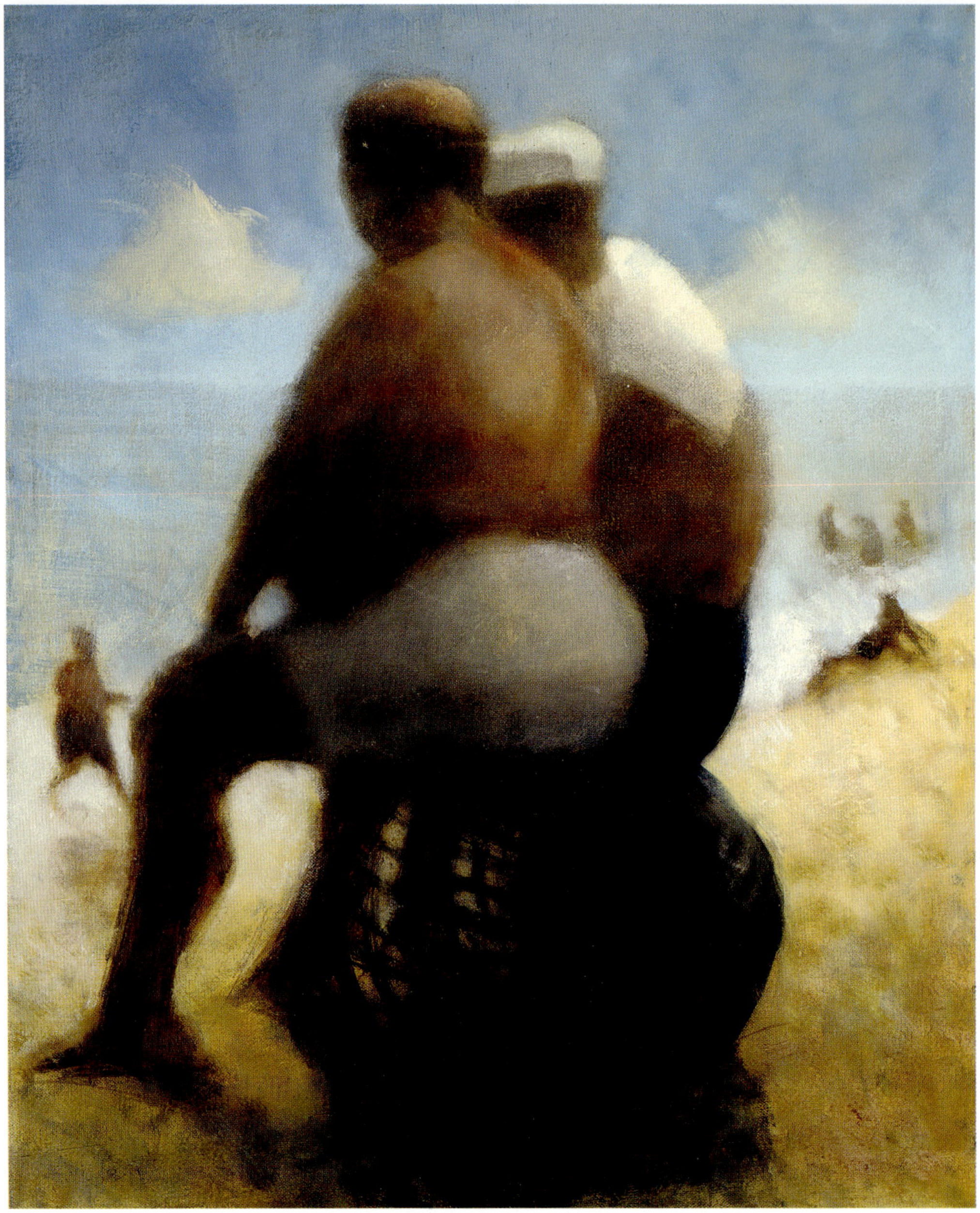

Two Men Talking, Coney Island
1992
Oil on canvas
50.8×40.6 cm.
20×16 in.

The Bather, Coney Island (Running Figure)
1992–99
Oil on canvas
152.4×106.7 cm.
60×42 in.

67

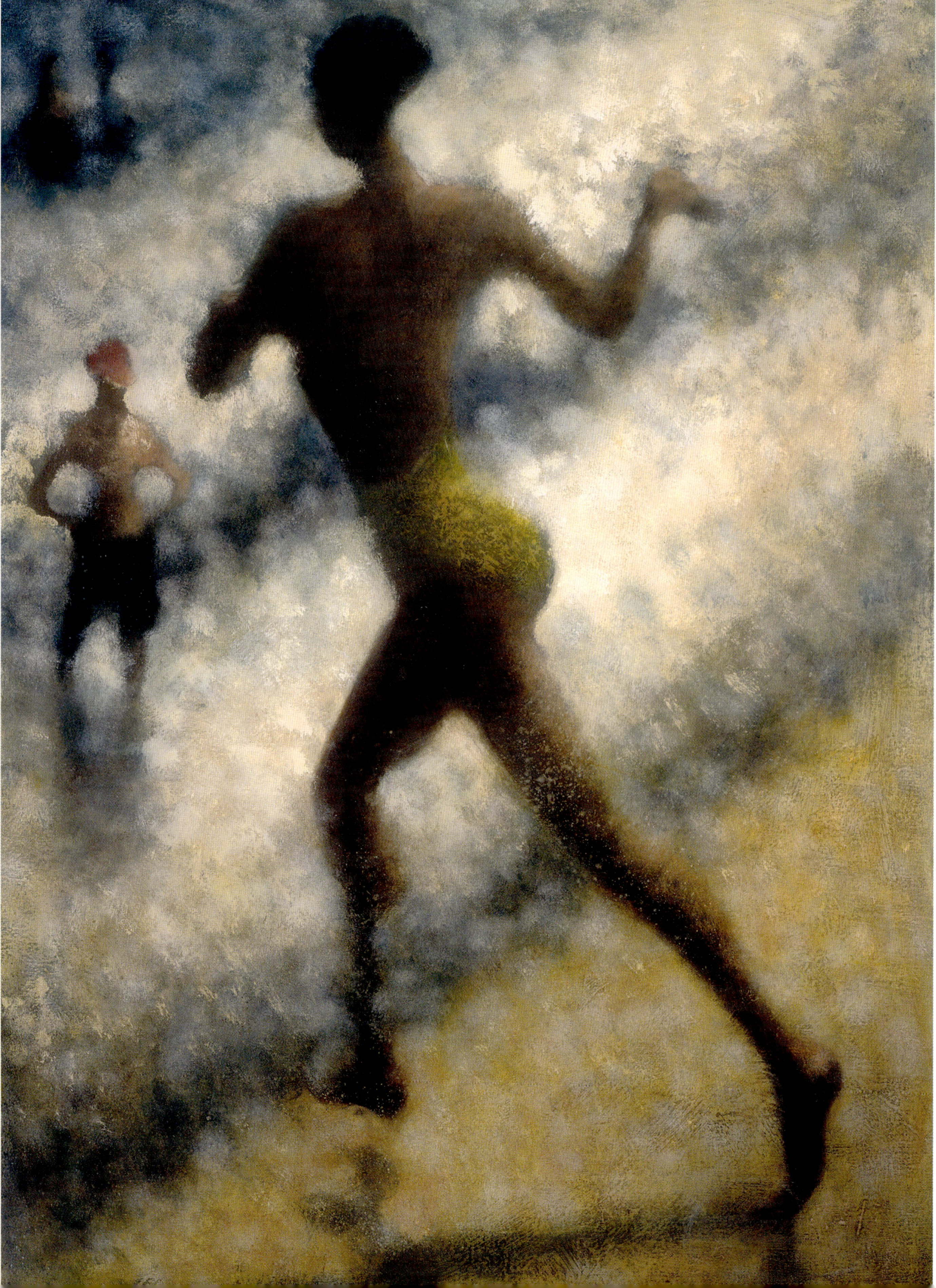

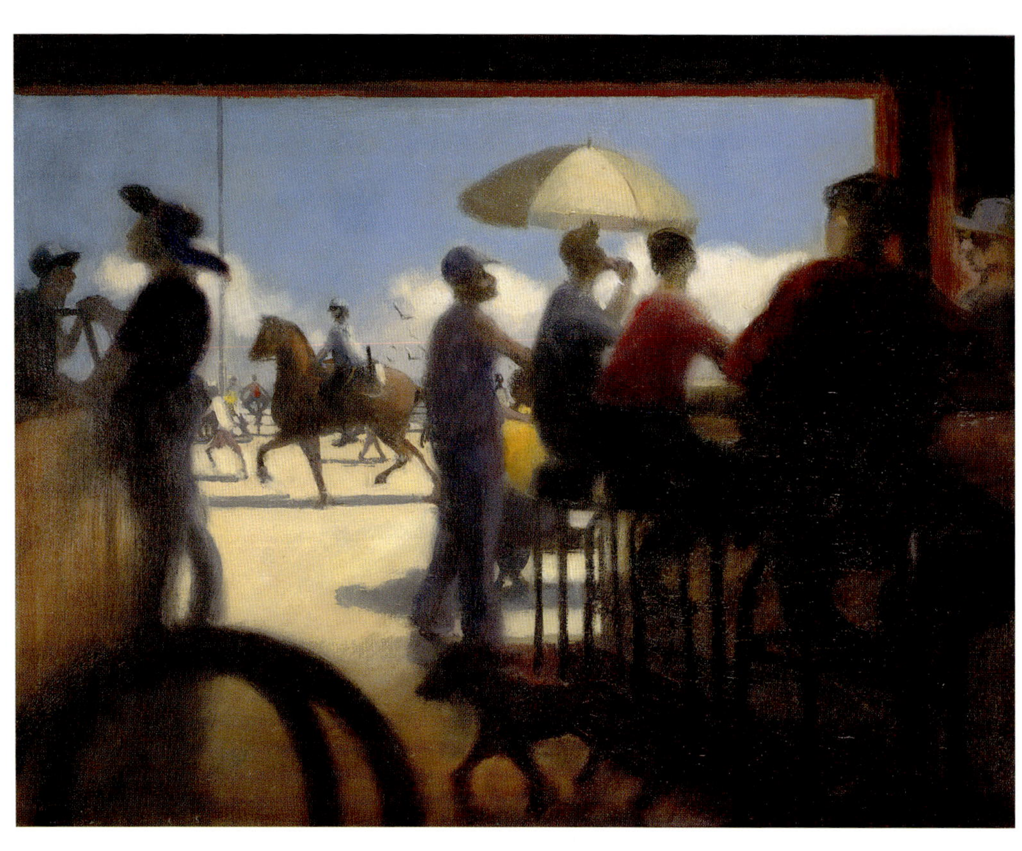

The Bar Coney Island I

1992
Oil on canvas
40.6×50.8 cm.
16×20 in.

Island Musée, Rape Of Reason I

1992–96
Oil on canvas
182.9×152.4 cm.
72×60 in.

RAND MUSSE
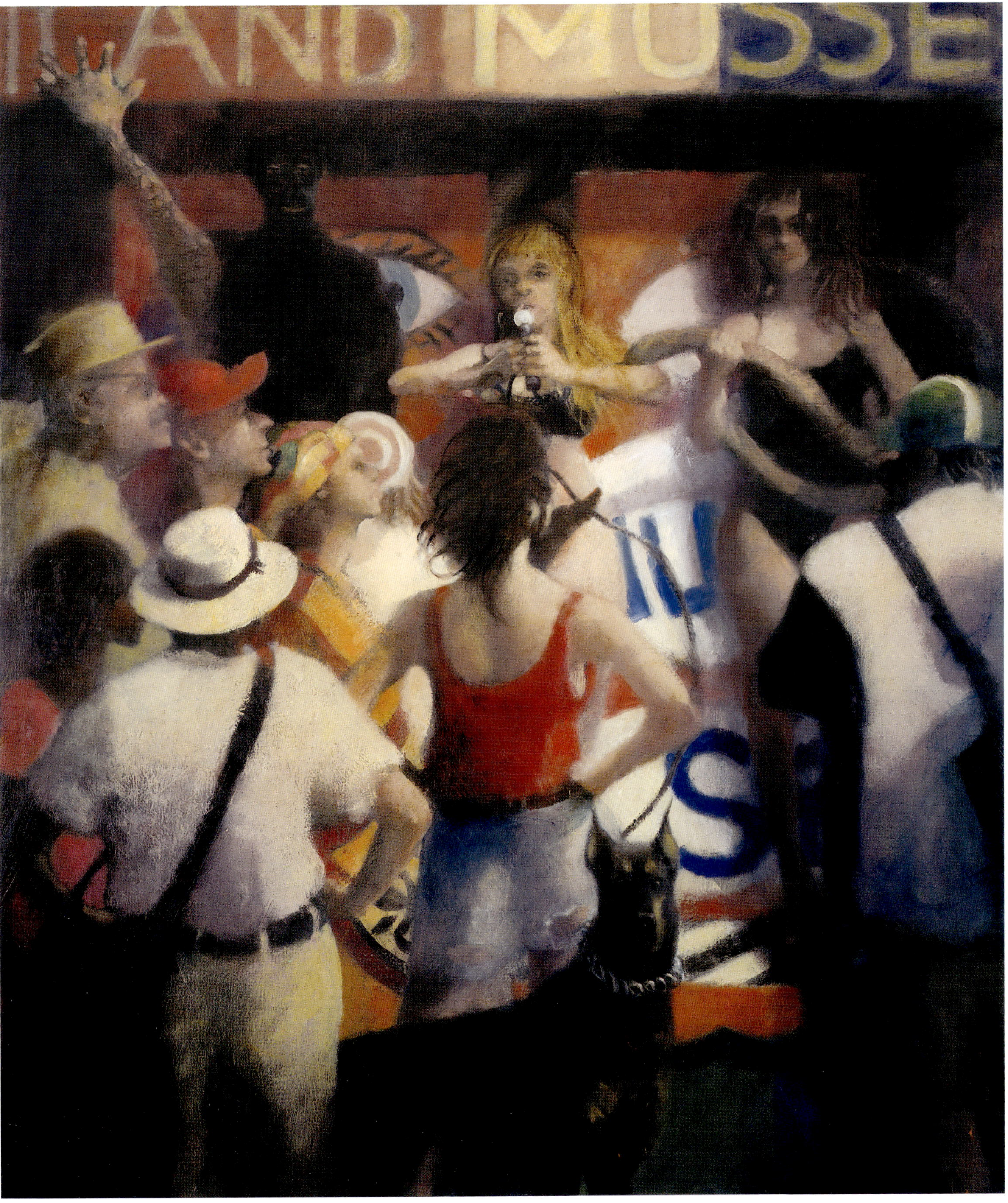

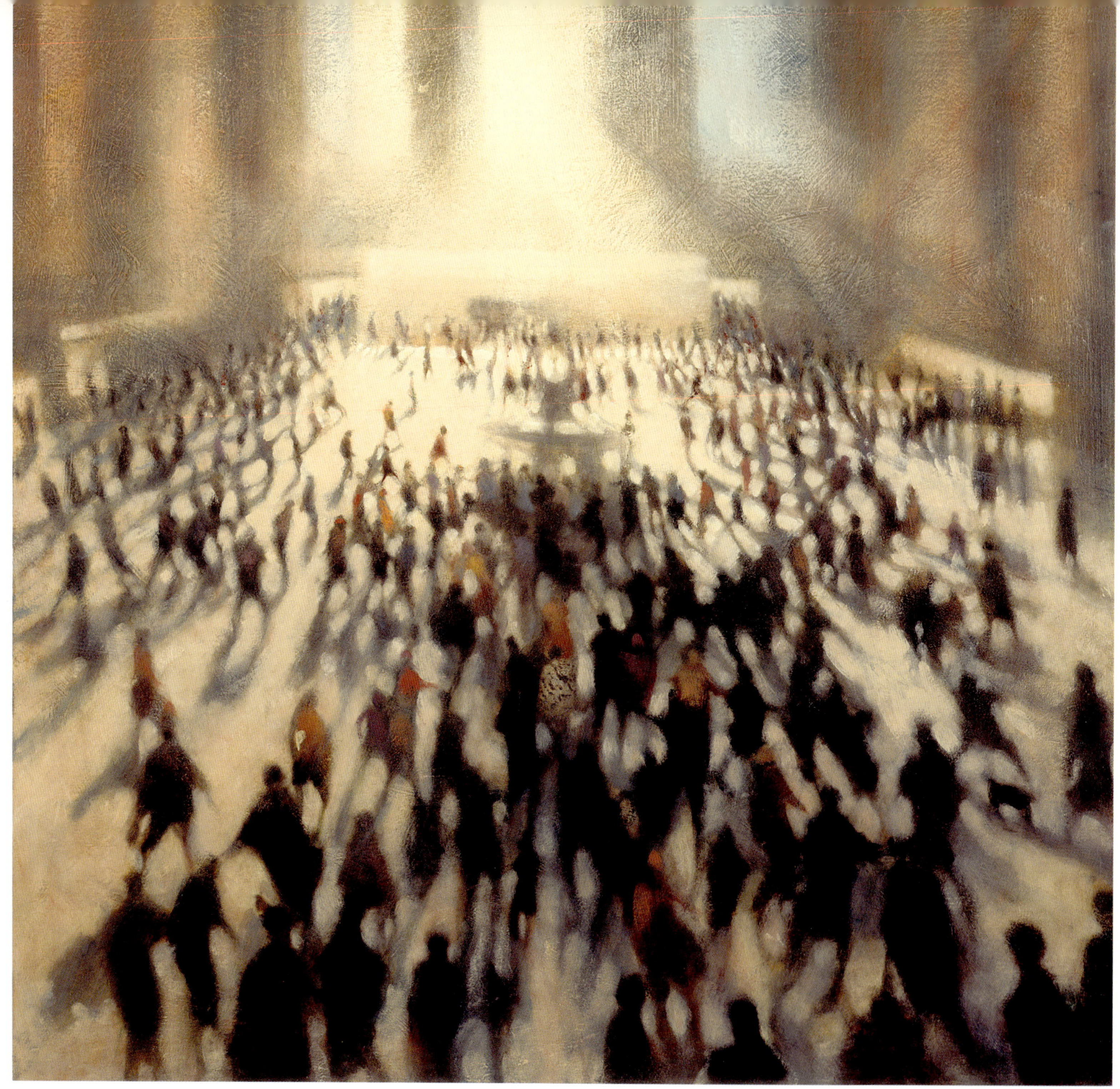

Concourse Grand Central Station II

1996
Oil on canvas
121.9 × 121.9 cm.
48 × 48 in.

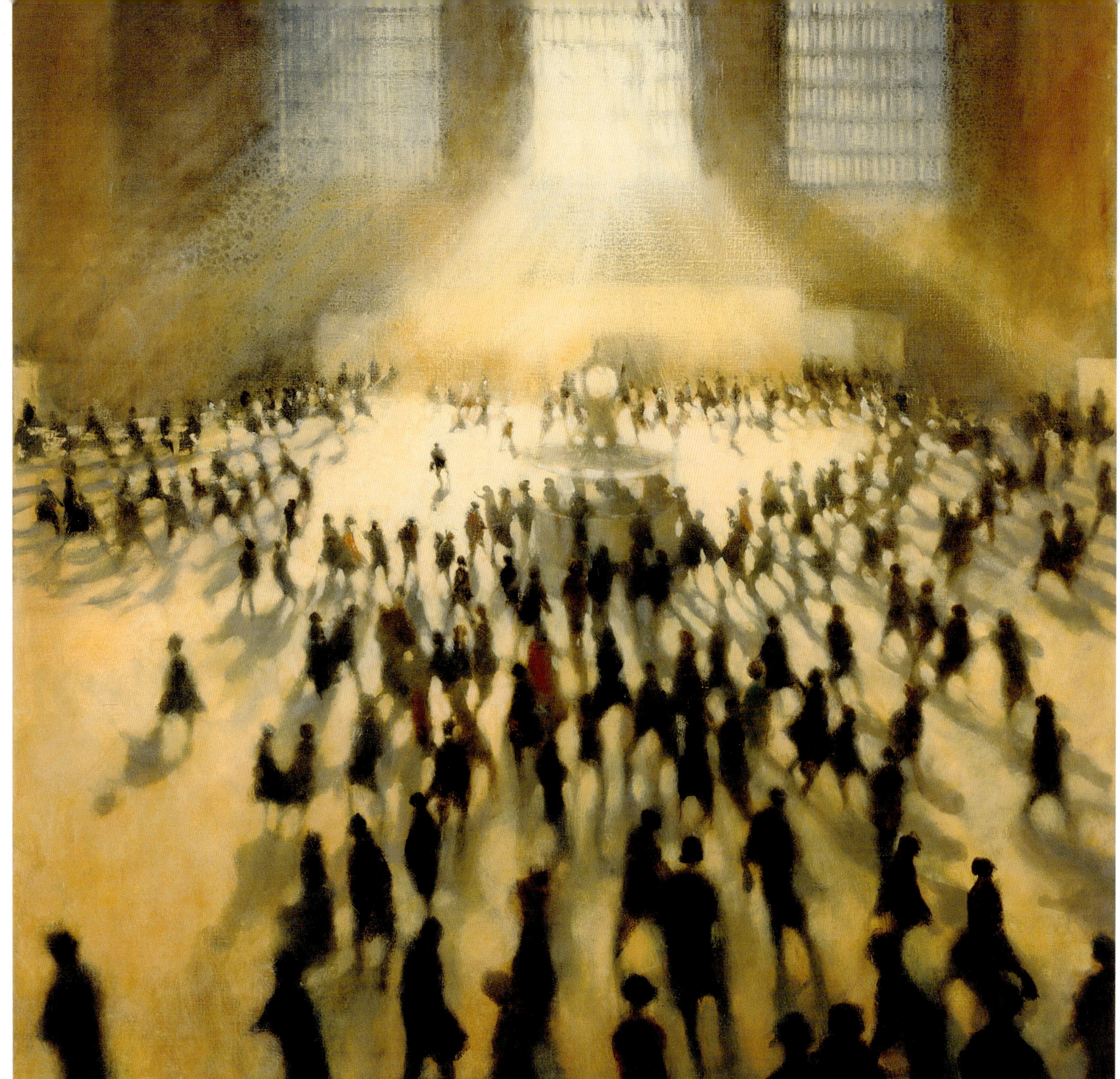

Incident Grand Central
1997
Oil on canvas
121.9 ×121.9 cm.
48×48 in.

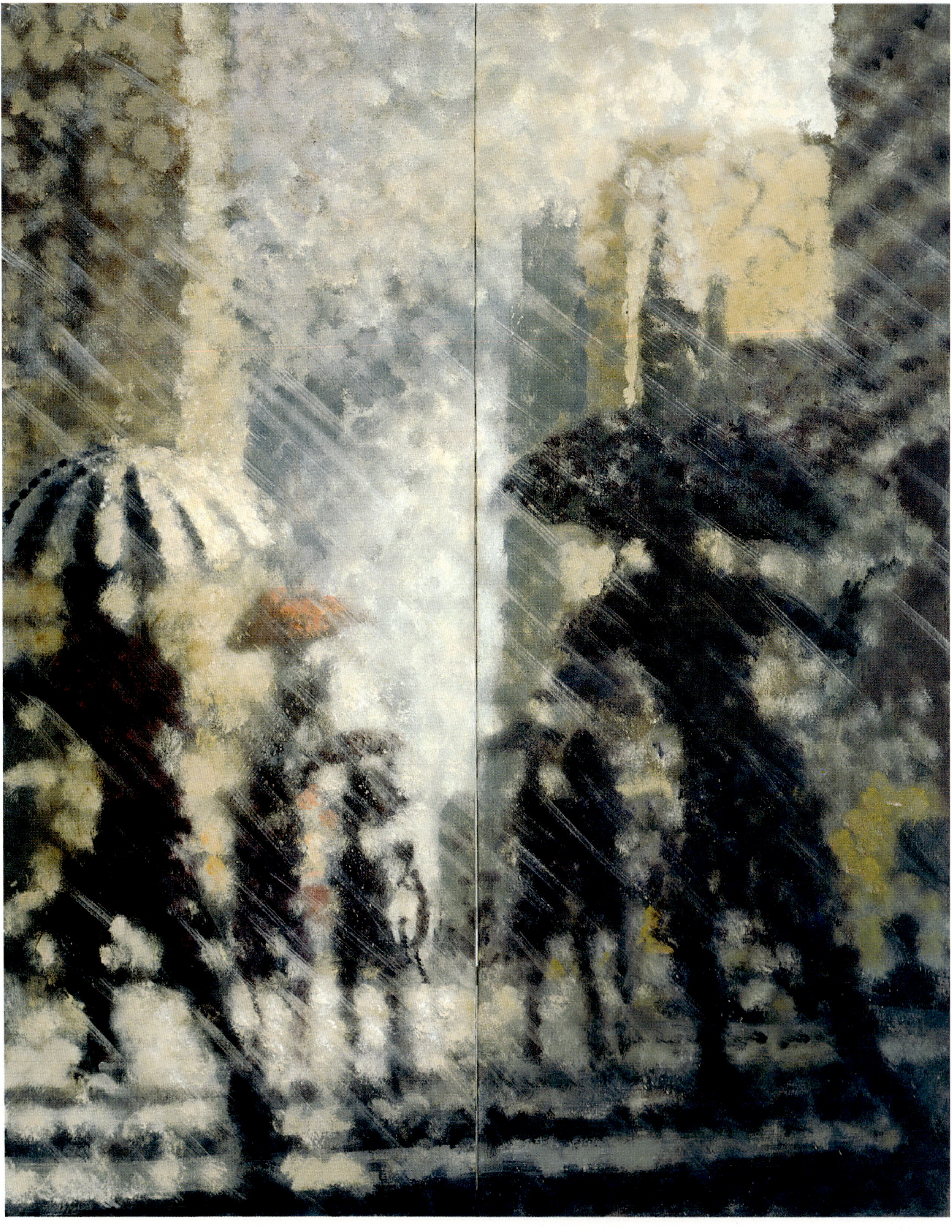

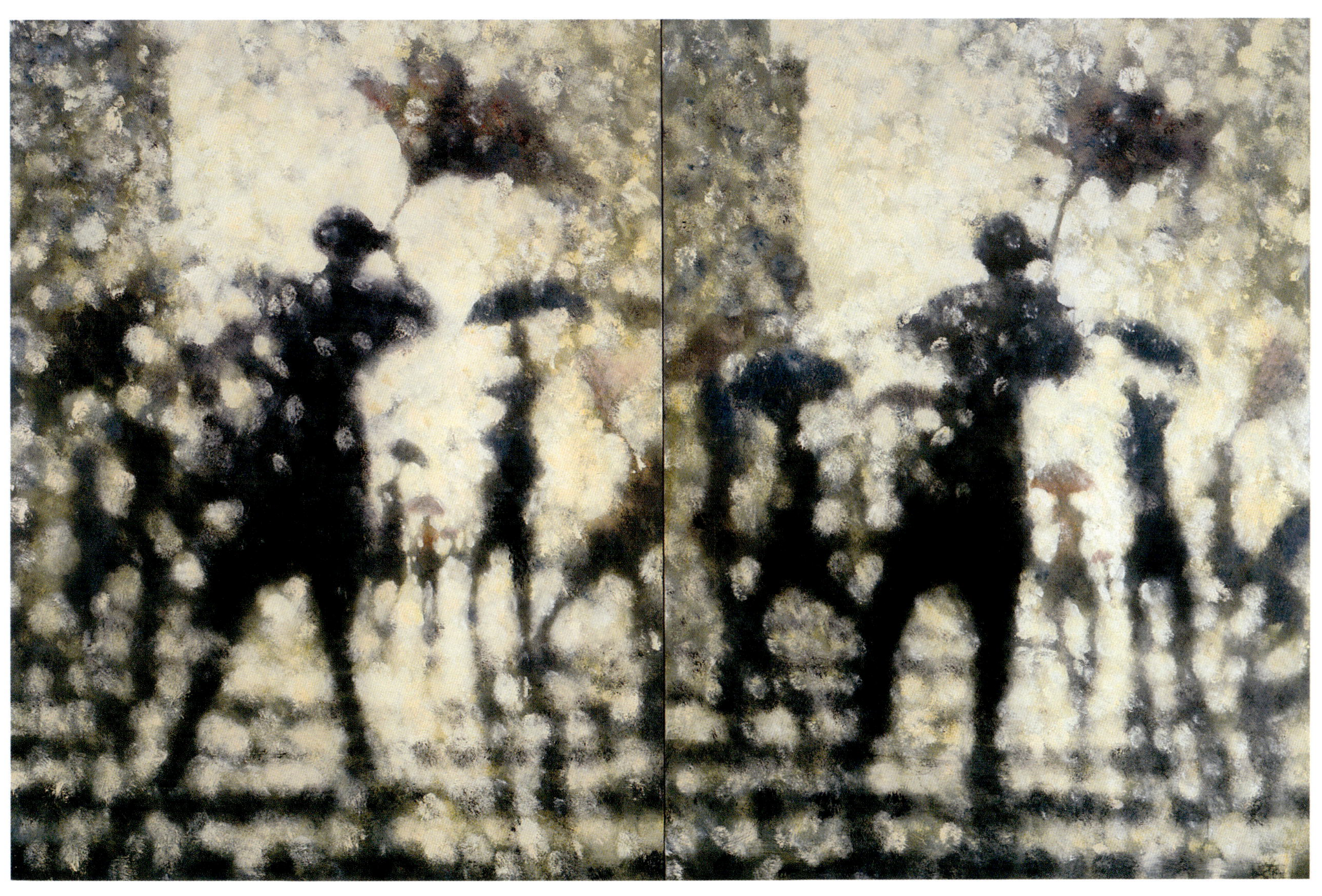

Crossing the Street In The Rain, 57th Street

1996
Oil on canvas
198.1×152.4 cm.
78×60 in.

Double Crossing NYC

1998
Oil on canvas
121.9×182.9 cm.
48×72 in.

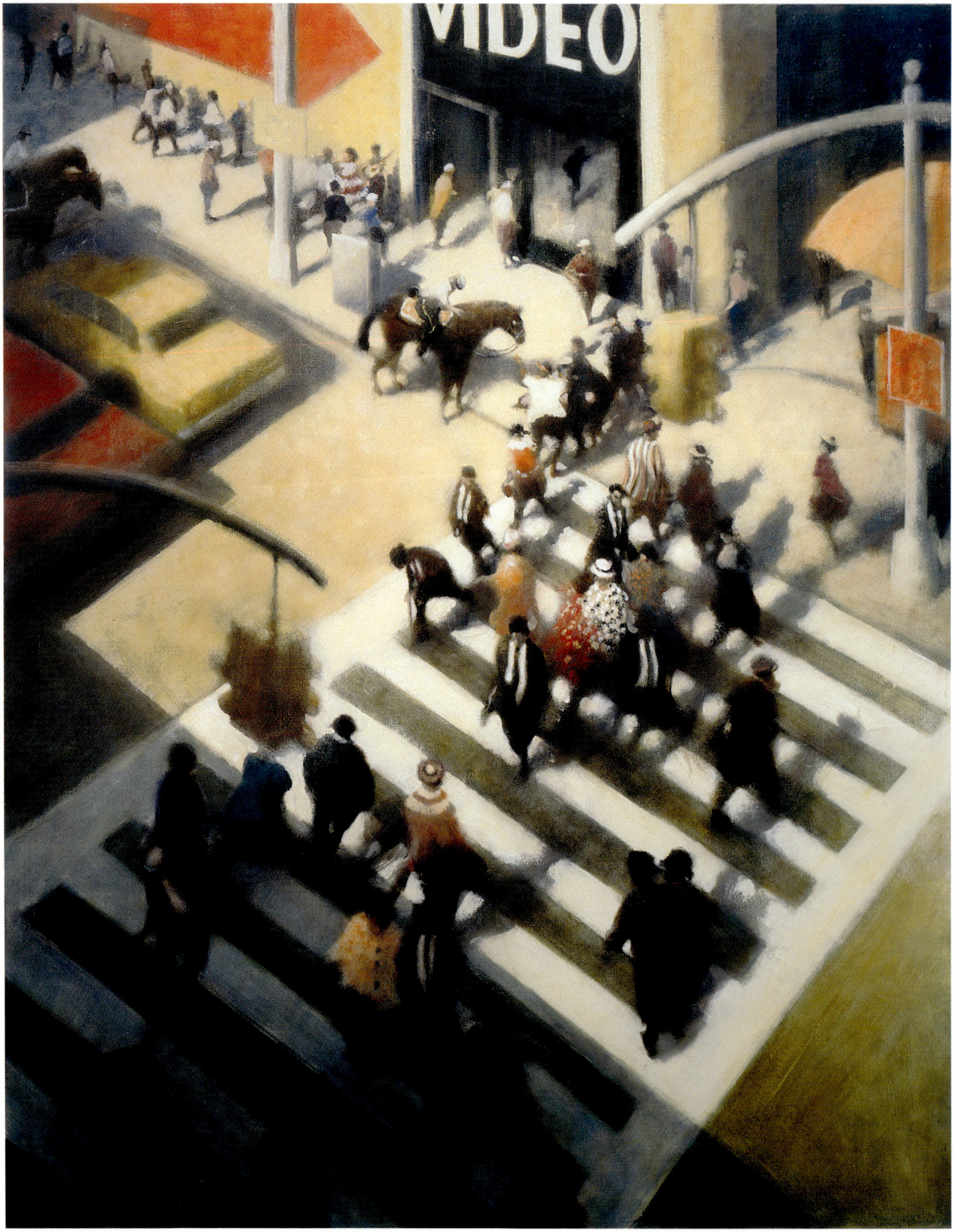

VIDEO

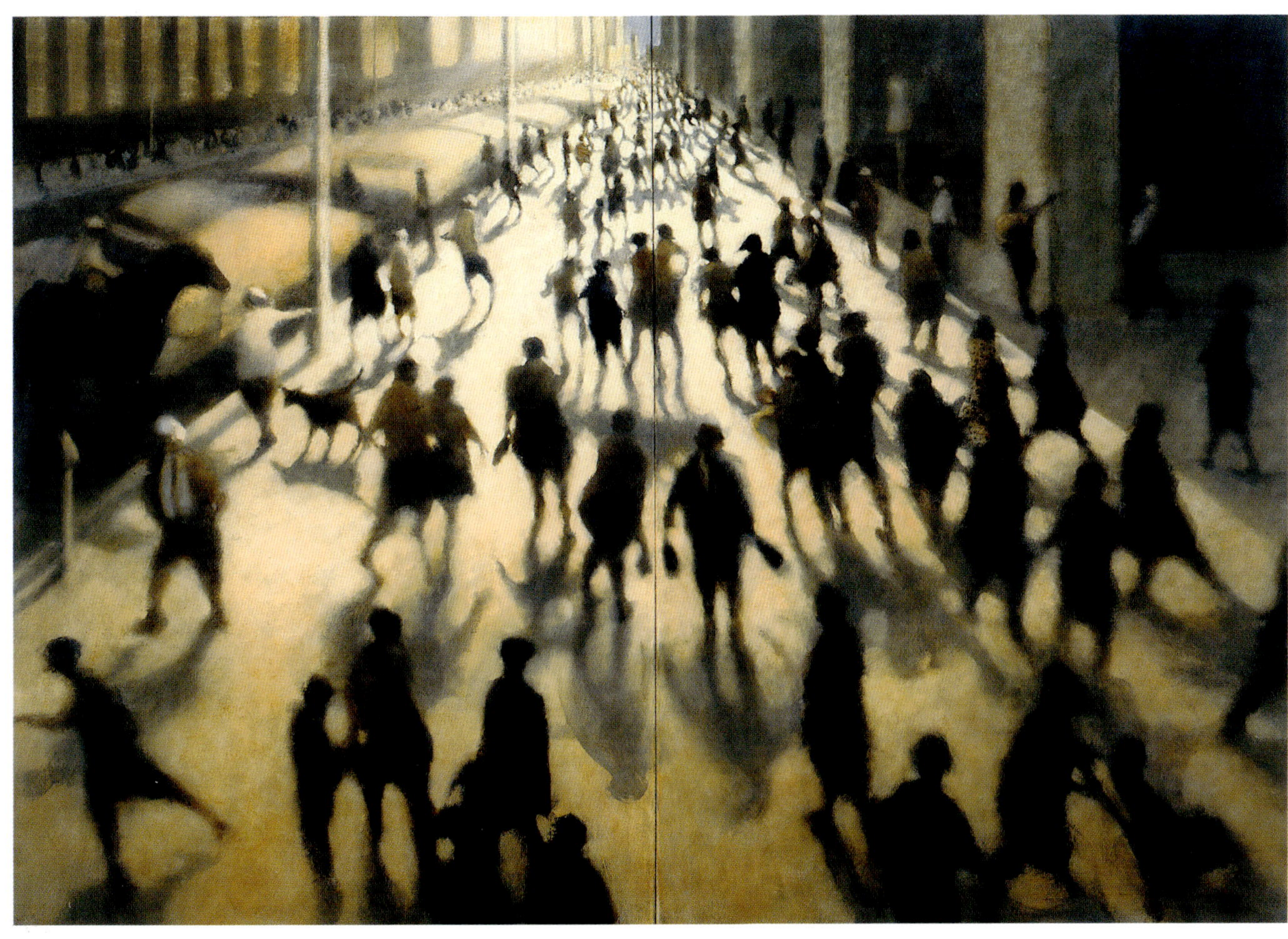

75

Times Square Incident I

1998

Oil on canvas

198.1×152.4 cm.

78×60 in.

Walking Down Broadway II

1998

Diptych; oil on canvas

152.4×213.4 cm.

60×84 in.

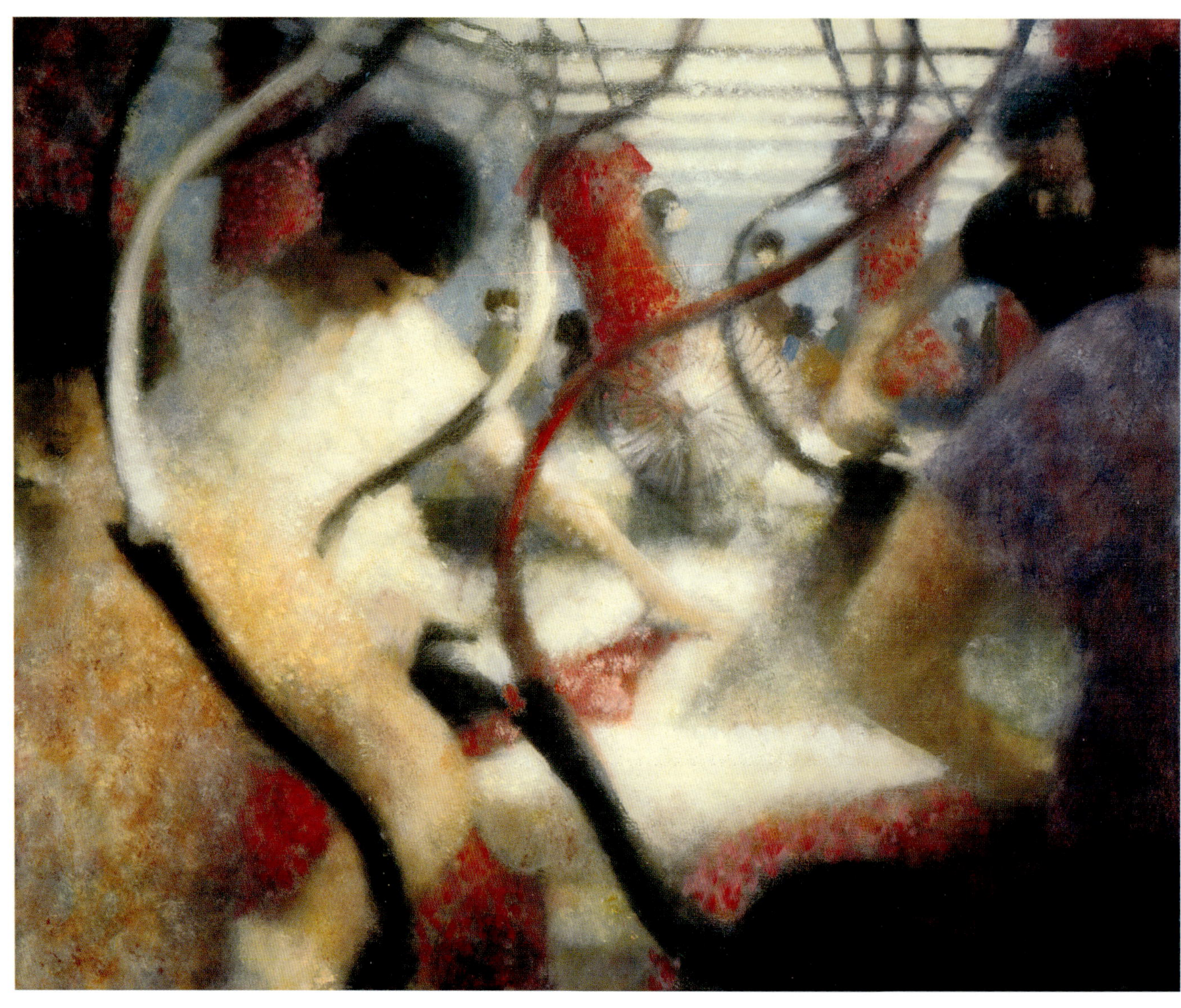

The Ironers, 36th Street II
1996
Oil on canvas
76.2×91.4 cm.
30×36 in.

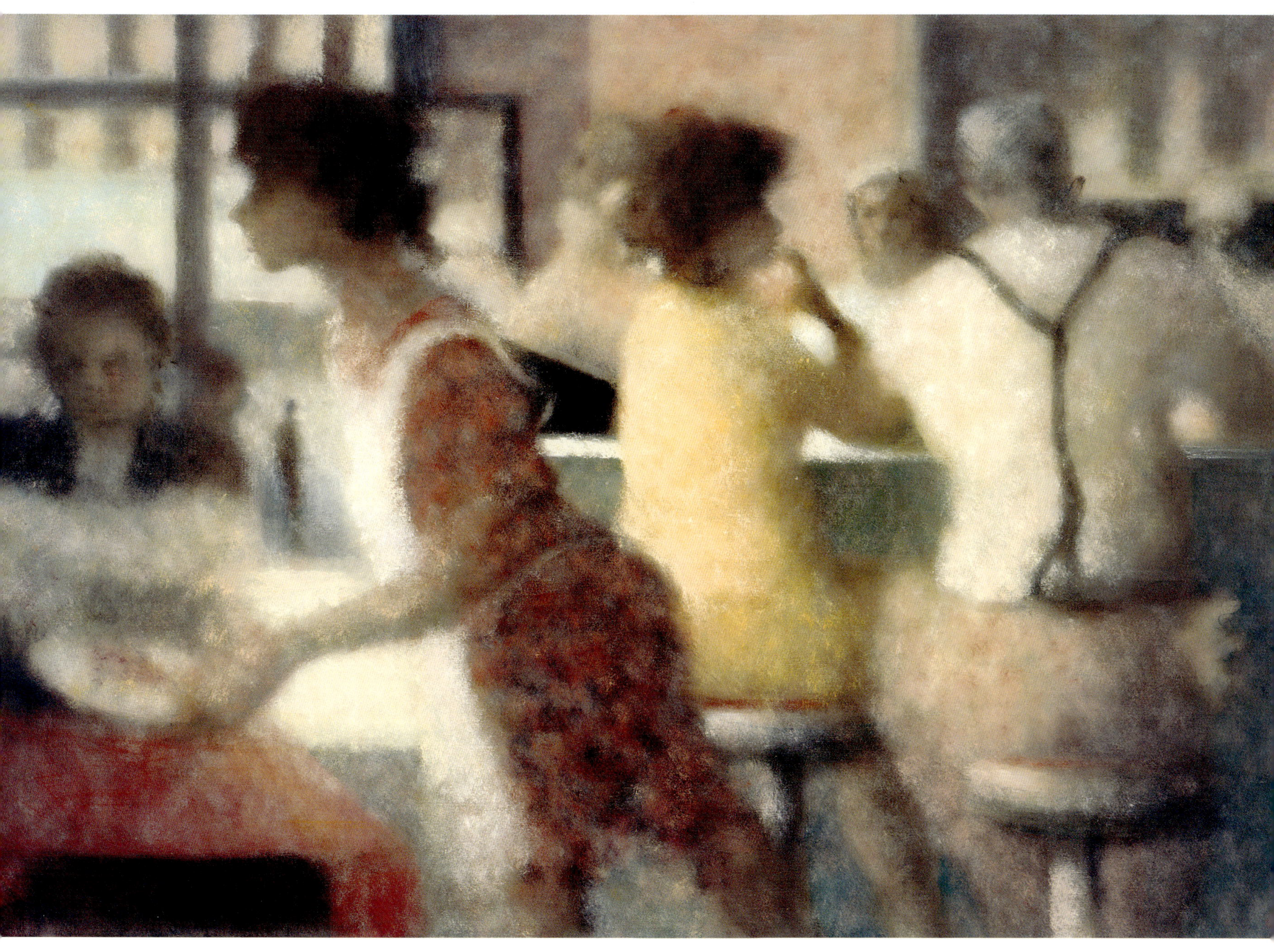

Matty's Diner II
1986
Oil on canvas
106.7×152.4 cm.
42×60 in.

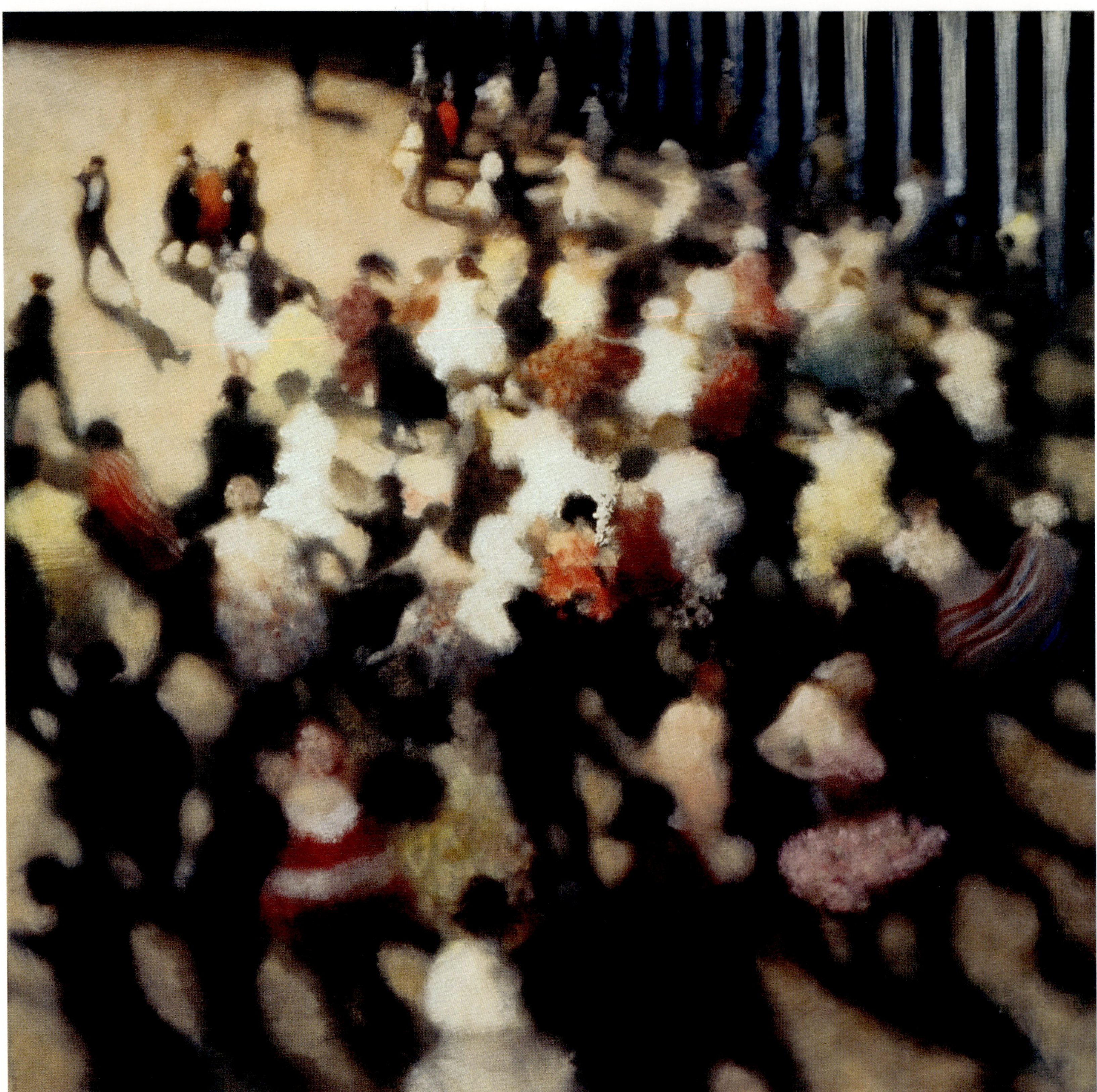

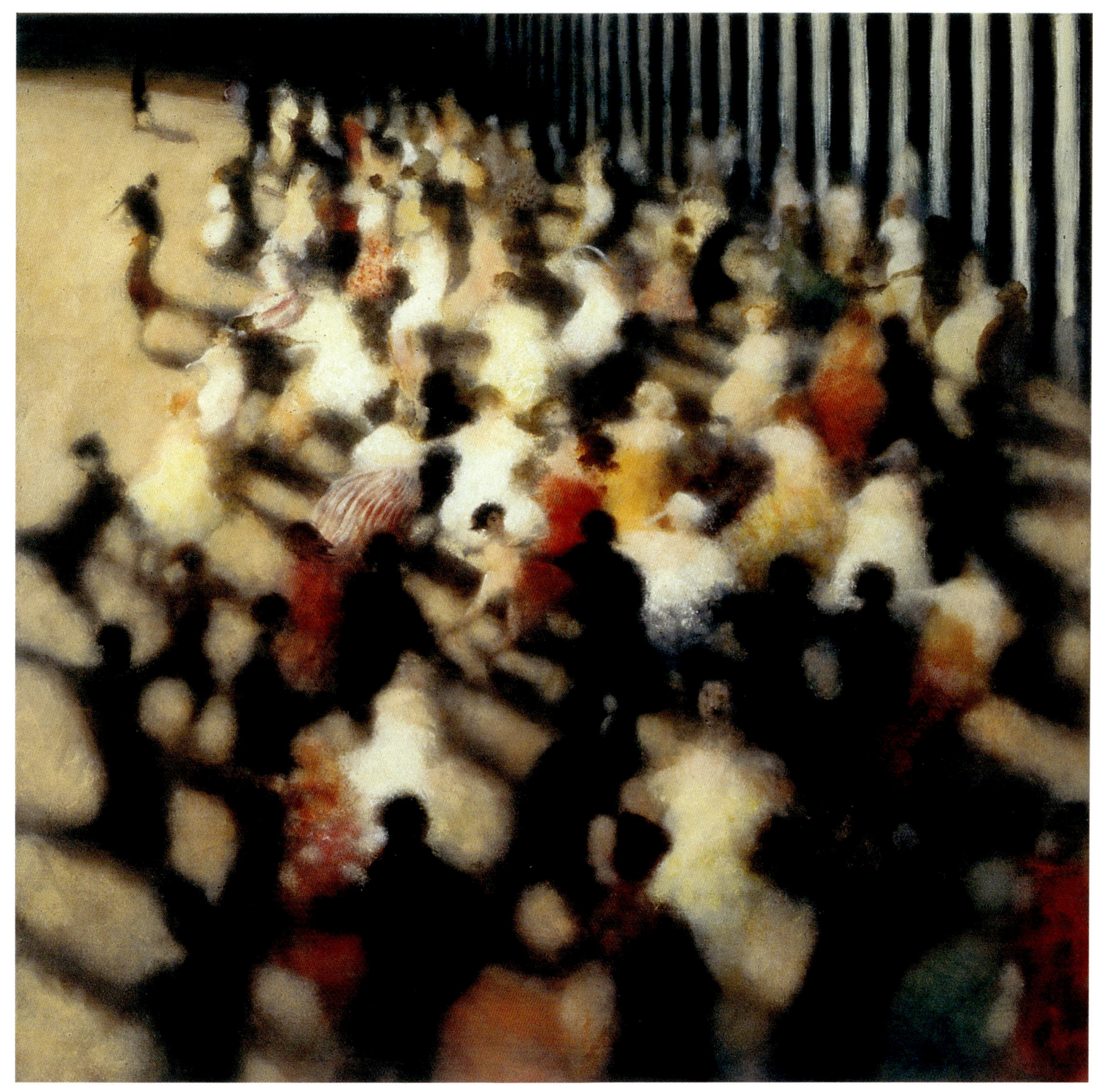

Roseland V

1998

Oil on canvas

152.4×152.4 cm.

60×60 in.

Roseland IV

1998

Oil on canvas

152.4×152.4 cm.

60×60 in.

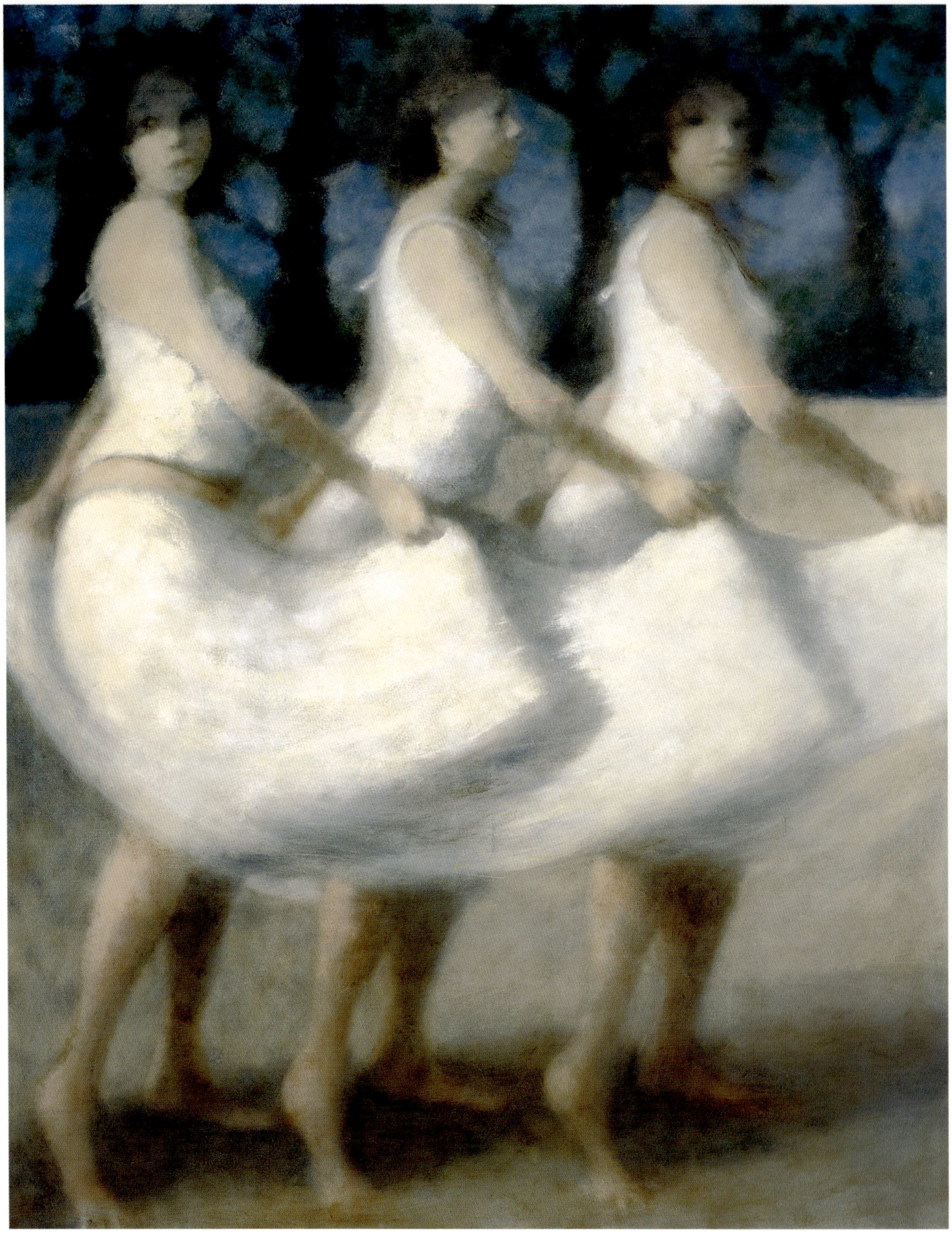

The Dancers, Washington Square
1999
Oil on canvas
198.1×152.4 cm.
78×60 in.

Before The Meeting, Great Lawn I
2000
Oil on canvas
121.9×121.9 cm.
48×48 in.

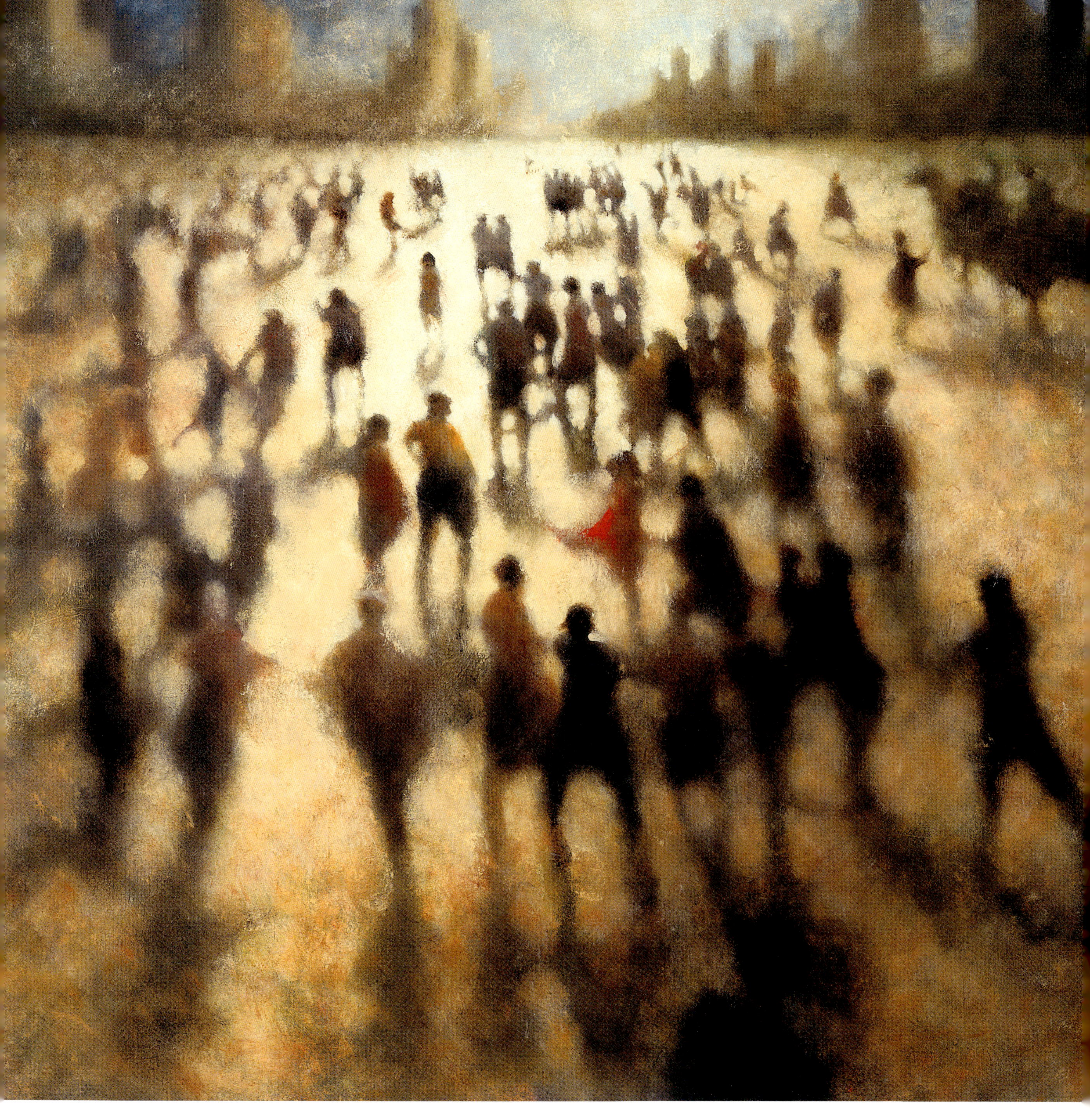

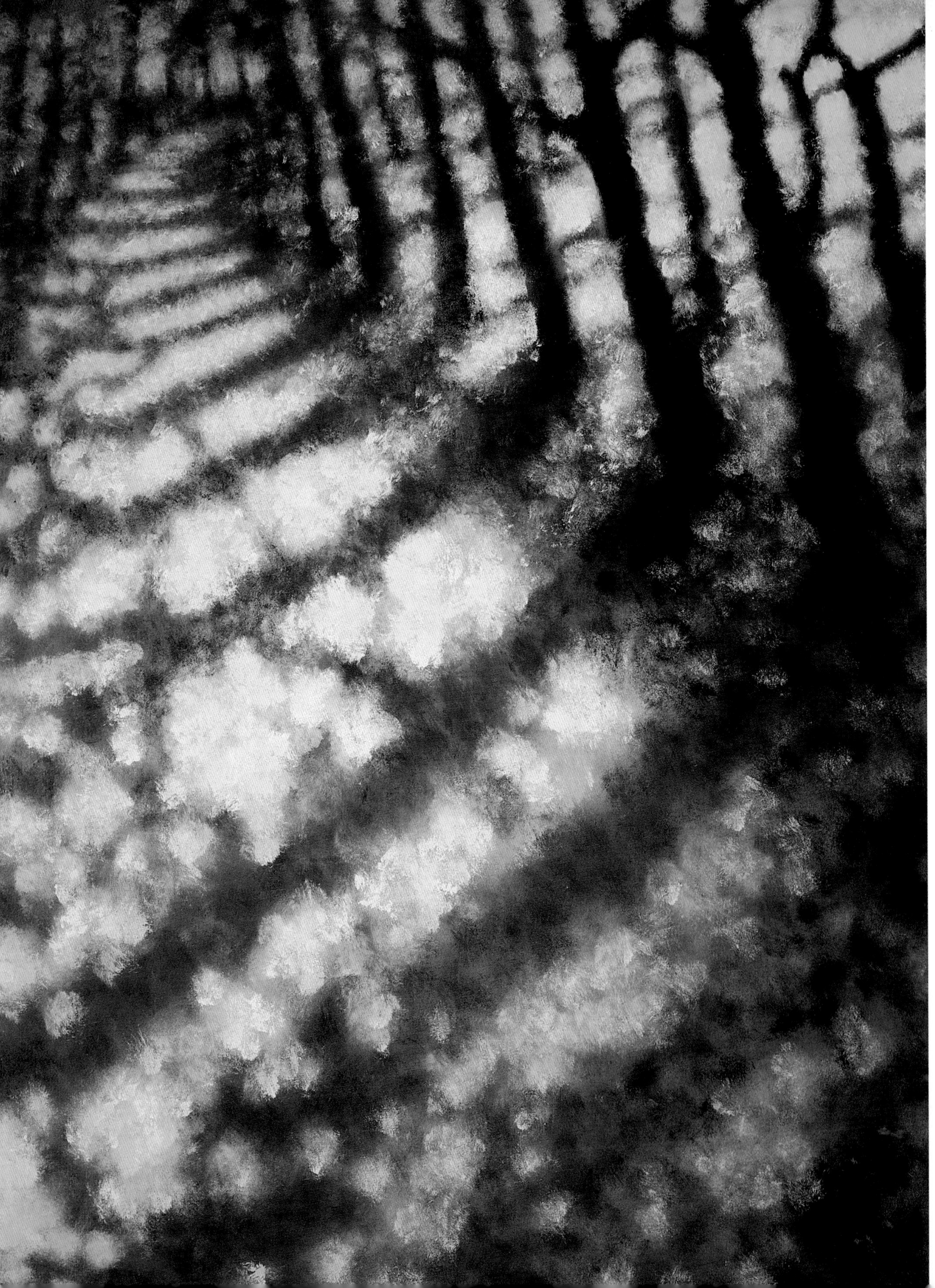

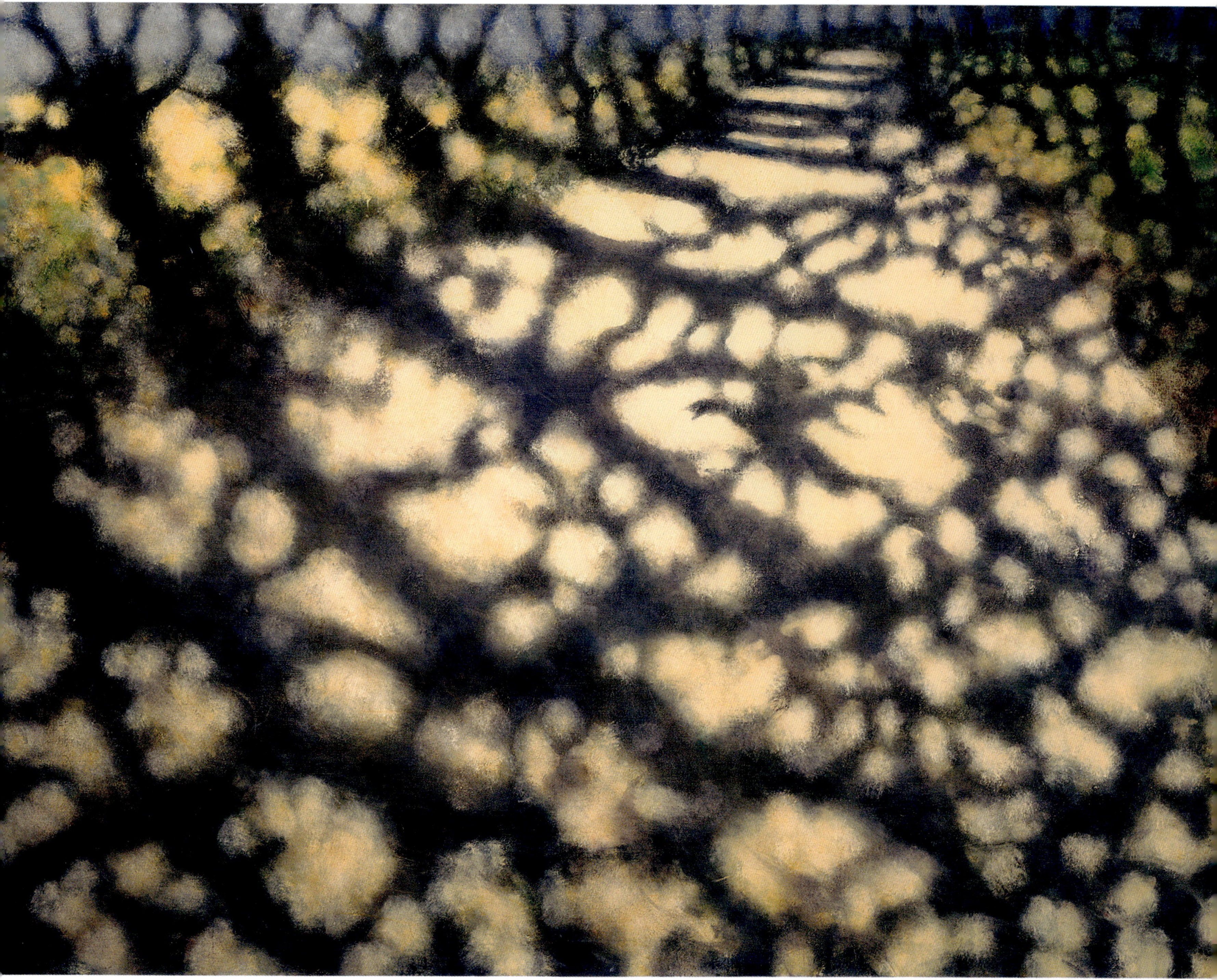

Into The Wood I

1999

Oil on canvas

182.9×127 cm.

72×50 in.

Out Of The Wood I

1999

Oil on canvas

152.4×198.1 cm.

60×78 in.

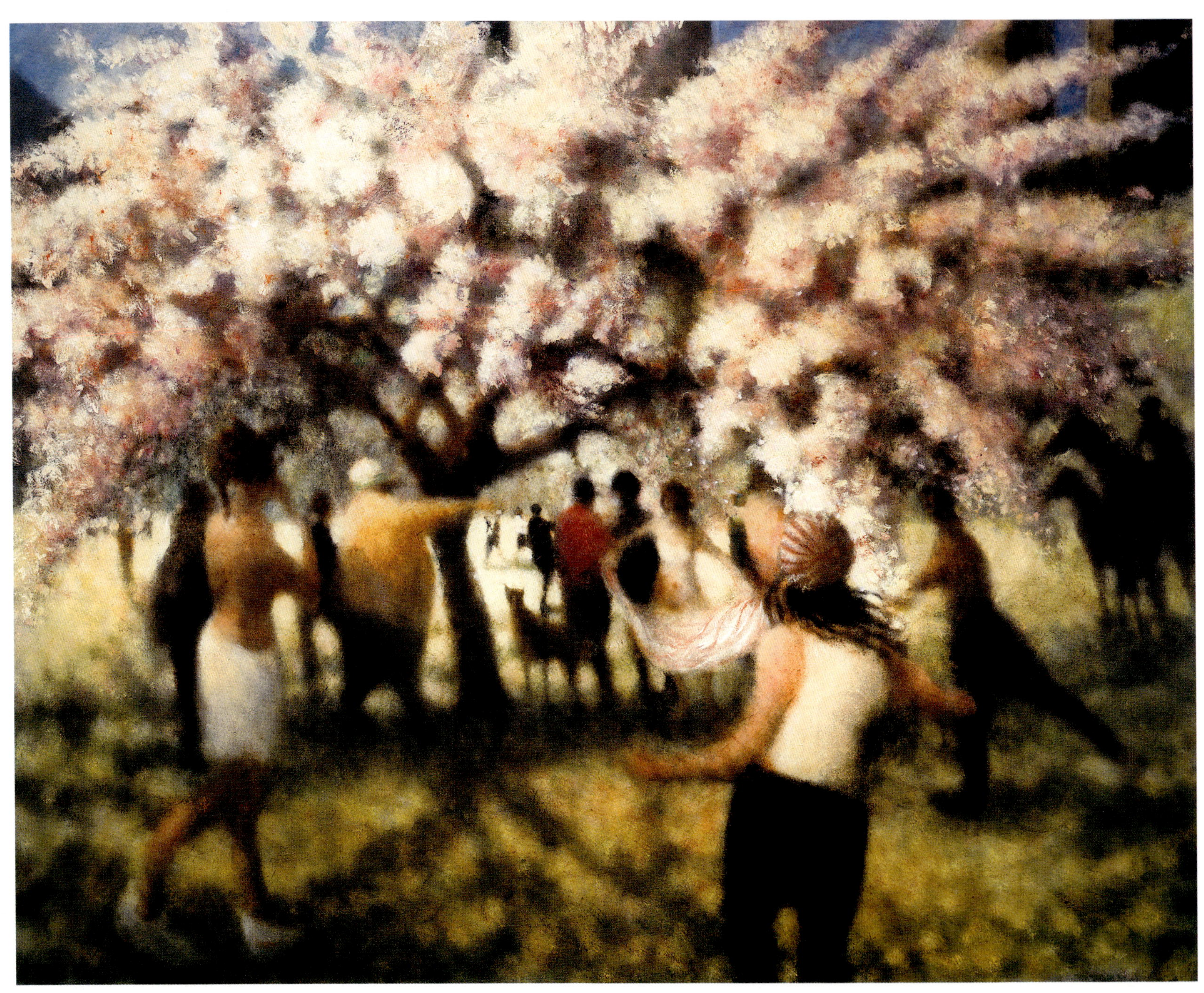

Cherry Tree With Dog, Great Lawn
2000
Oil on canvas
198.2×243.8 cm.
78×96 in.

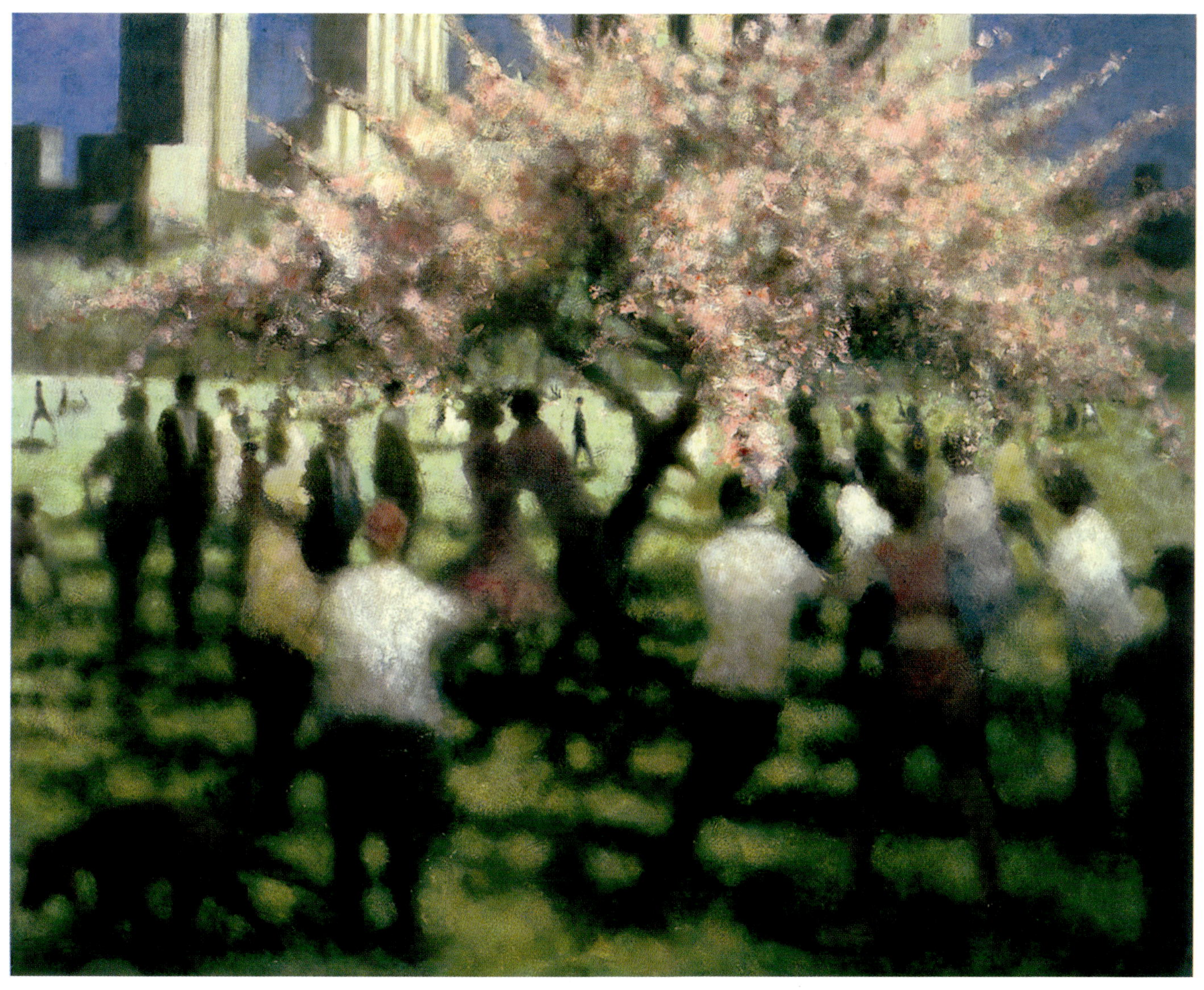

Underneath The Cherry Tree NYC
1999
Oil on canvas
198.2 × 243.8 cm.
78 x 96 in.

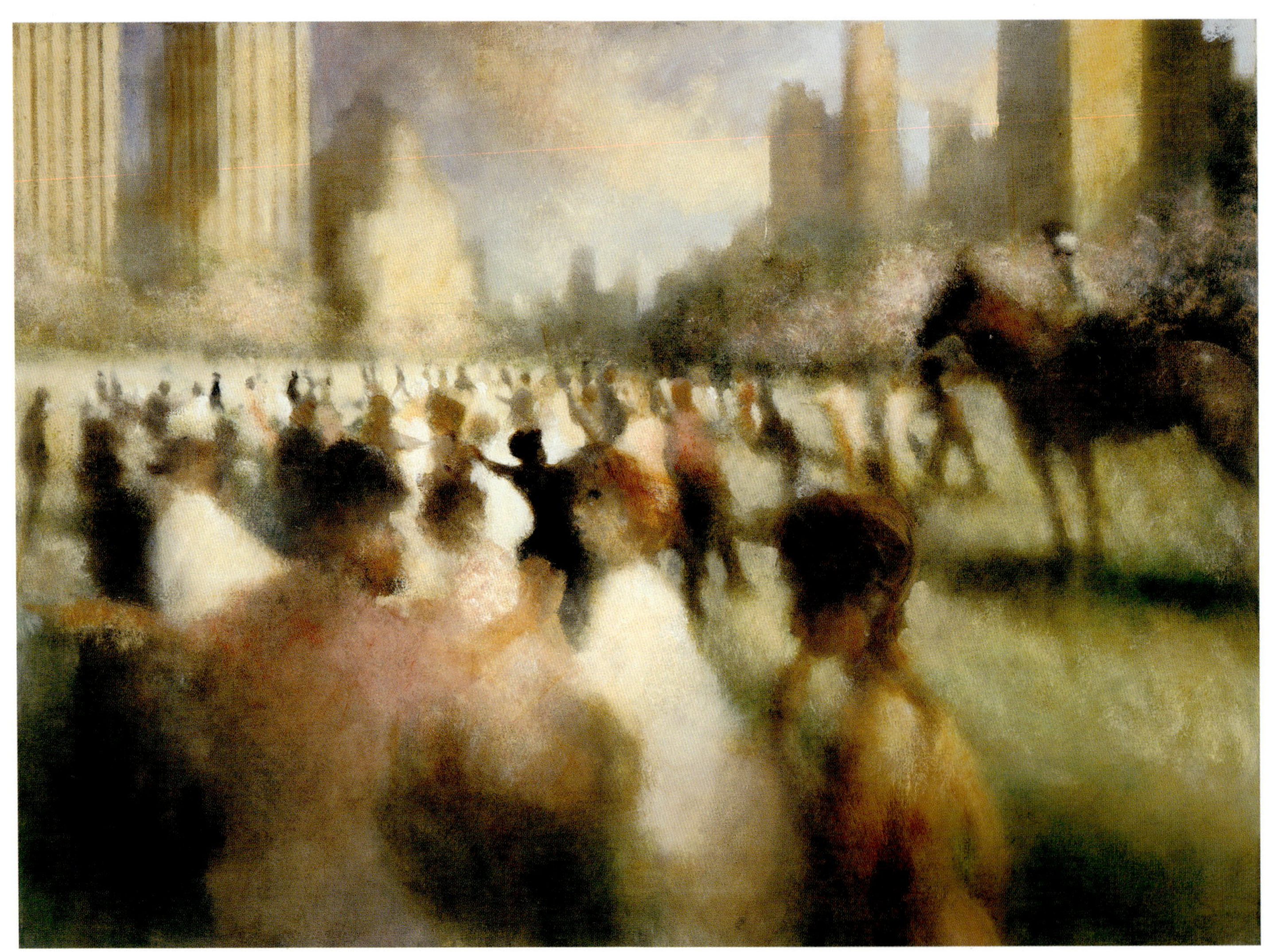

After The Event Great Lawn I

2000

Oil on canvas

91.4×121.9 cm.

36×48 in.

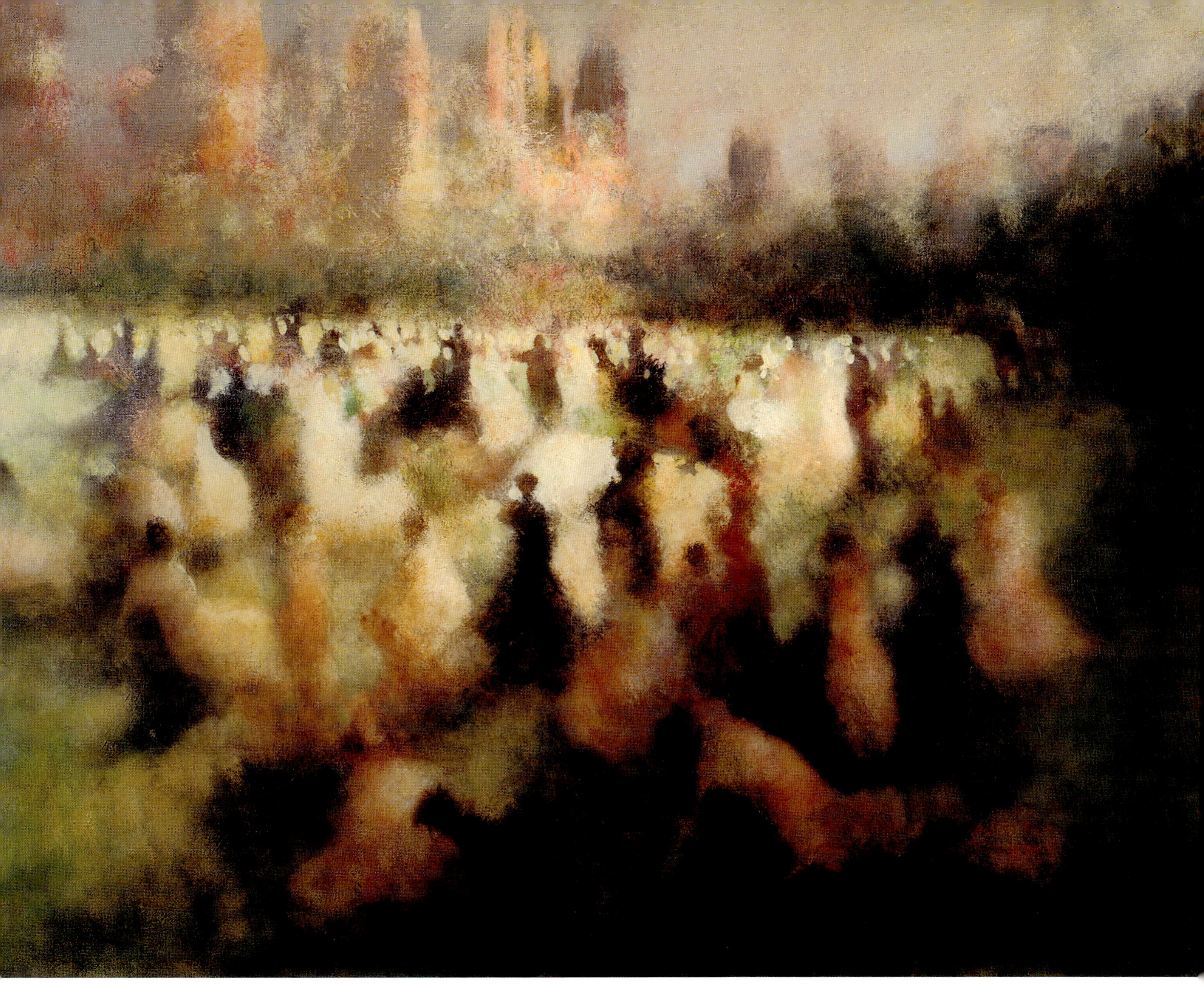

Gathering Central Park II
2000
Oil on canvas
121.9×152.4 cm.
48×60 in.

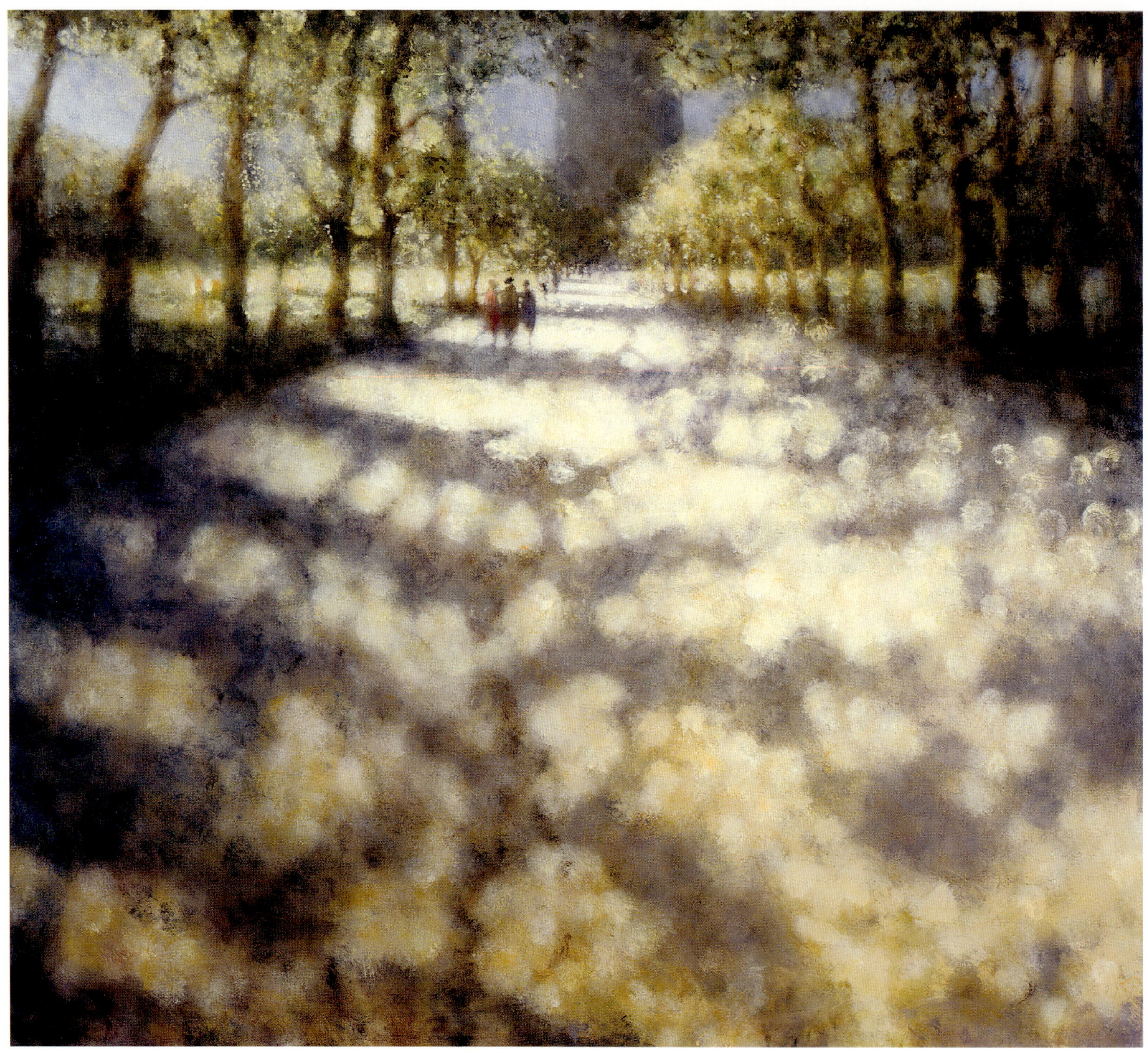

Literature Walk, Central Park I
2001
Oil on canvas
152.4×167.6 cm.
60×66 in.

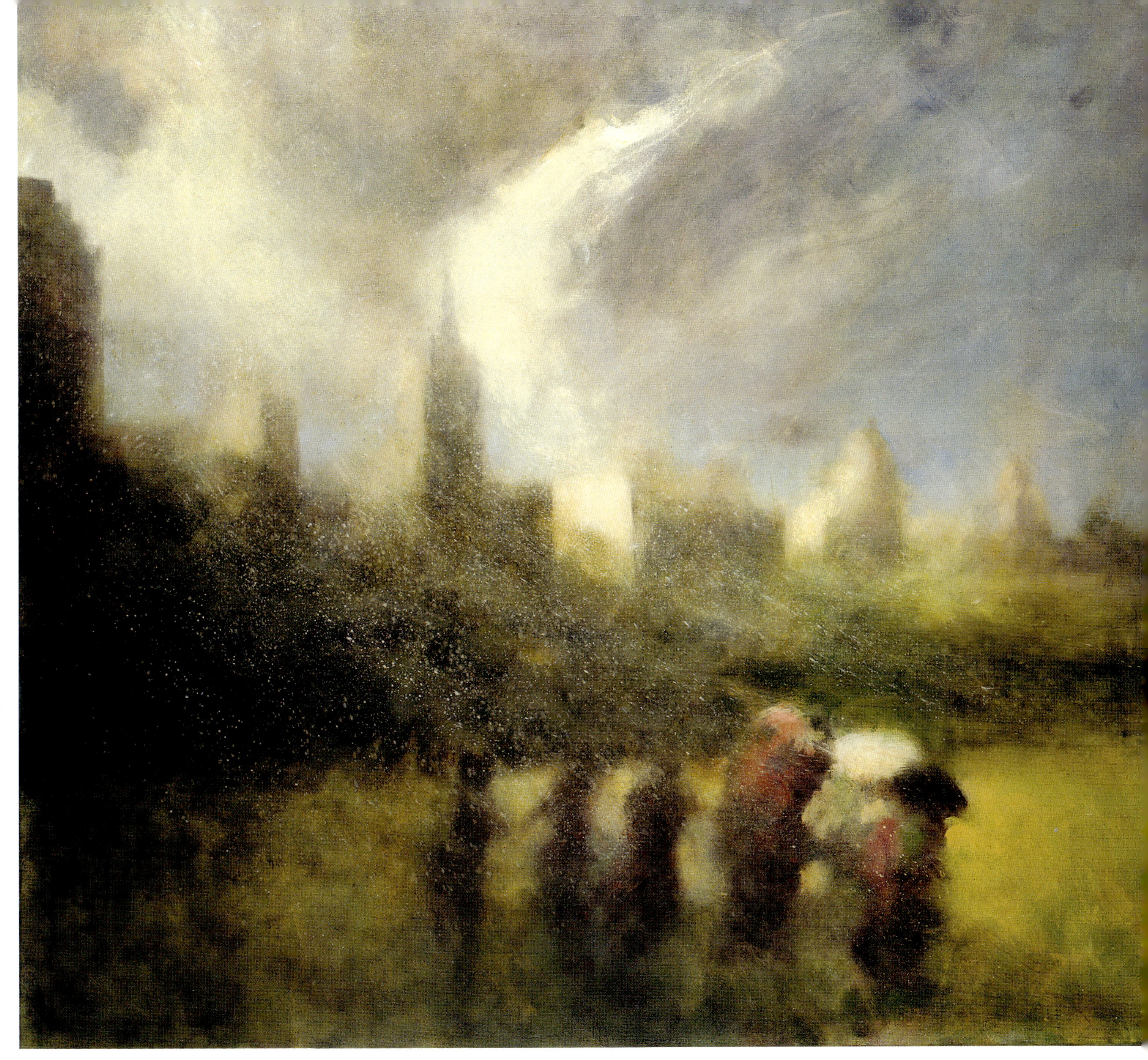

89

Increase NYC I
2001
Oil on canvas
182.8×198.1 cm.
72×78 in.

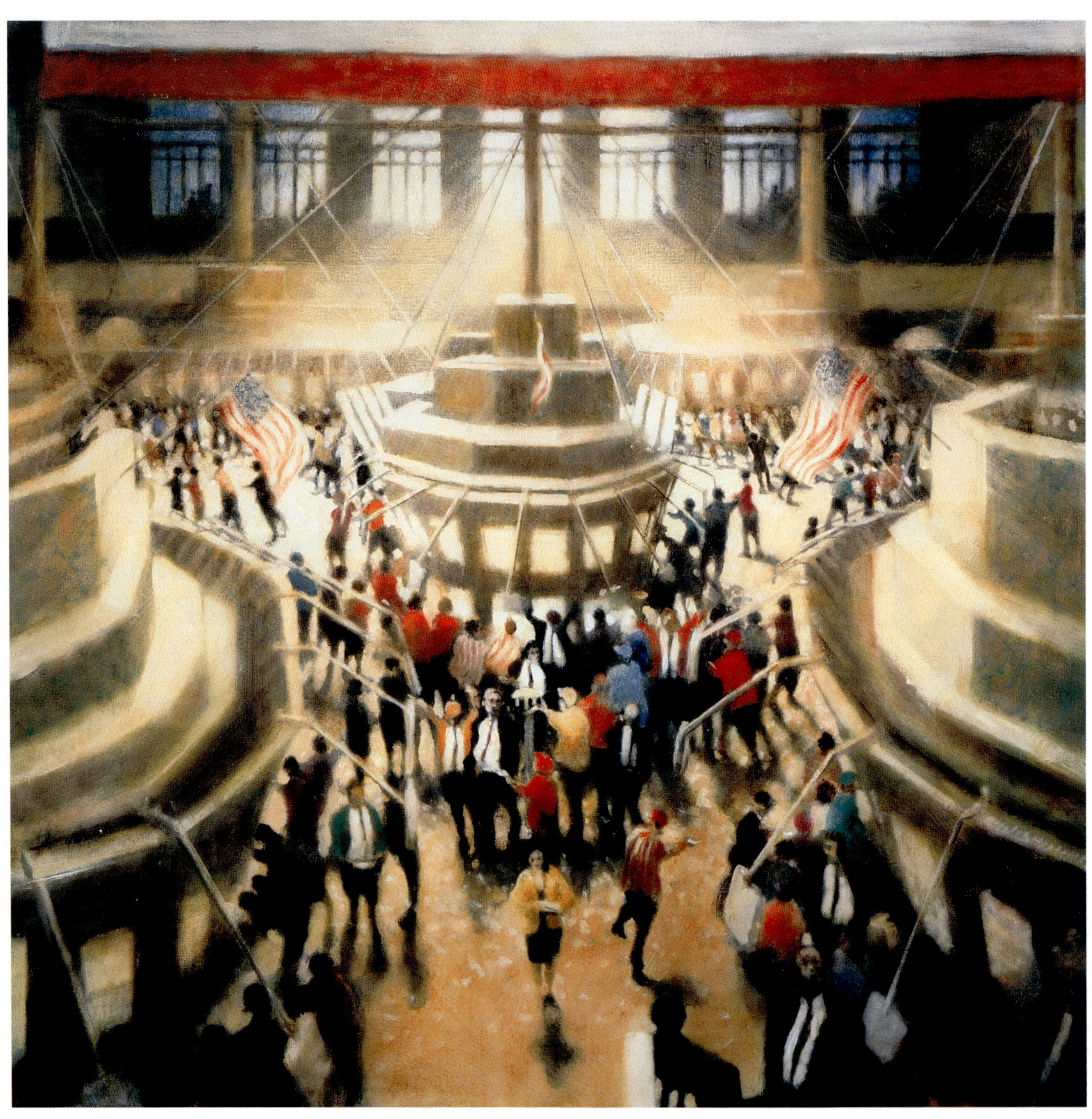

New York Stock Exchange Floor I
1998
Oil on canvas
152.4 × 152.4 cm.
60 × 60 in.

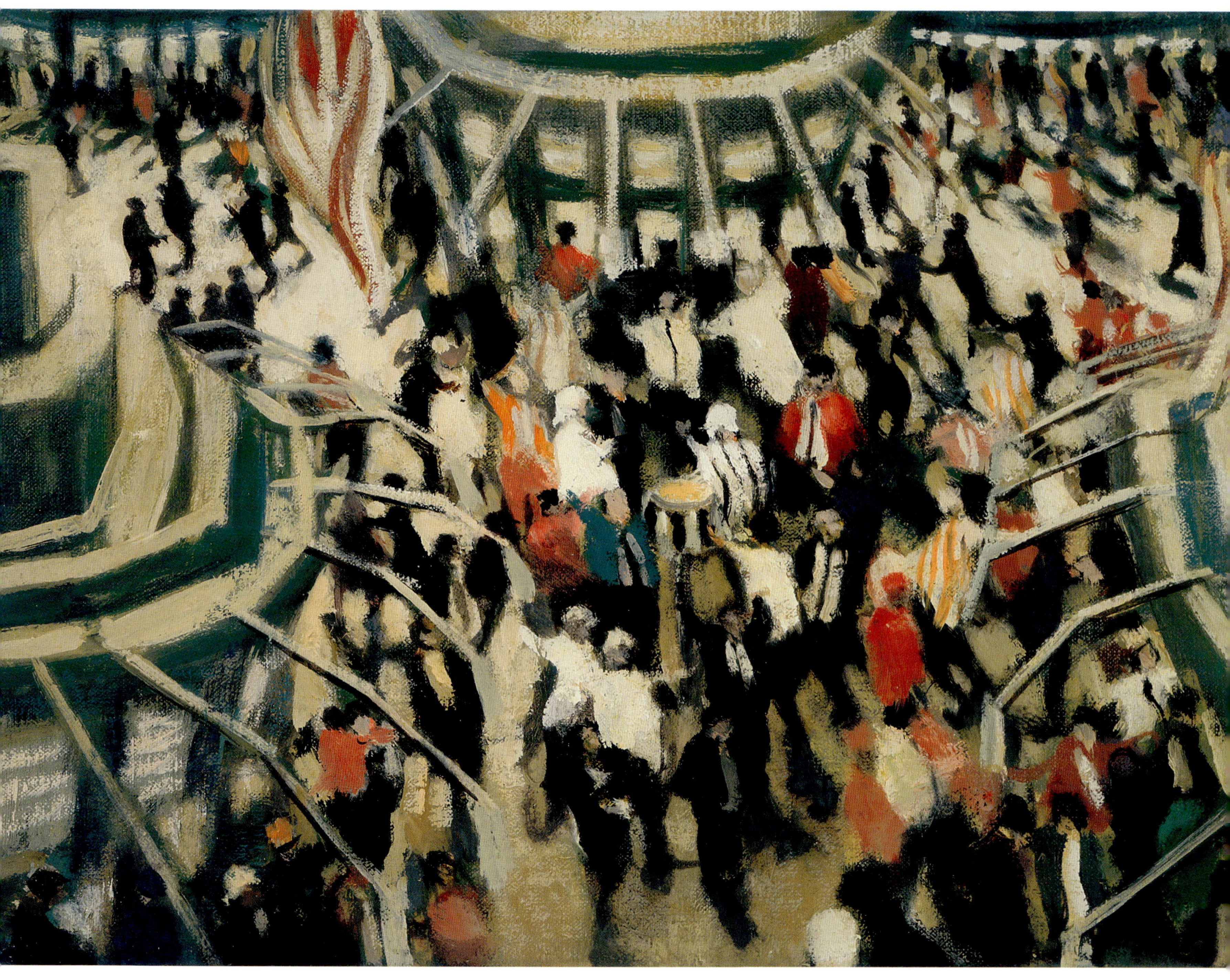

NYC Stock Exchange Study I
1999
Oil on canvas
30.4×40.6 cm.
12×16 in.

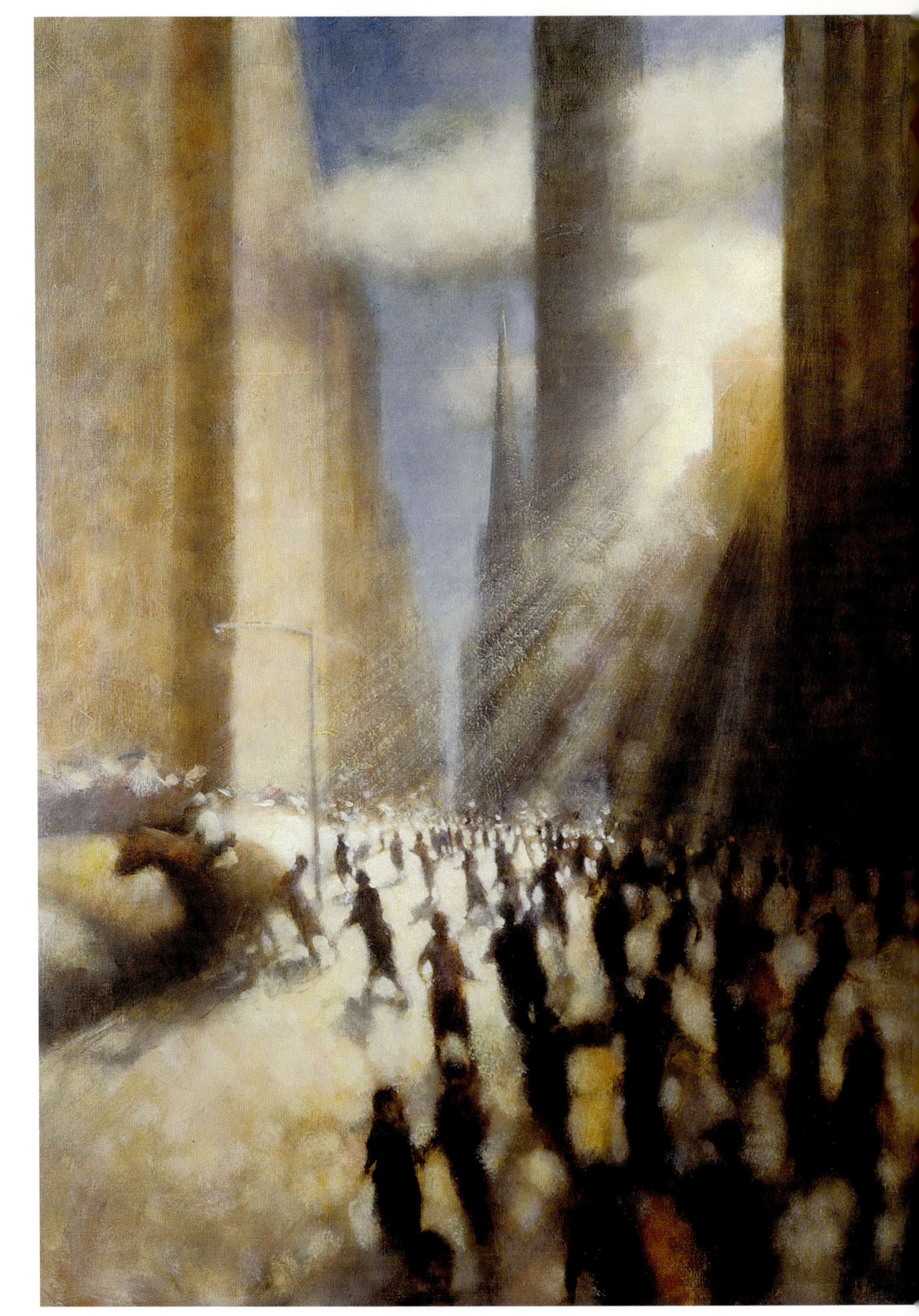

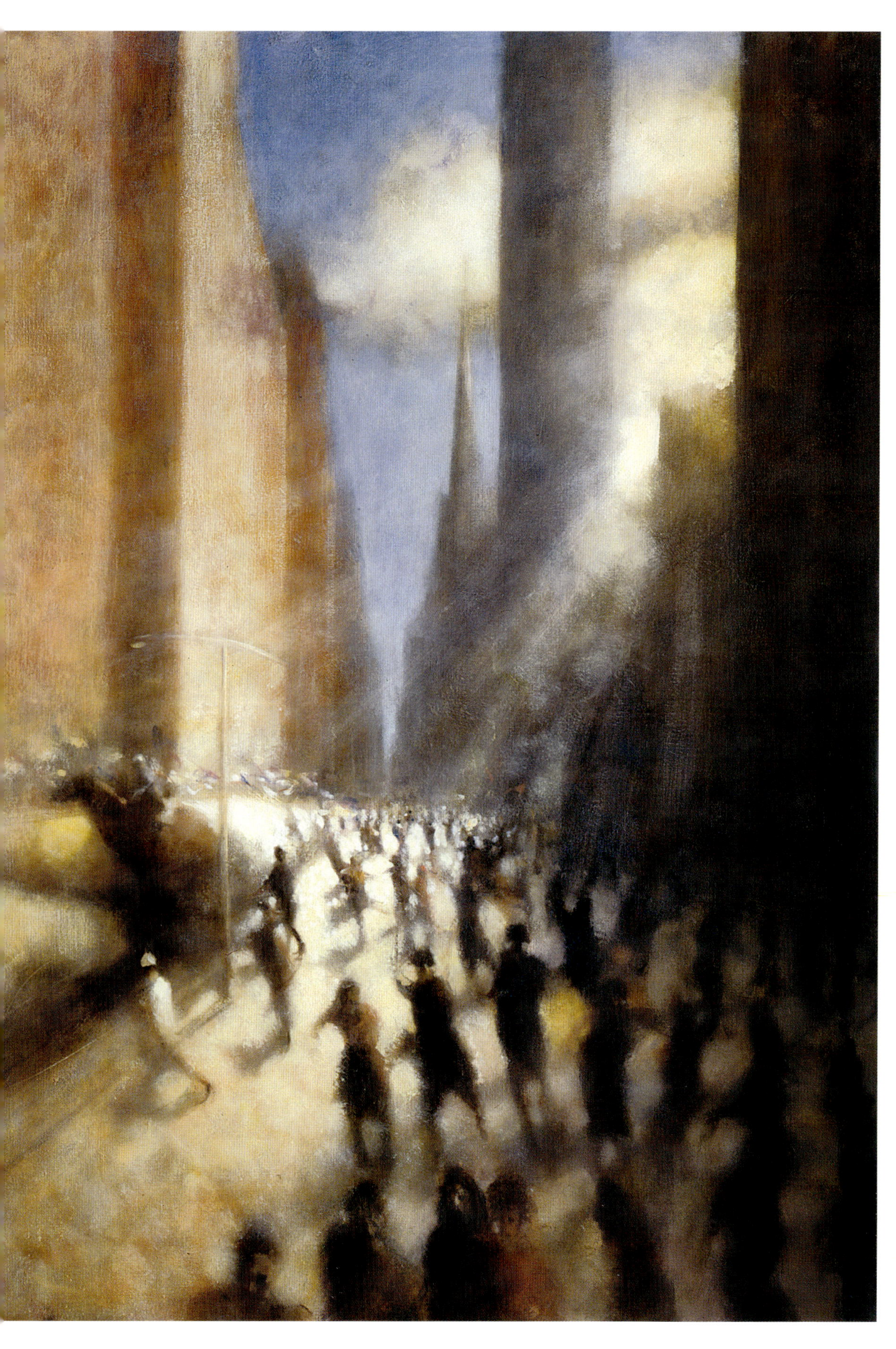

Sun And Clouds Over Broadway

2003
Diptych; oil on canvas
Each panel 127×182.9 cm.
50×72 in.

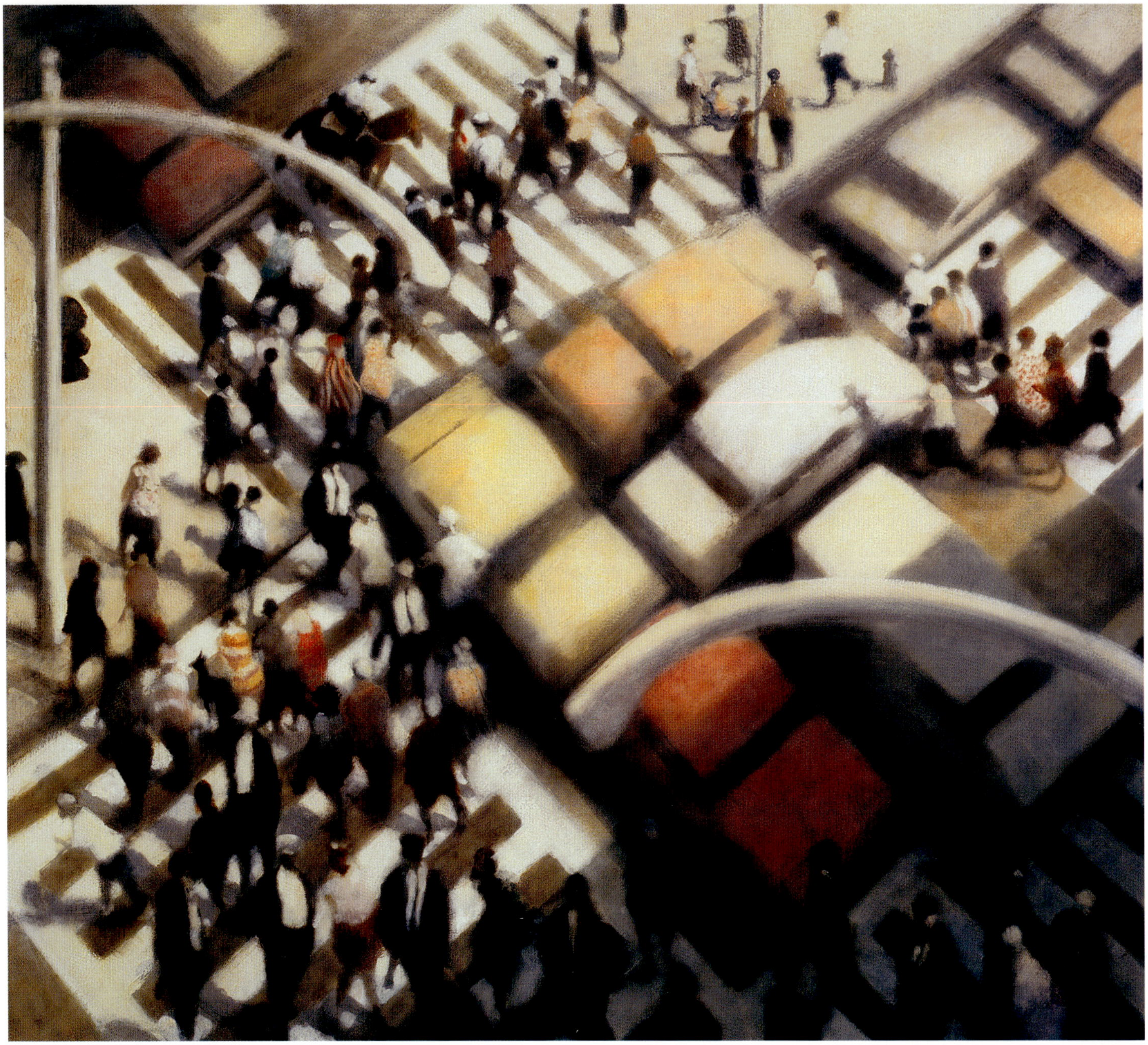

Gridlock NYC
1998
Oil on canvas
152.4×167.6 cm.
60×66 in.

Times Square Incident II
1998
Oil on canvas
198.1×152.4 cm.
78×60 in.

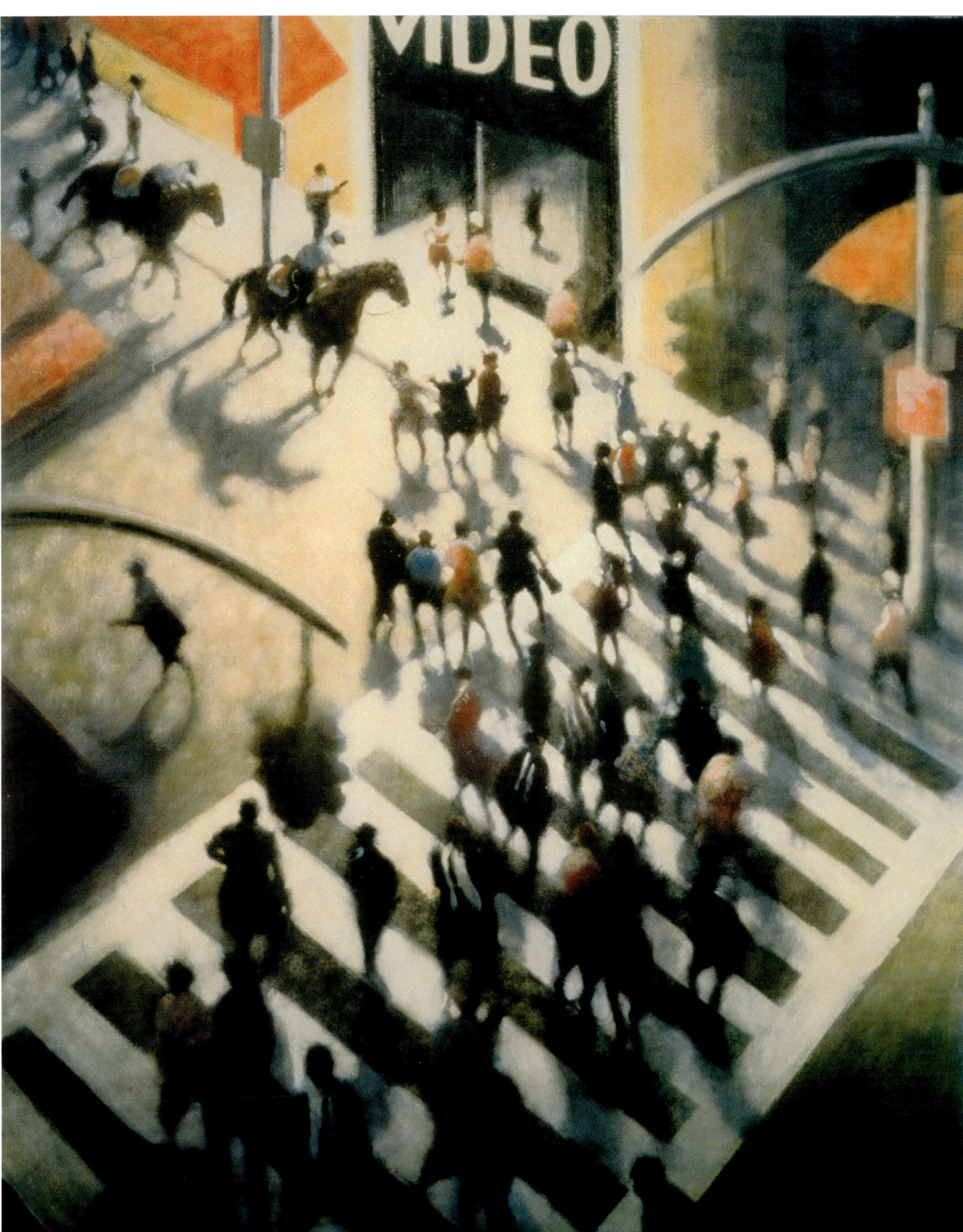
VIDEO

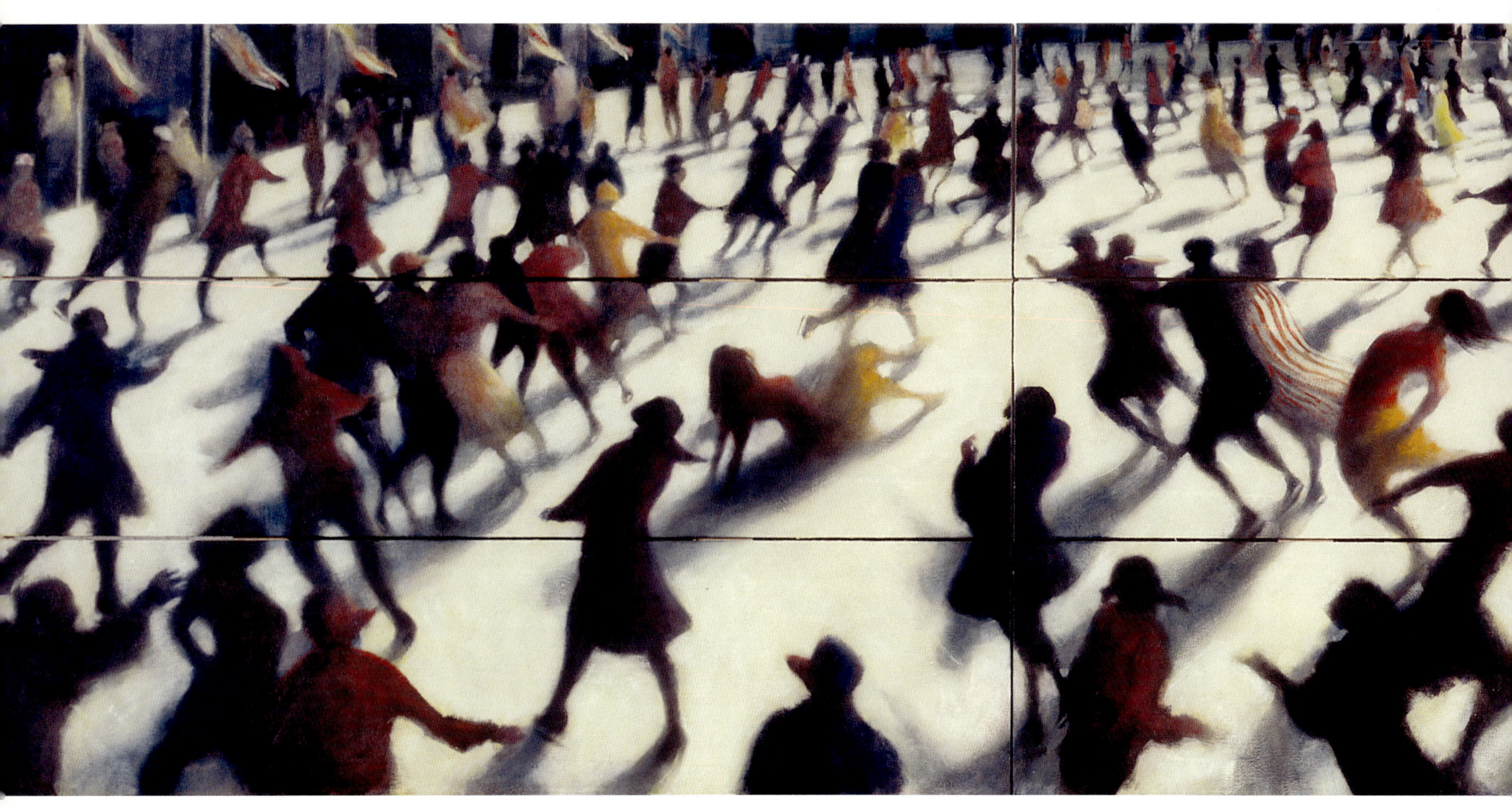

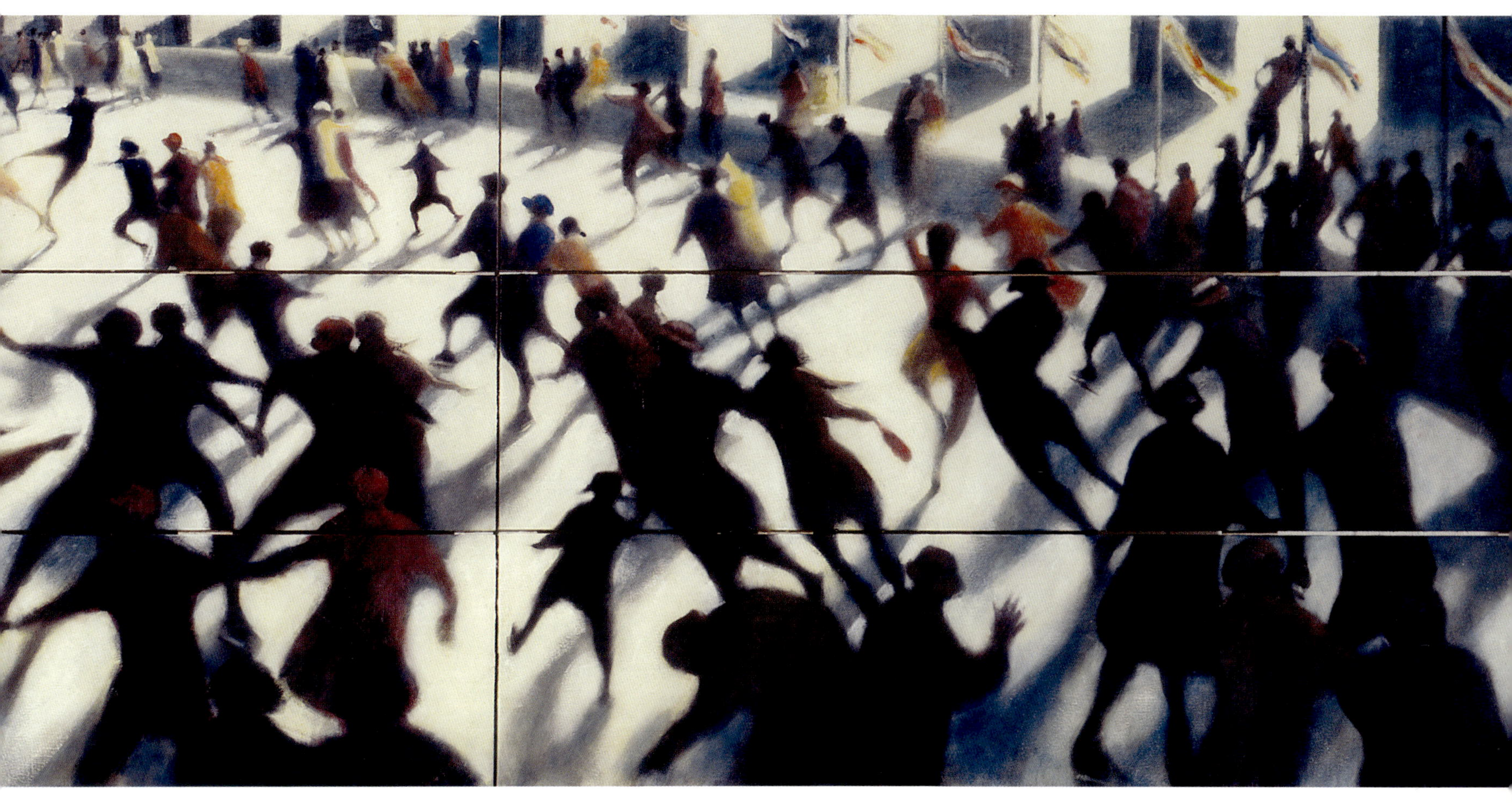

The Rink

1996
Triptych; oil on canvas
182.8×731.5 cm.
72×288 in.

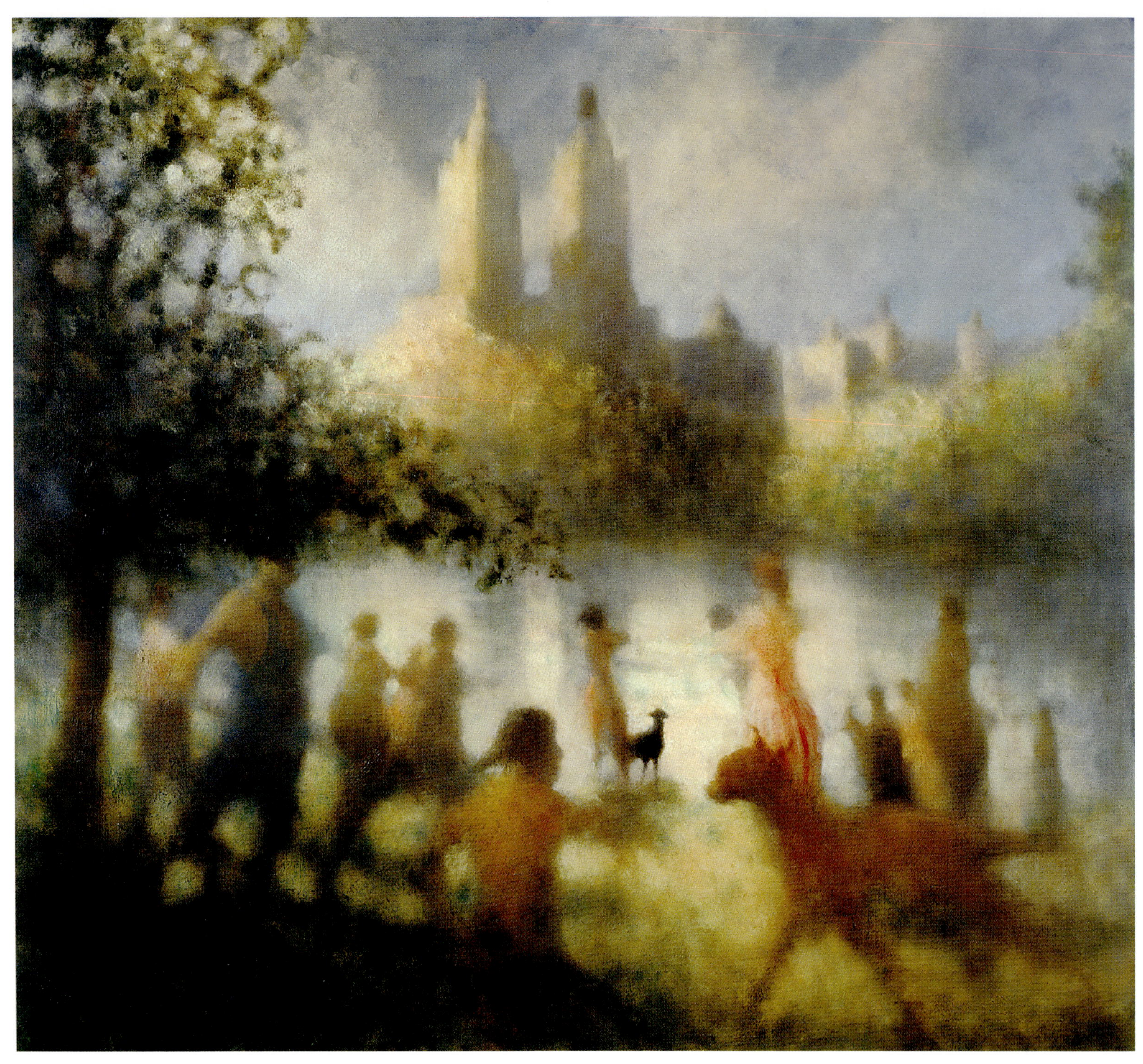

Down By The Water, Central Park

2001
Oil on canvas
182.9 × 198.1 cm.
72 × 78 in.

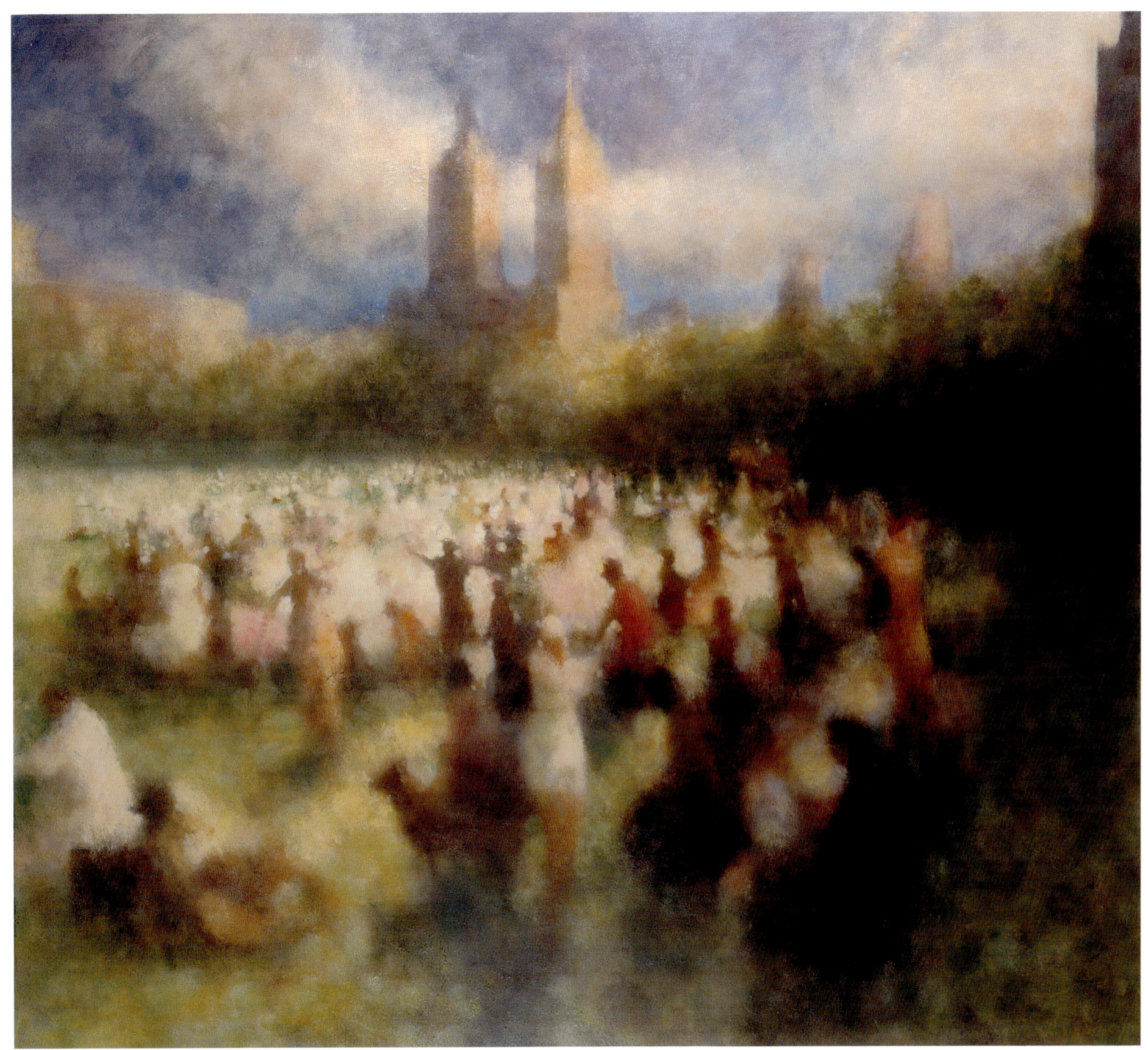

Gathering, Central Park IV
2001
Oil on canvas
182.9×198.1 cm.
72×78 in.

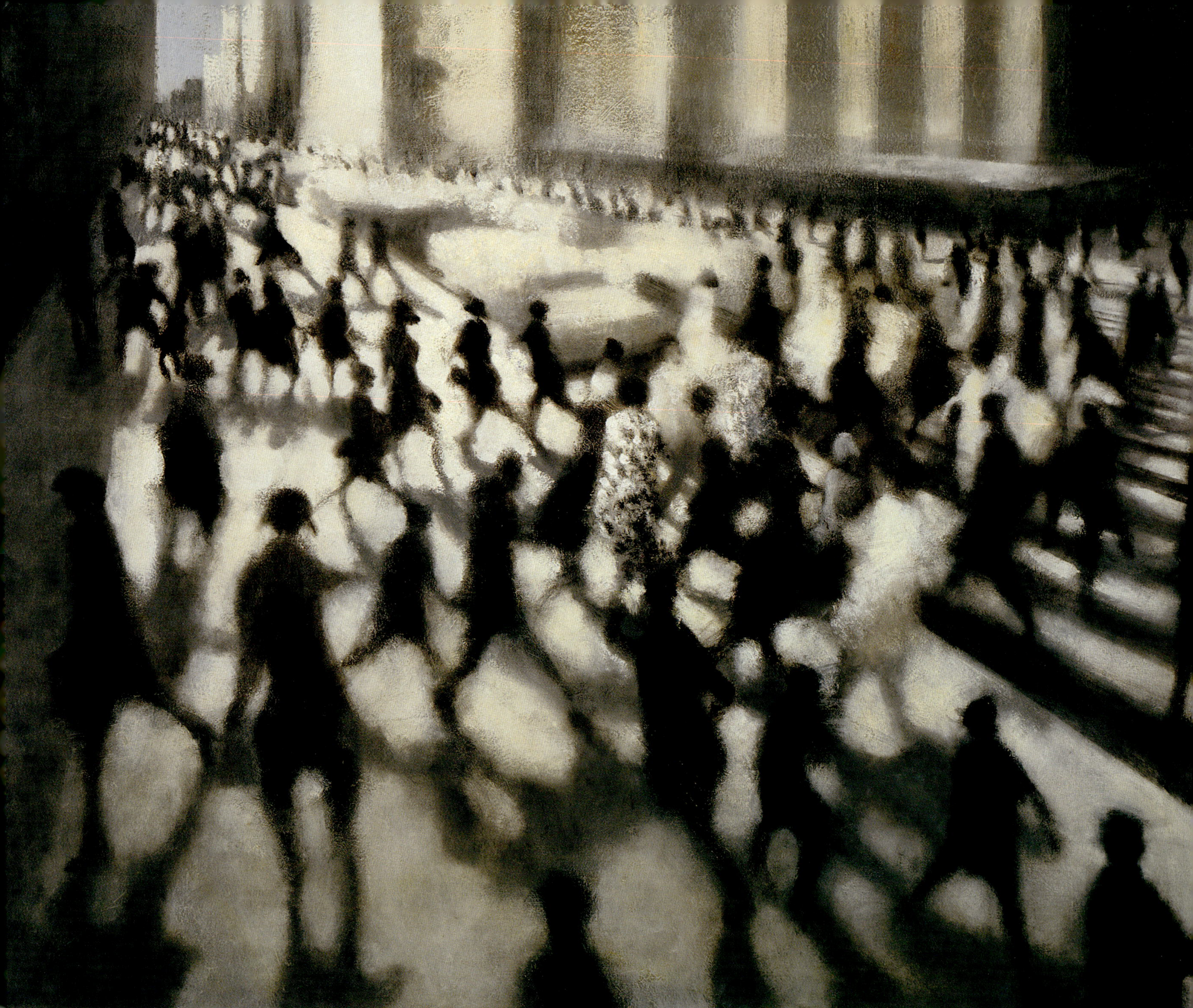

Walking Down Broadway III

1998
Oil on canvas
121.9×144.8 cm.
48×57 in.

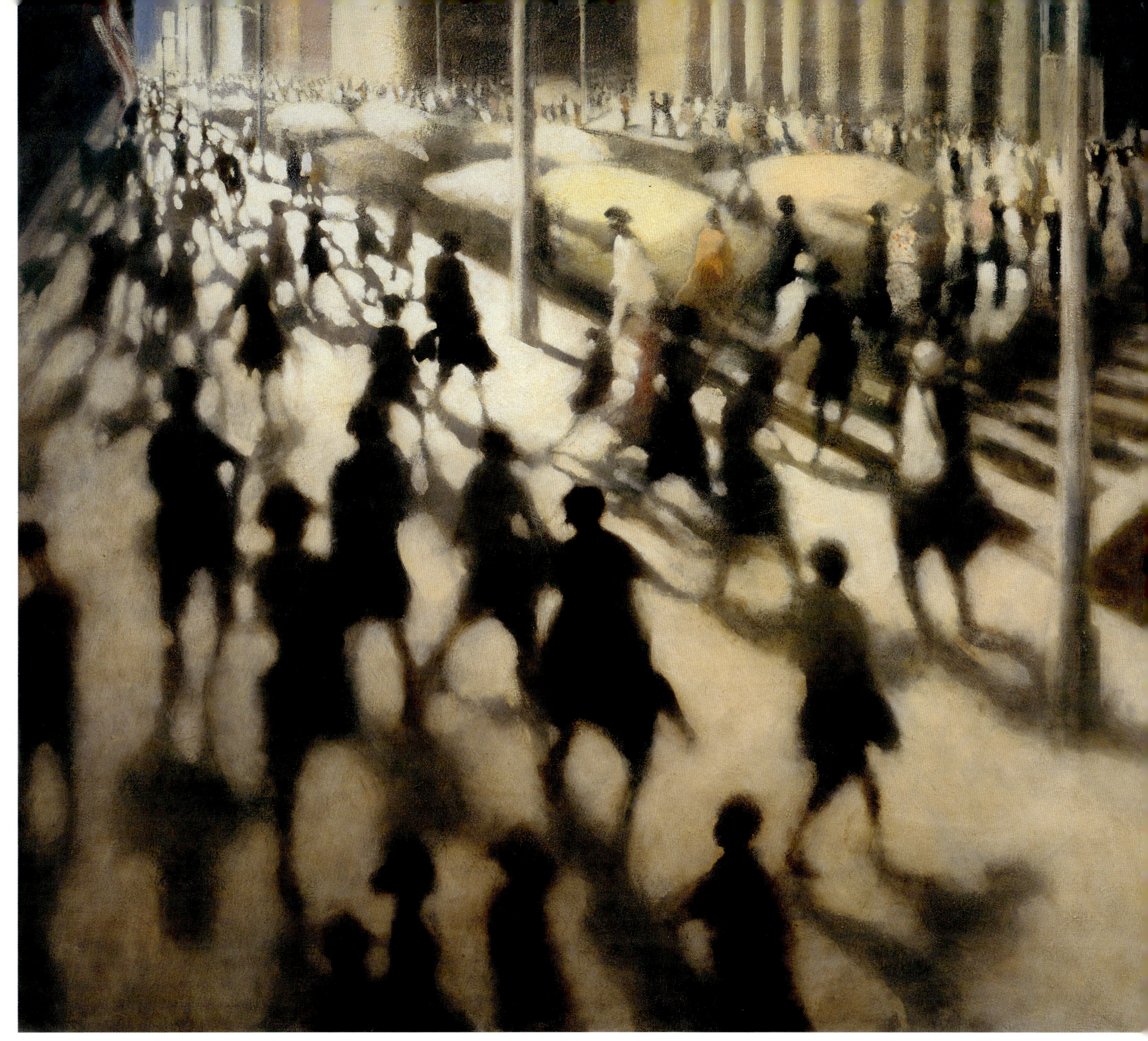

Walking Down Broadway I
1998
Oil on canvas
152.4×167.6 cm.
60×66 in.

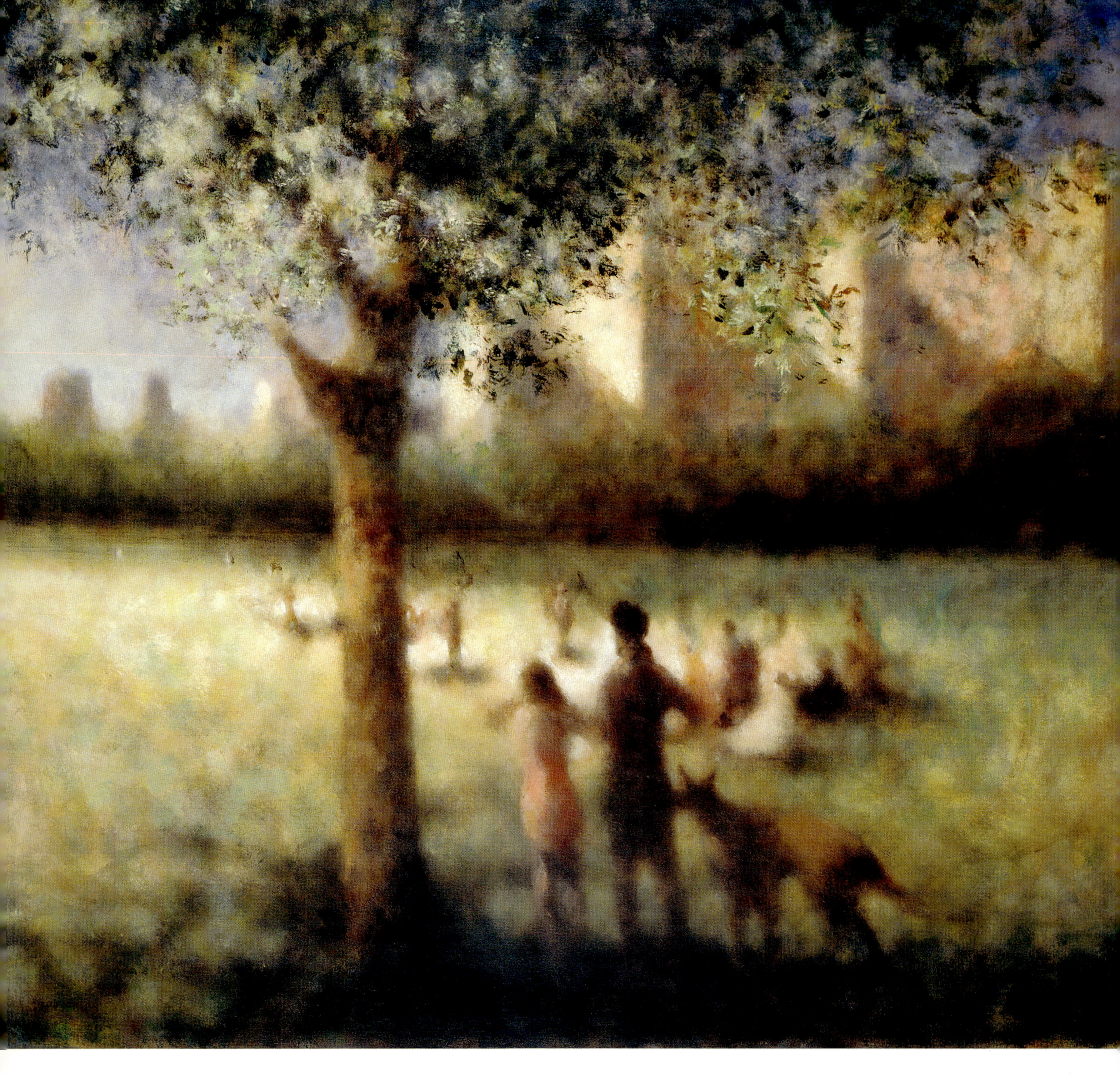

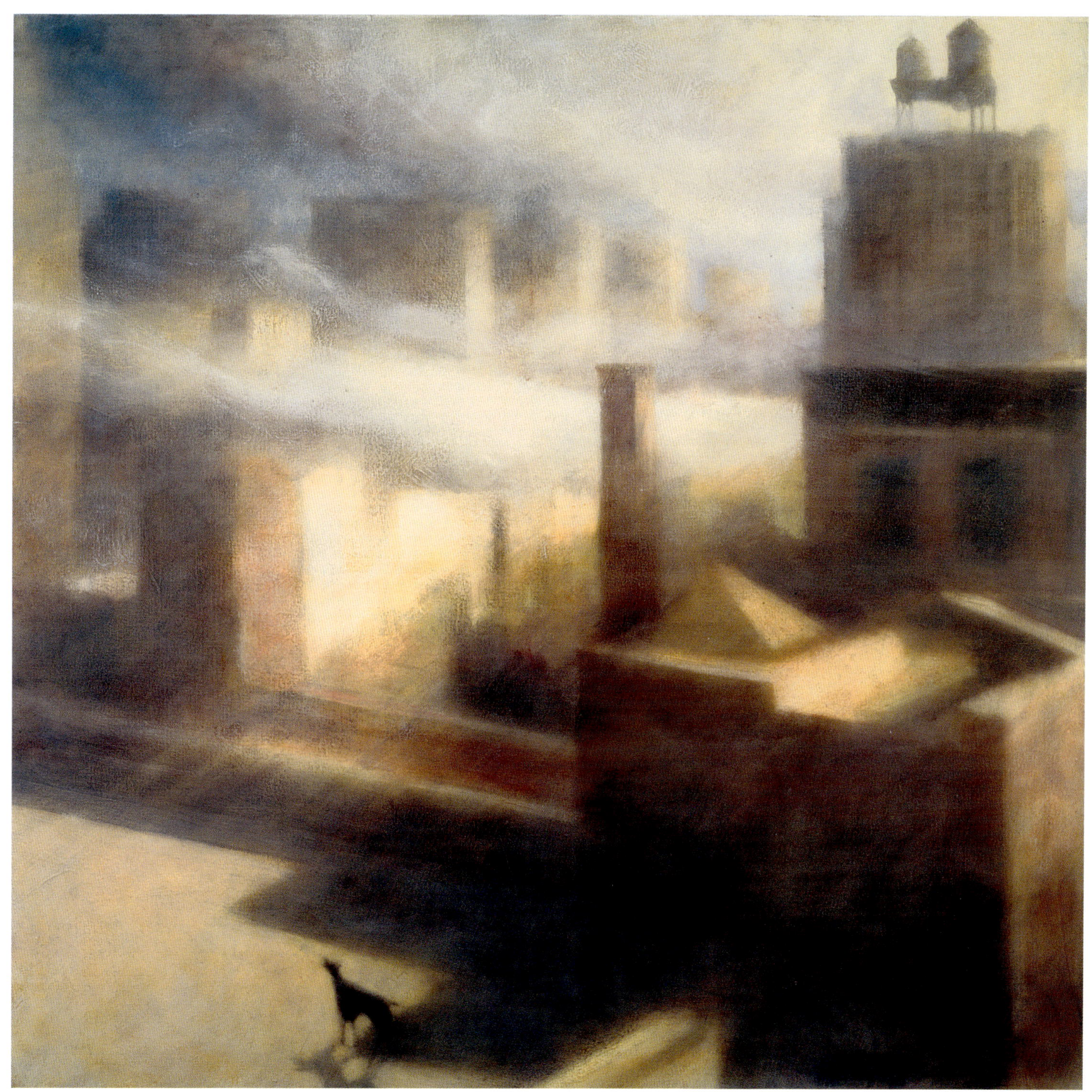

Muse, Central Park

2002

Oil on canvas

152.4×167.6 cm.

72×78 in.

Sun And Fog With Dog, Roof Top

1998

Oil on canvas

152.4×152.4 cm.

60×60 in.

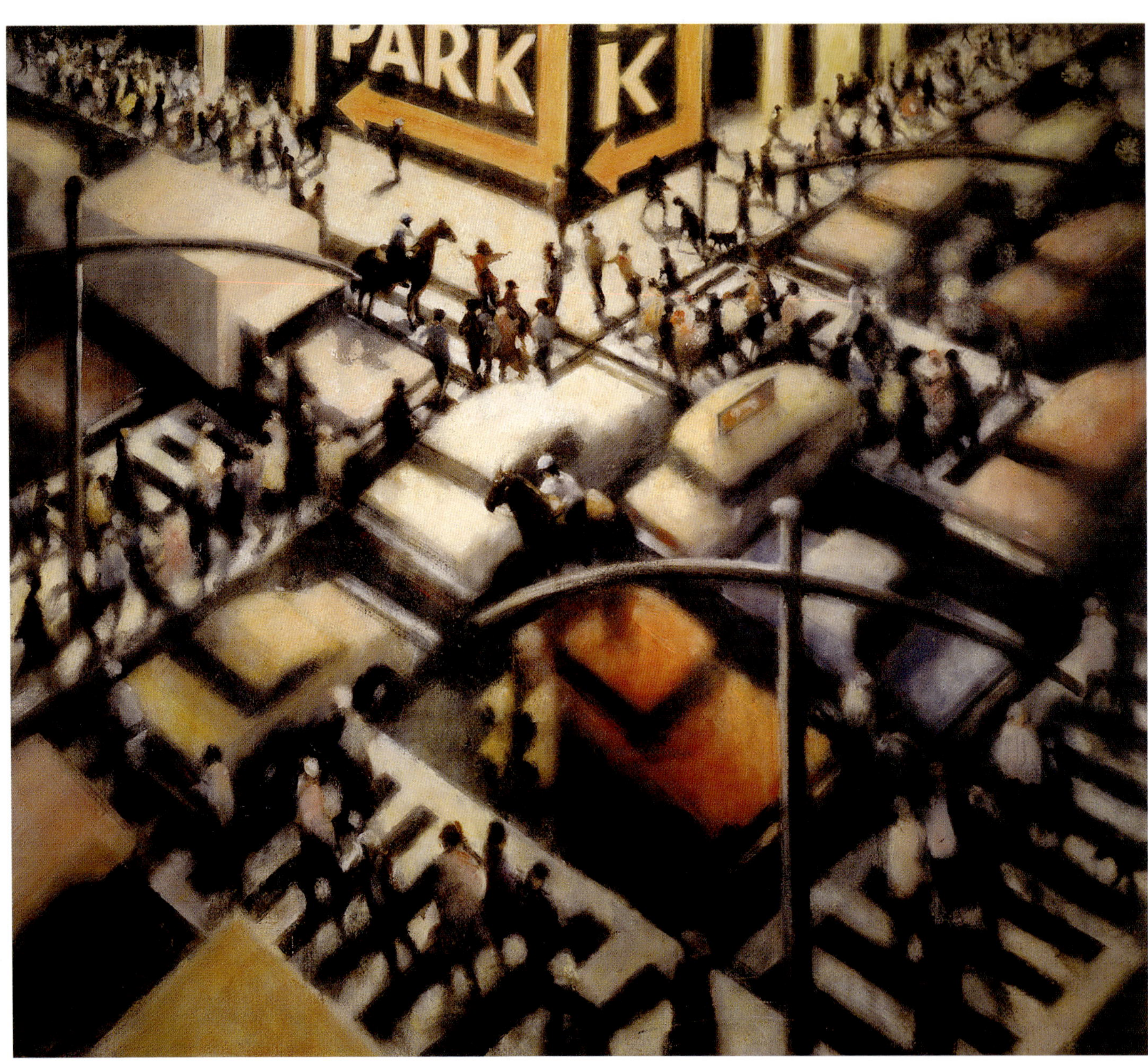

Gridlock II
2005
Oil on canvas
152.4×167.6 cm.
60×66 in.

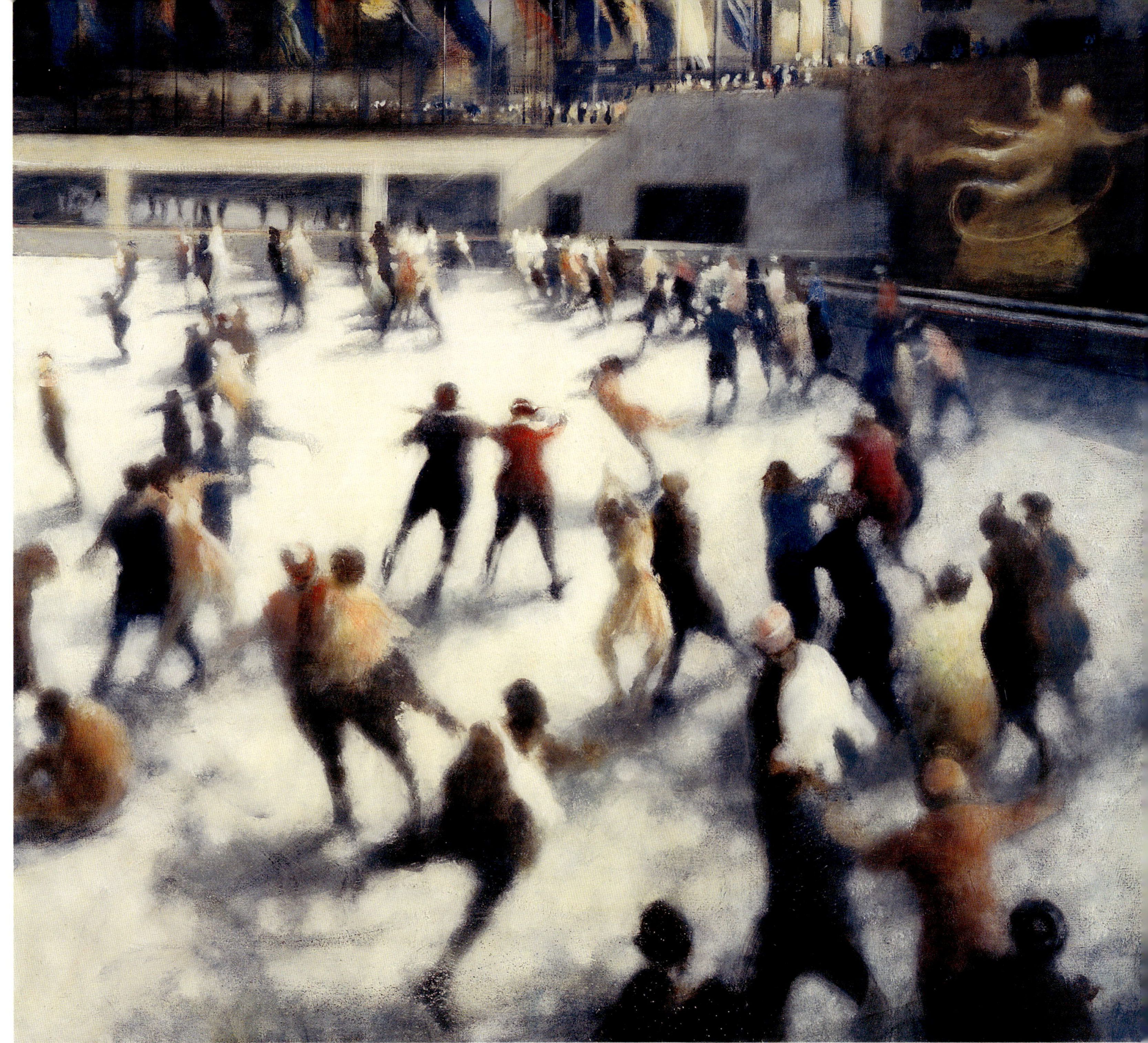

Rockefeller Skaters VI
2006
Oil on canvas
182.9×198.1 cm.
72×78 in.

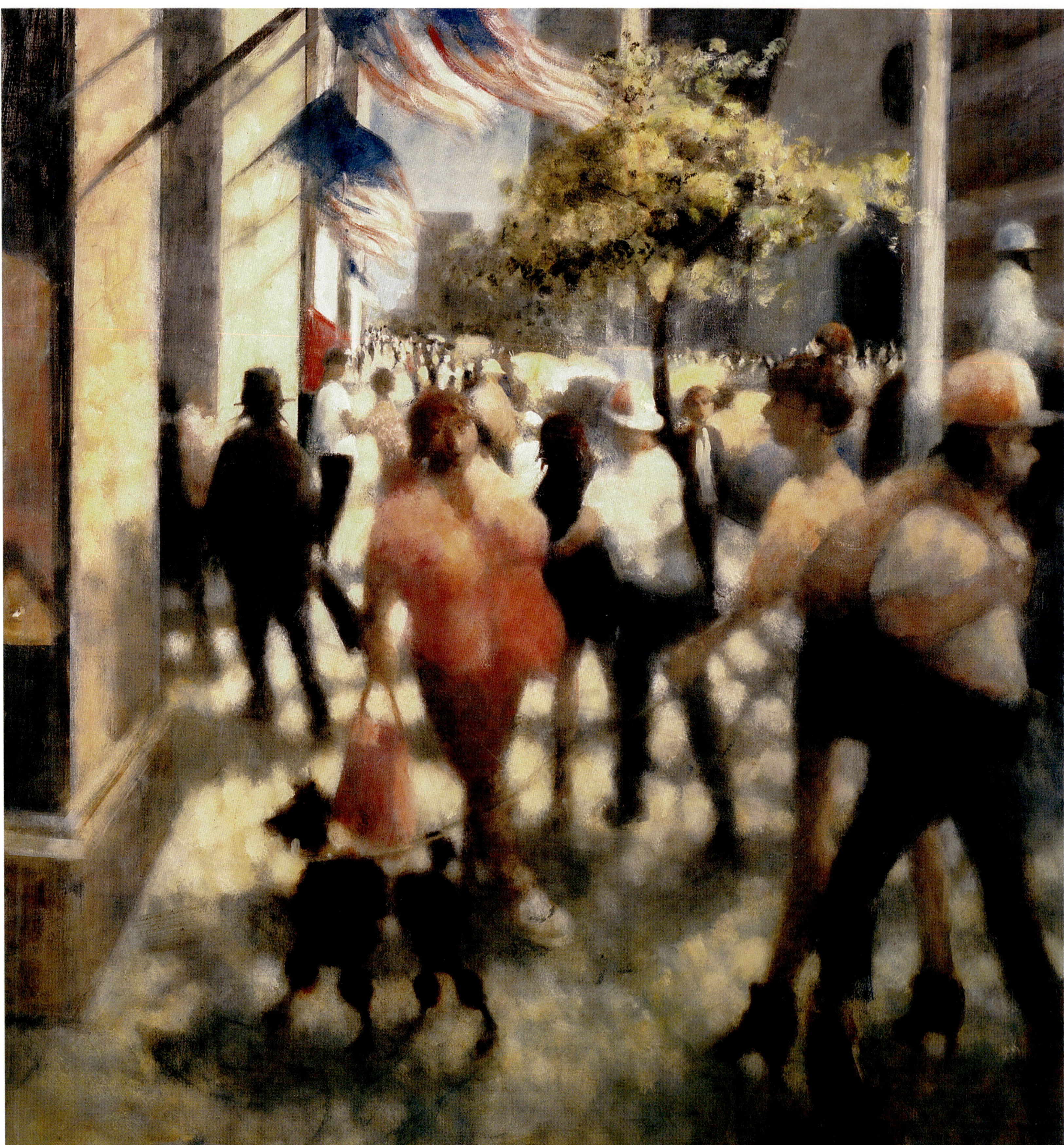

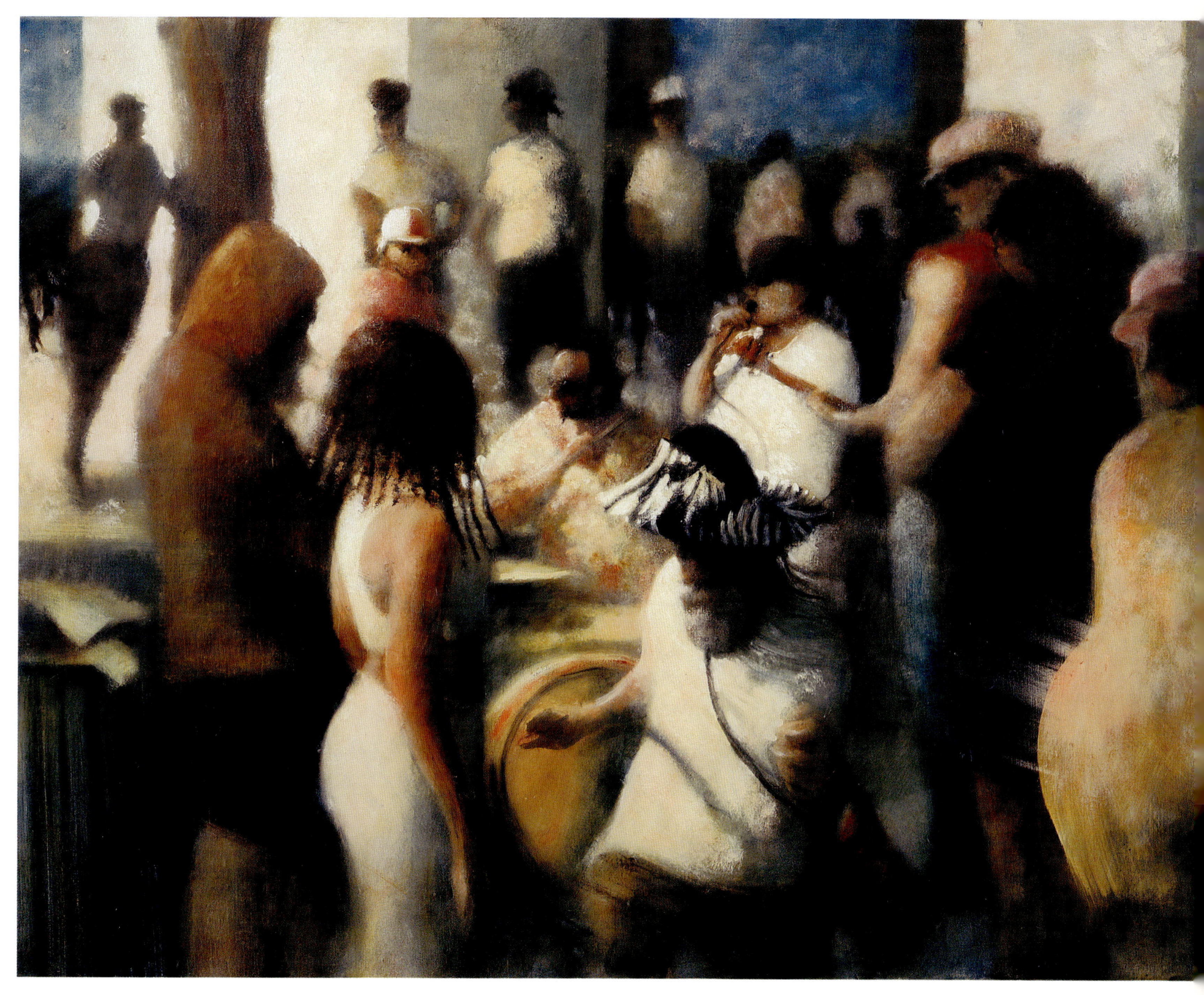

Walking Up Fifth Avenue I

2007
Oil on canvas
198.1×182.9 cm.
78×72 in.

Onlookers 05 Washington Square II

2006
Oil on canvas
121.9×152.4 cm.
48×60 in.

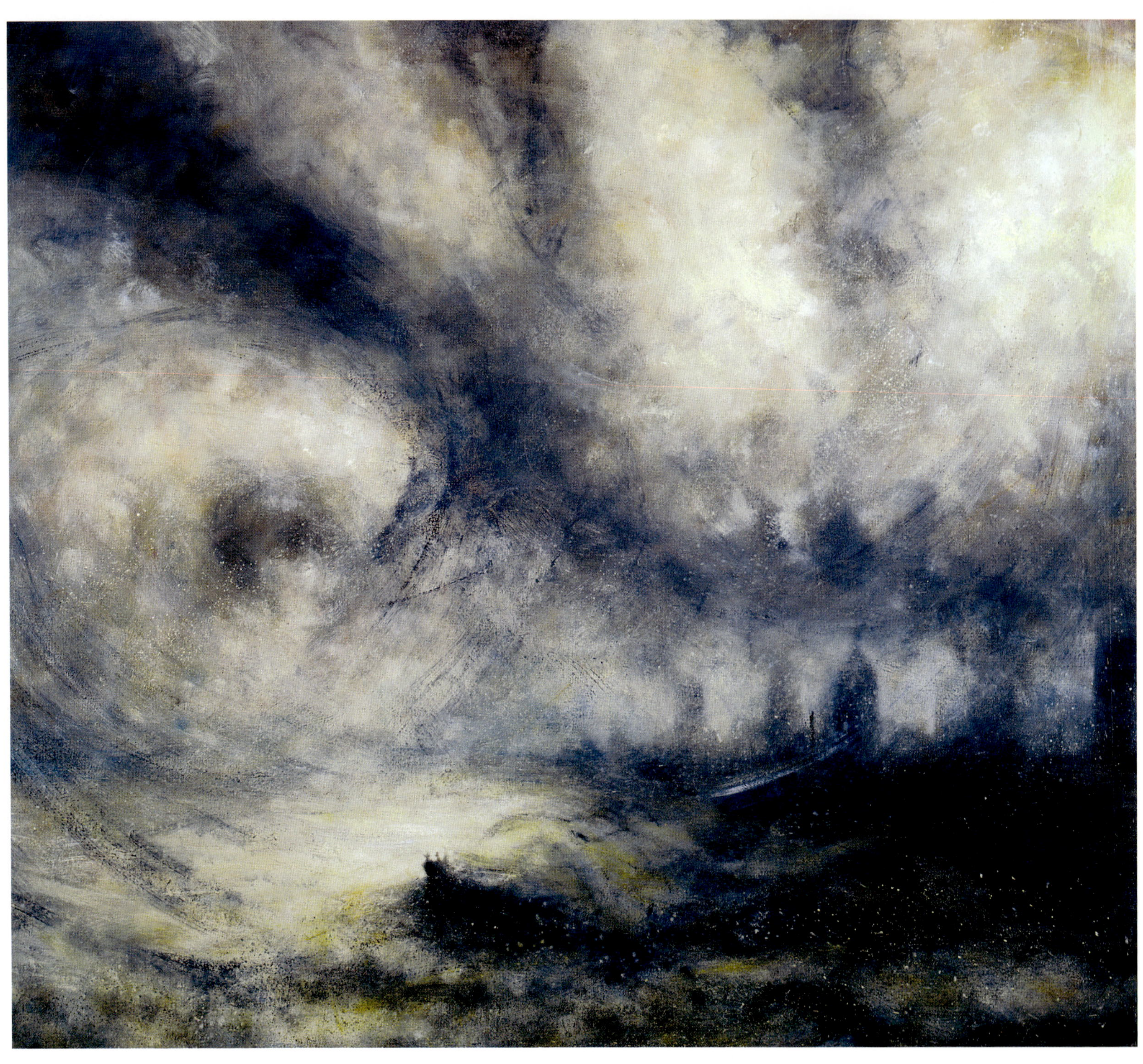

Tempest I
2008
Oil on canvas
182.9 × 198.1 cm.
72 × 78 in.

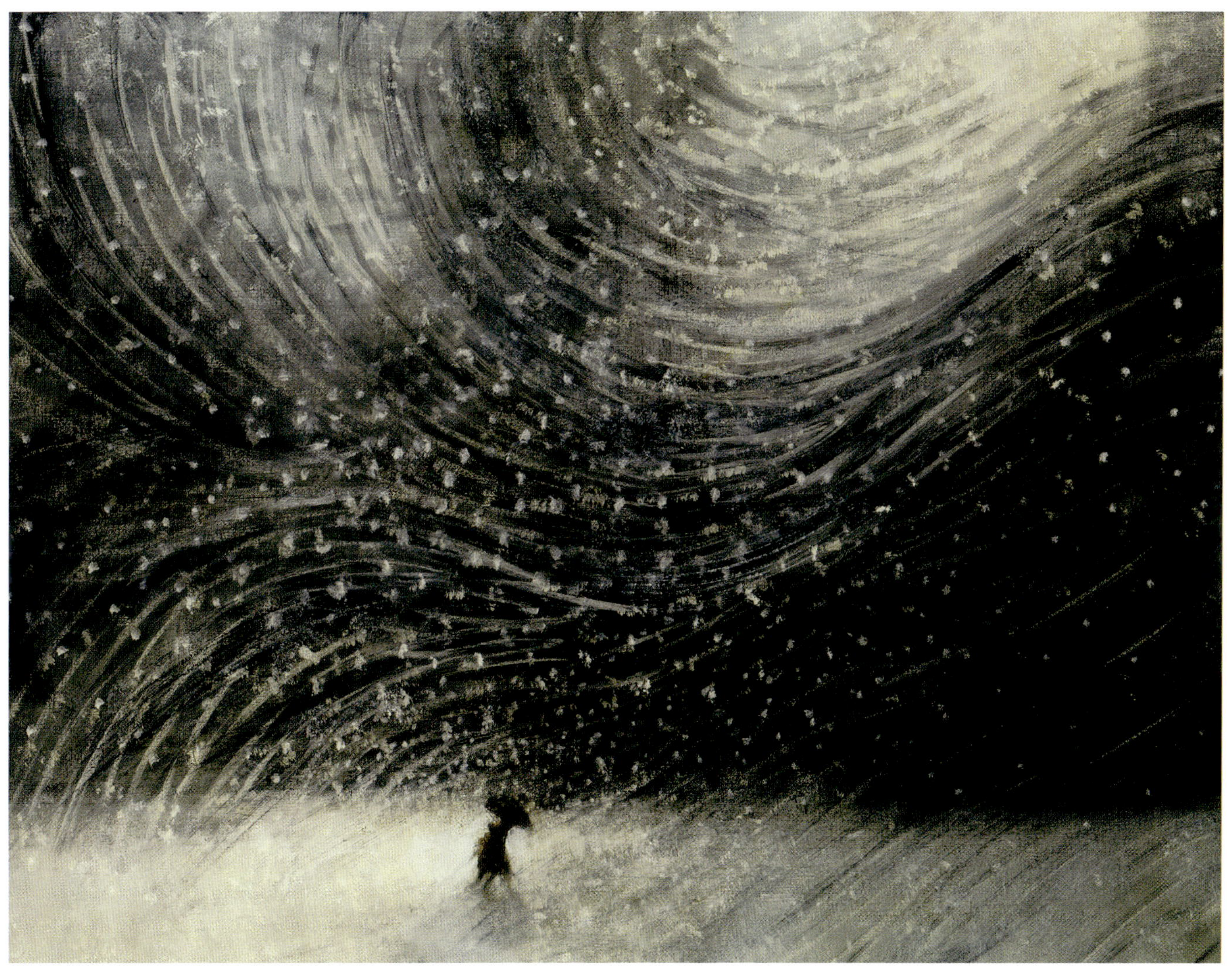

Snowy Night
2008
Oil on canvas
61×76.2 cm.
24×30 in.

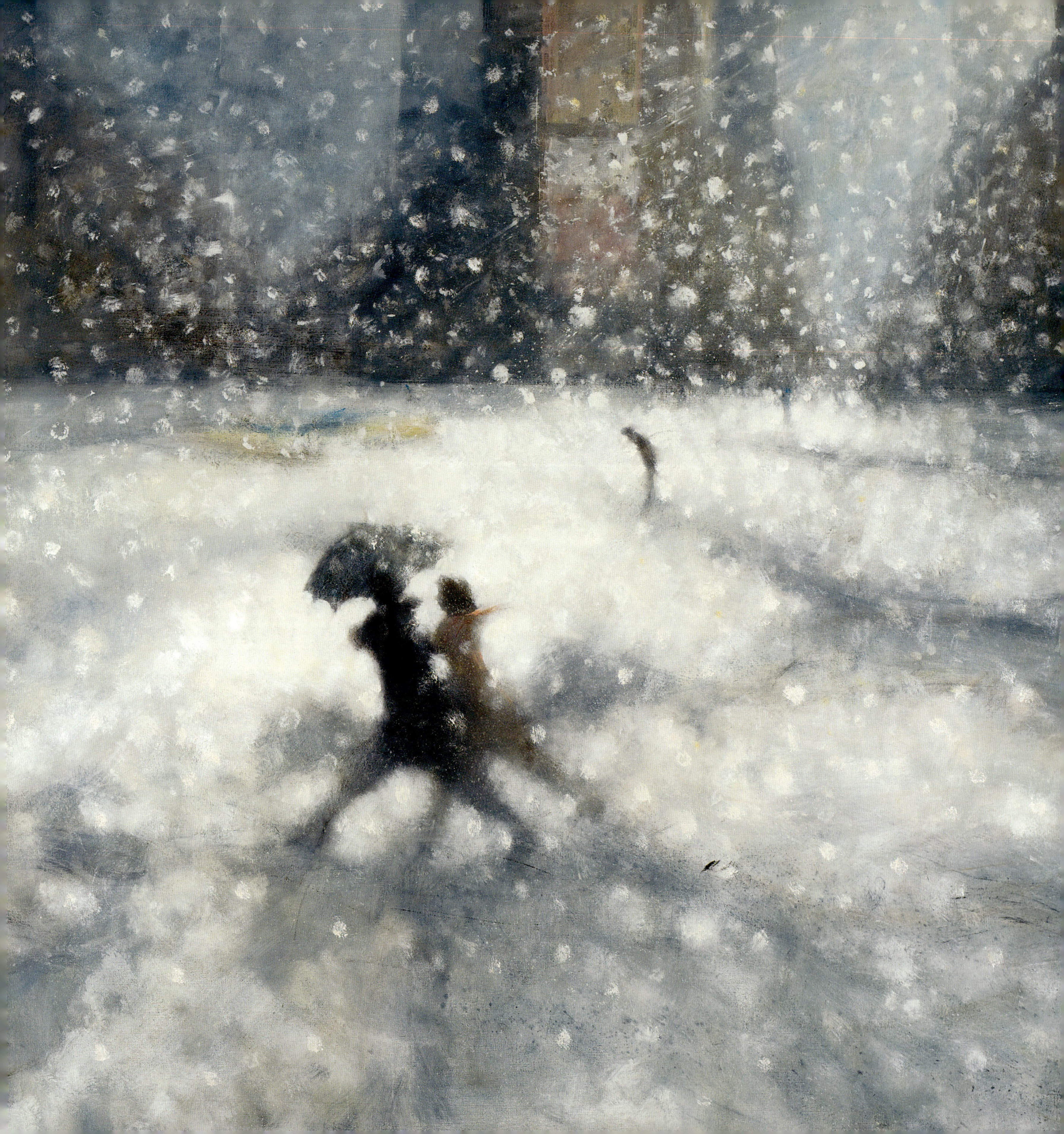

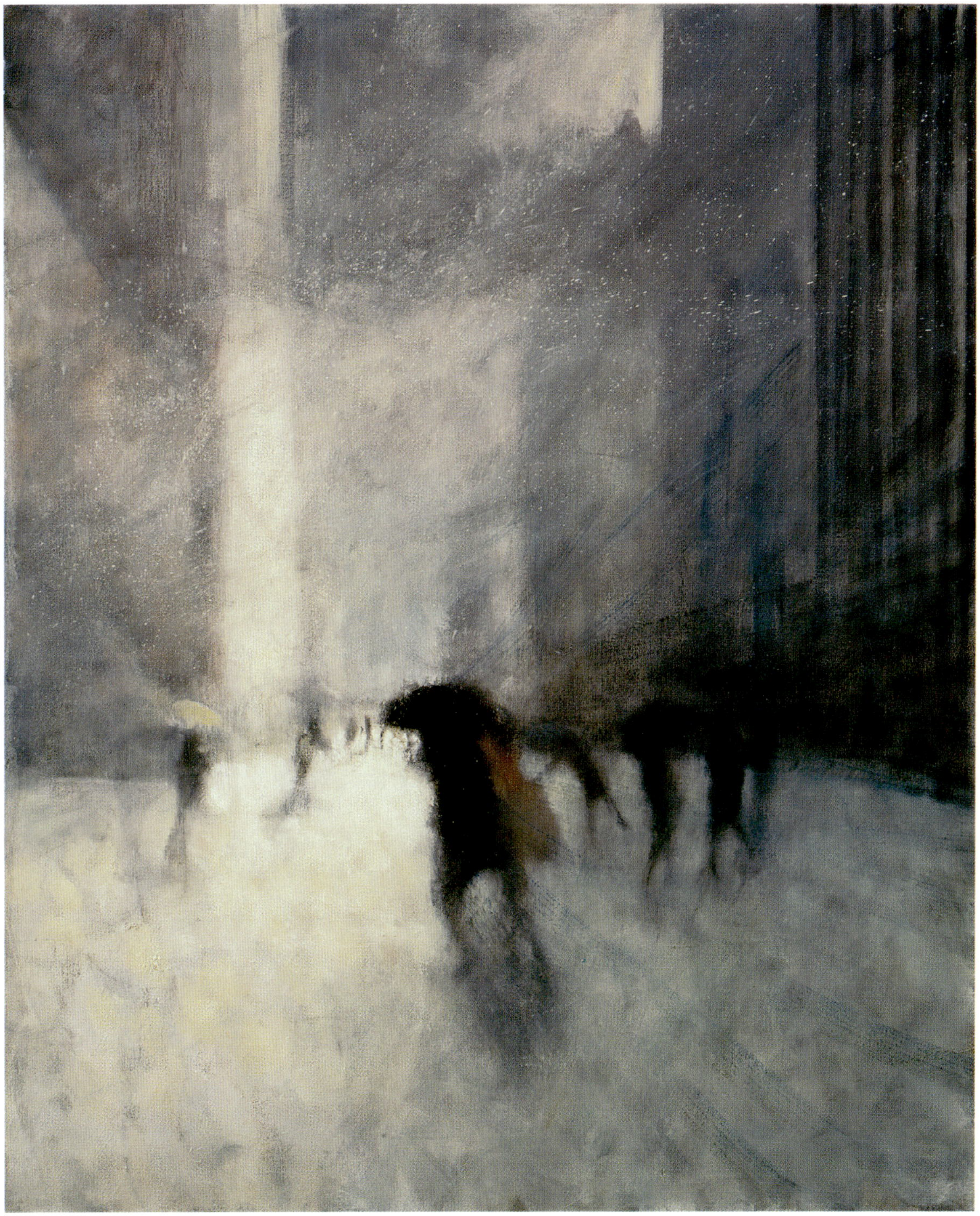

Snow, Times Square II
2008
Oil on canvas
198.1×152.4 cm.
78×60 in.

The Black Umbrella, Times Square
2007
Oil on canvas
152.4×121.9 cm.
60×48 in.

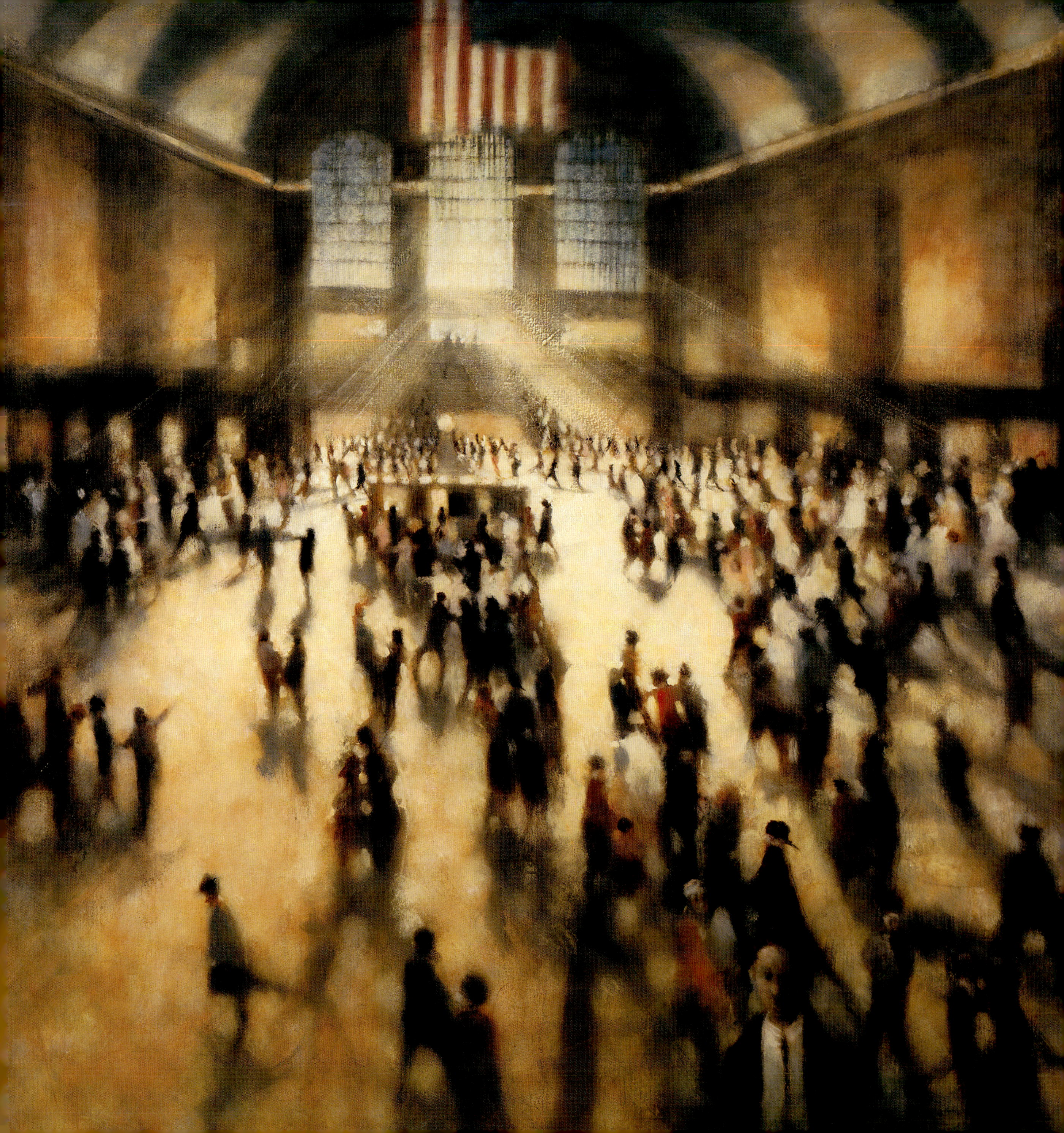

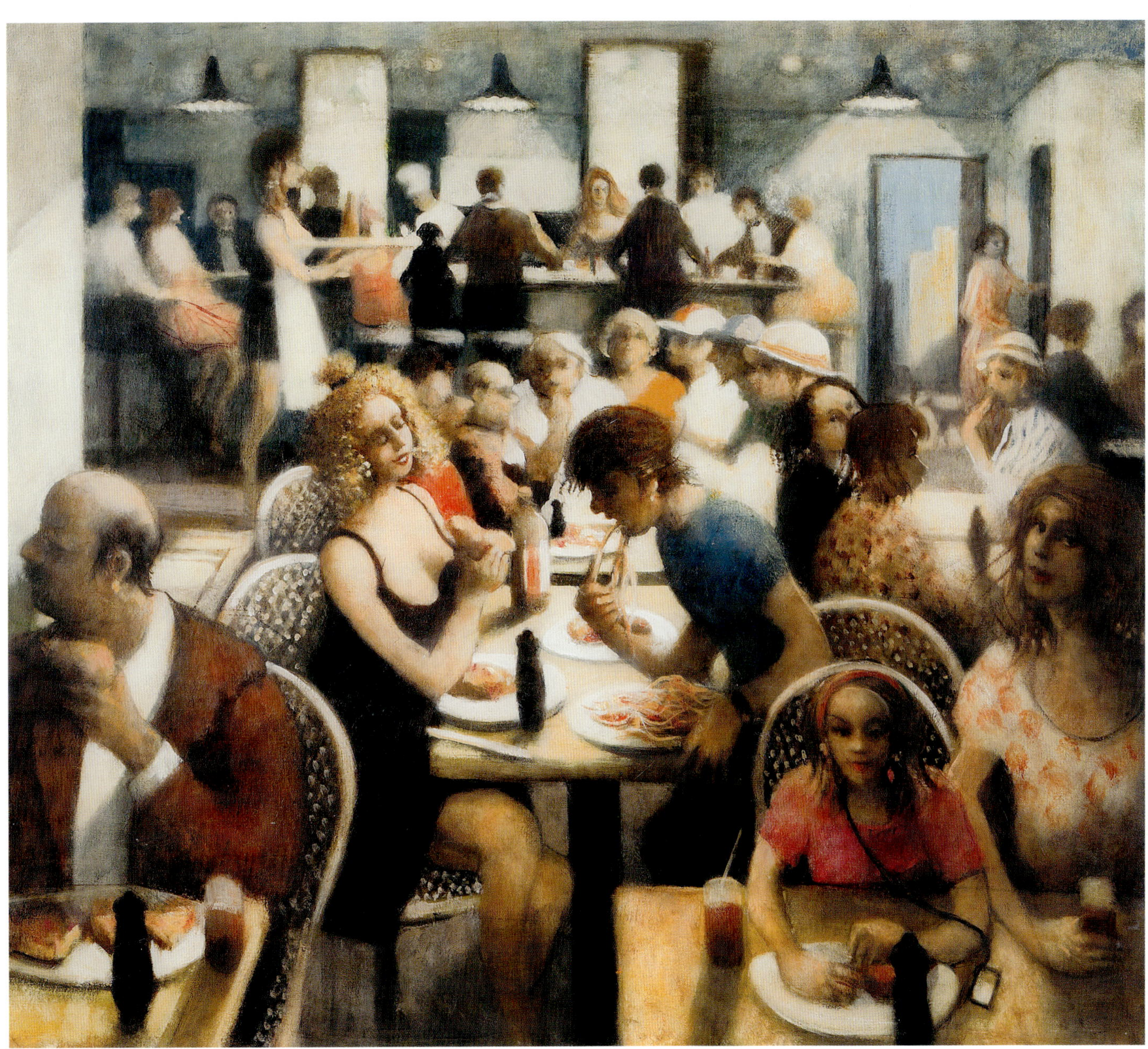

Chance Encounter, Grand Central II
2006
Oil on canvas
198.1×182.9 cm.
78×72 in.

Little Italy II
2010
Oil on canvas
152.4×167.6 cm.
60×66 in.

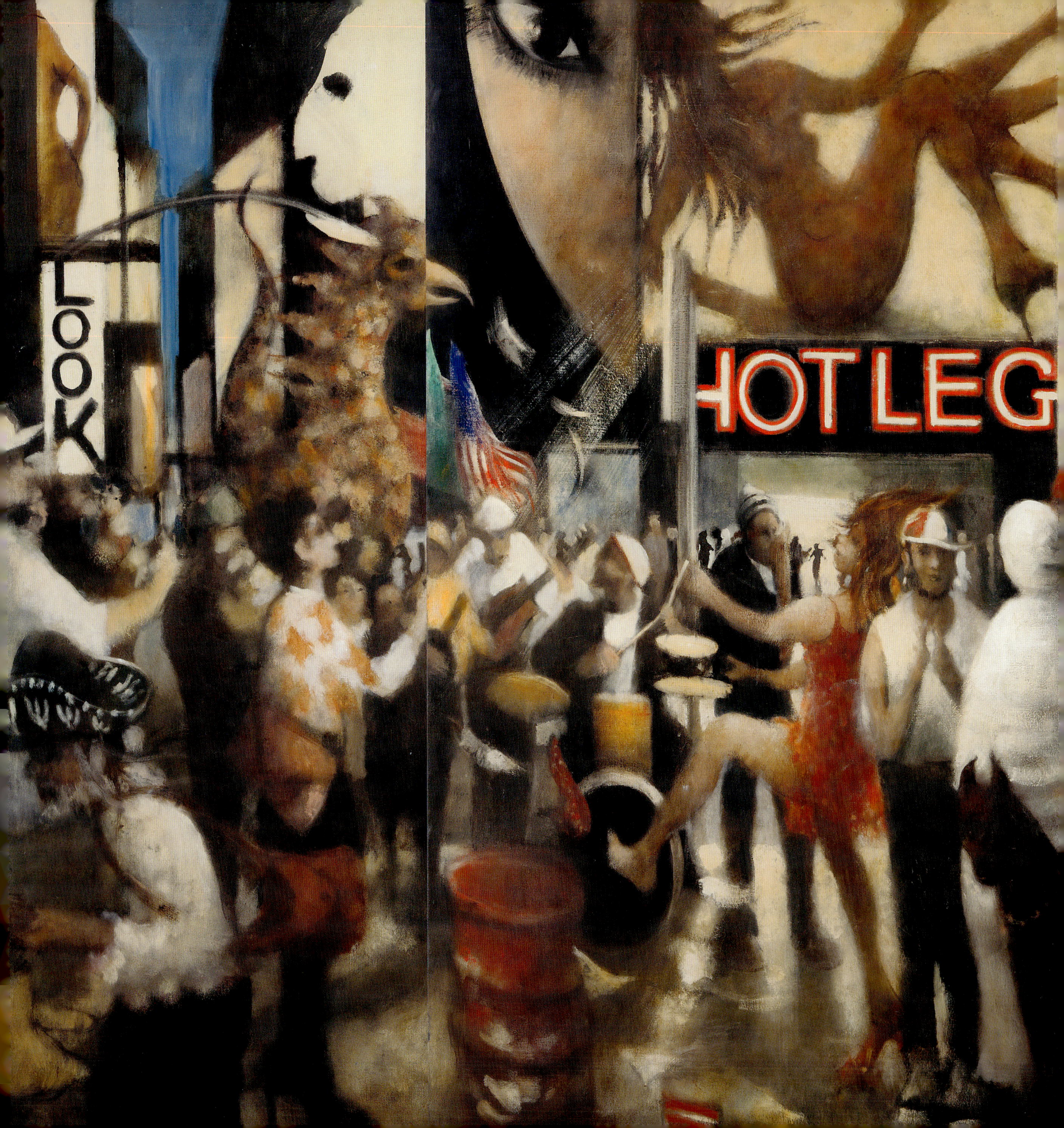
LOOK
HOT LEG

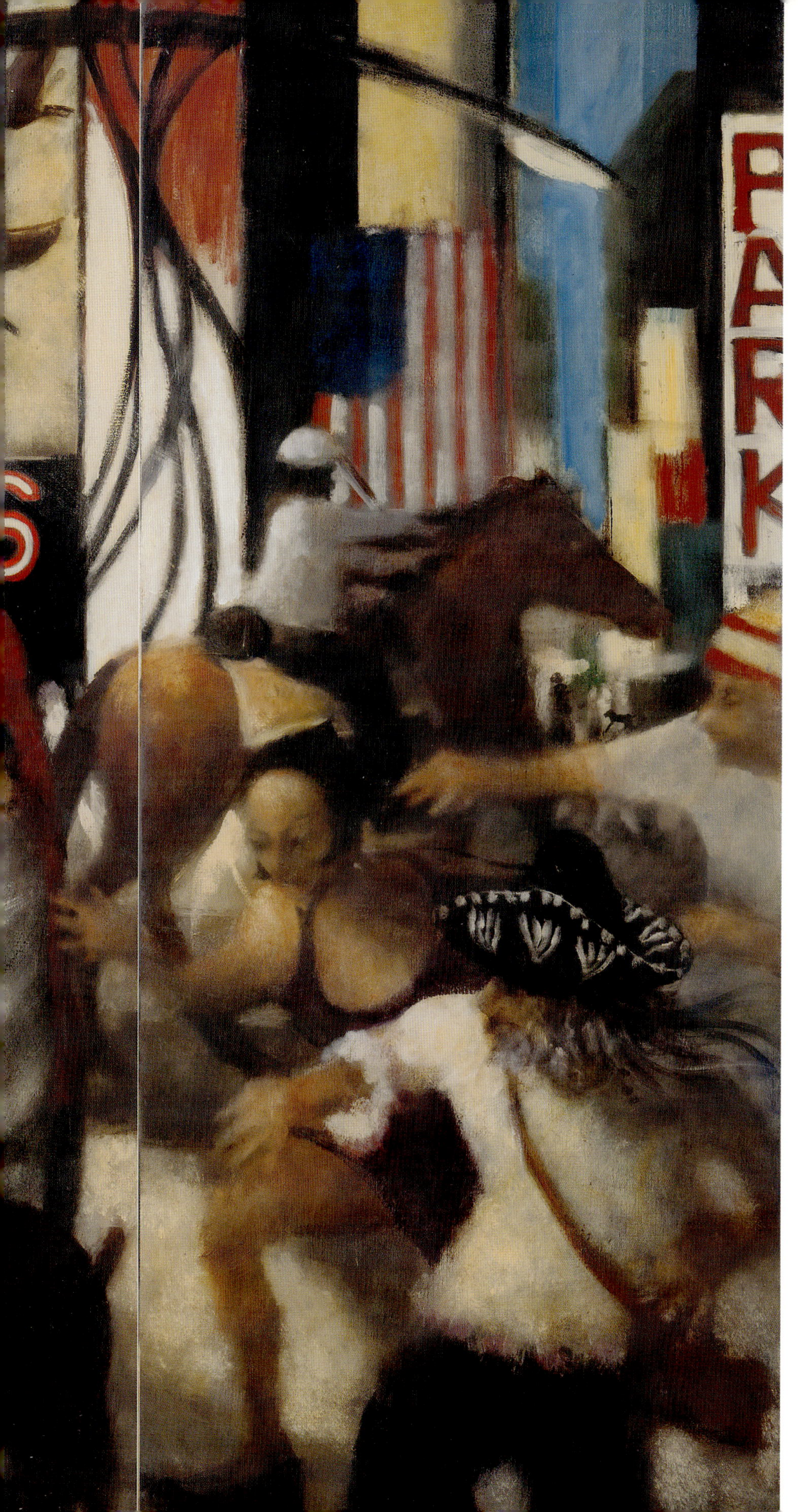

Hot Legs, Times Square

2011
Triptych; oil on canvas
198.1×76.2, 198.1×152.4, 198.1×76.2 cm.
78×30, 78×60, 78×30 in.

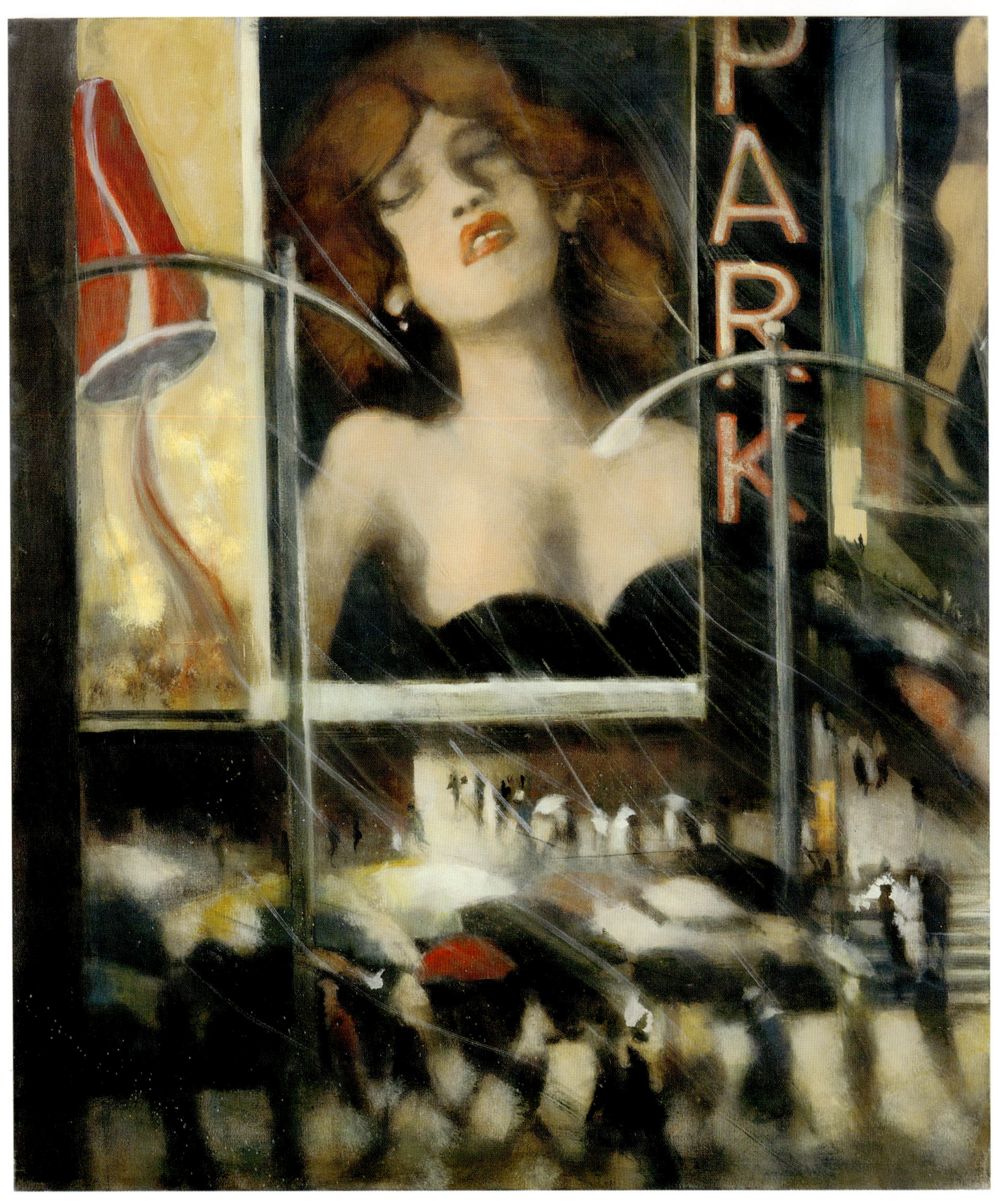

Times Square In The Rain

2011
Oil on canvas
167.6×142.2 cm.
66×56 in.

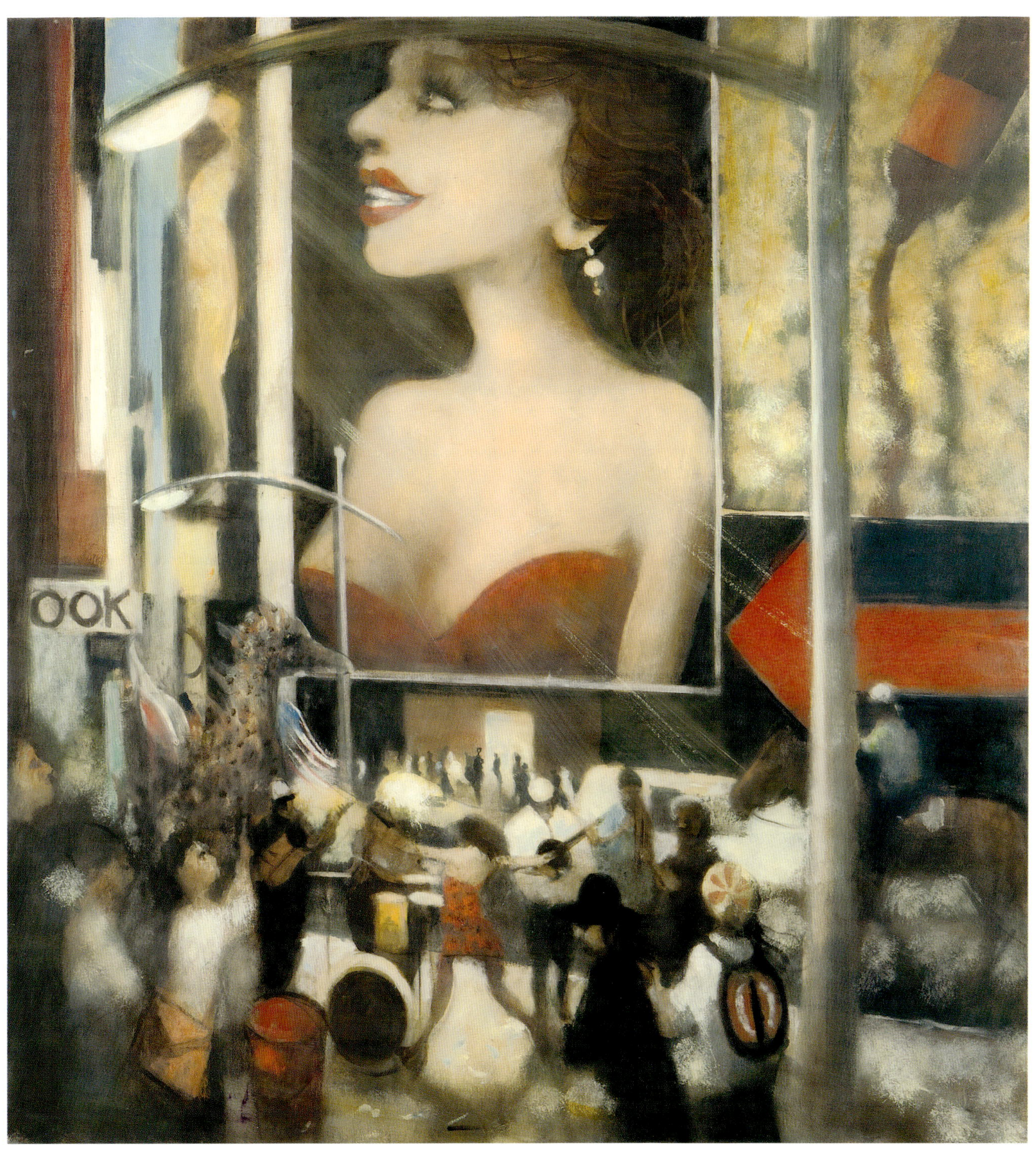

Times Square Musicians

2011
Oil on canvas
167.6×152.4 cm.
66×60 in.

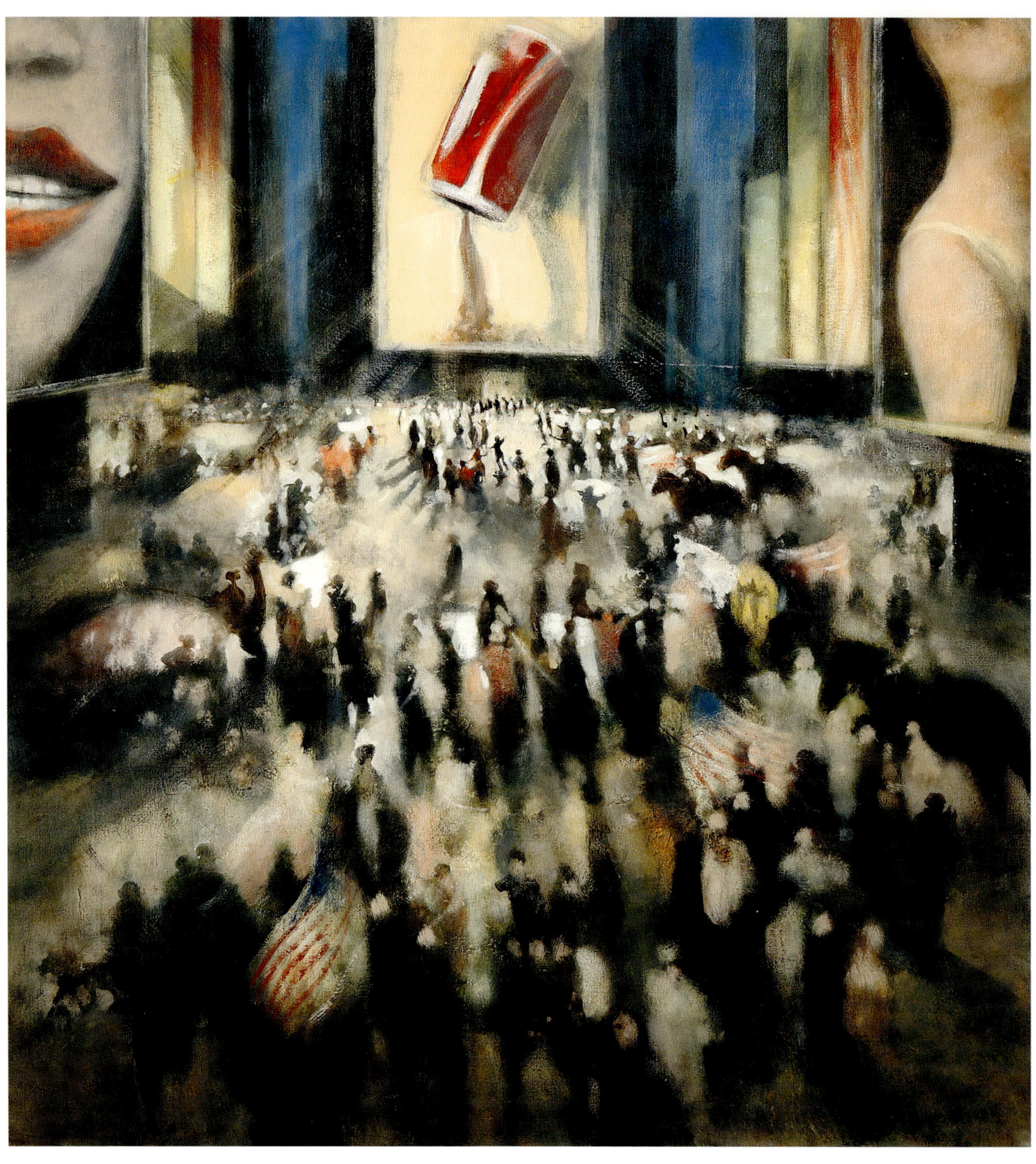

Times Square At Night I

2011
Oil on canvas
167.6×152.4 cm.
66×60 in.

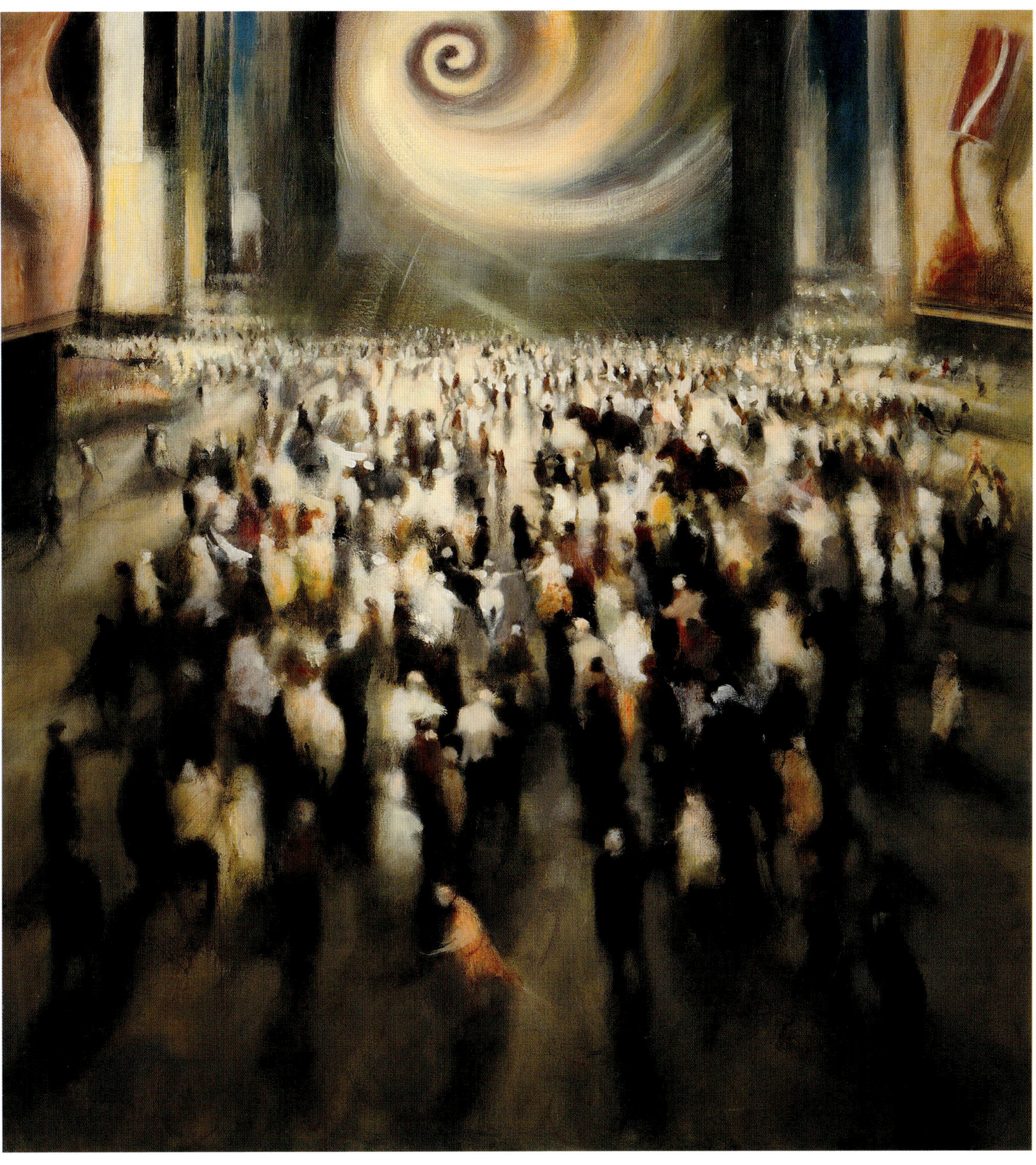

Times Square At Night III
2012–13
Oil on canvas
167.6×152.4 cm.
66×60 in.

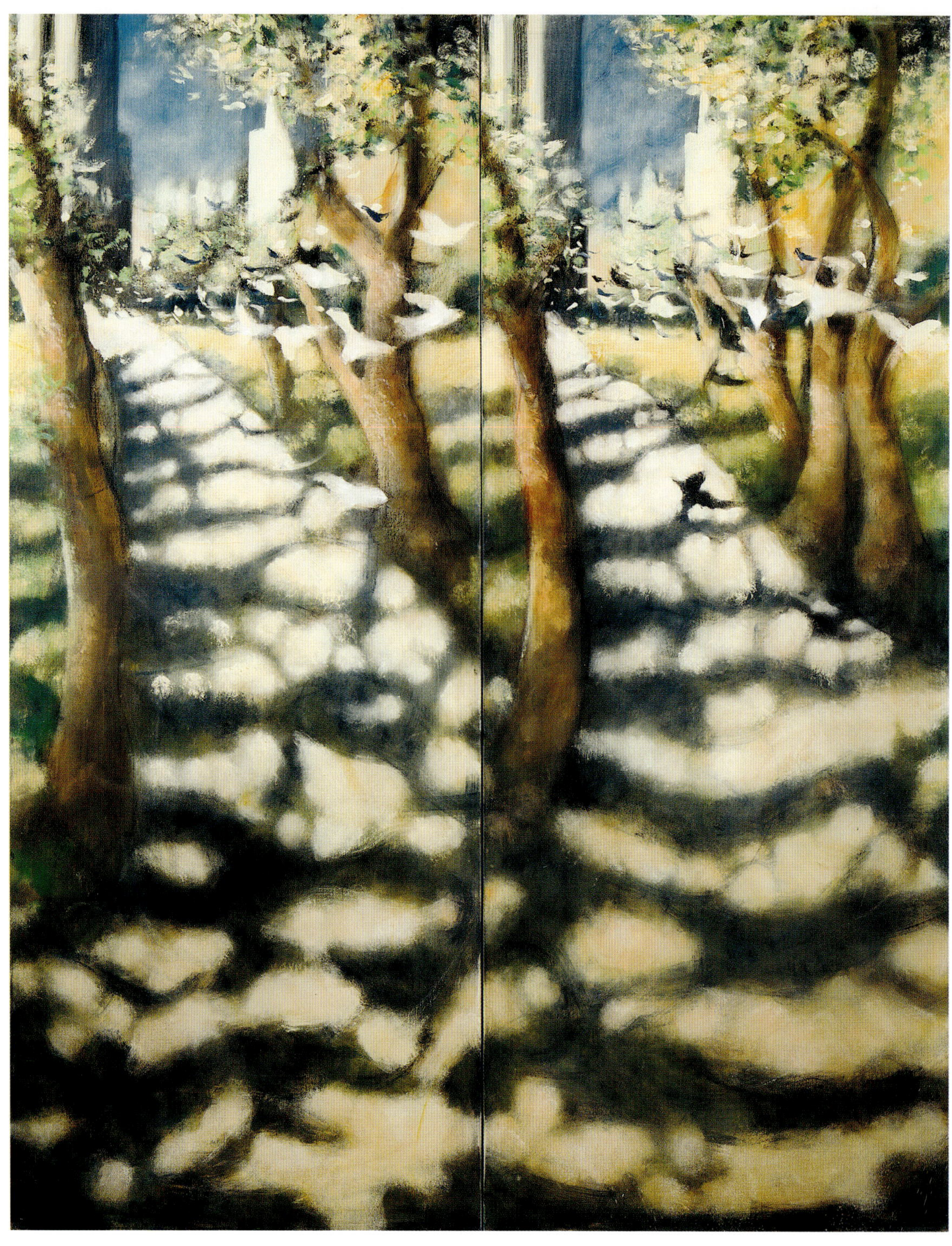

Double Road With Birds

2012
Diptych; oil on canvas
198.1×152.4 cm.
78×60 in.

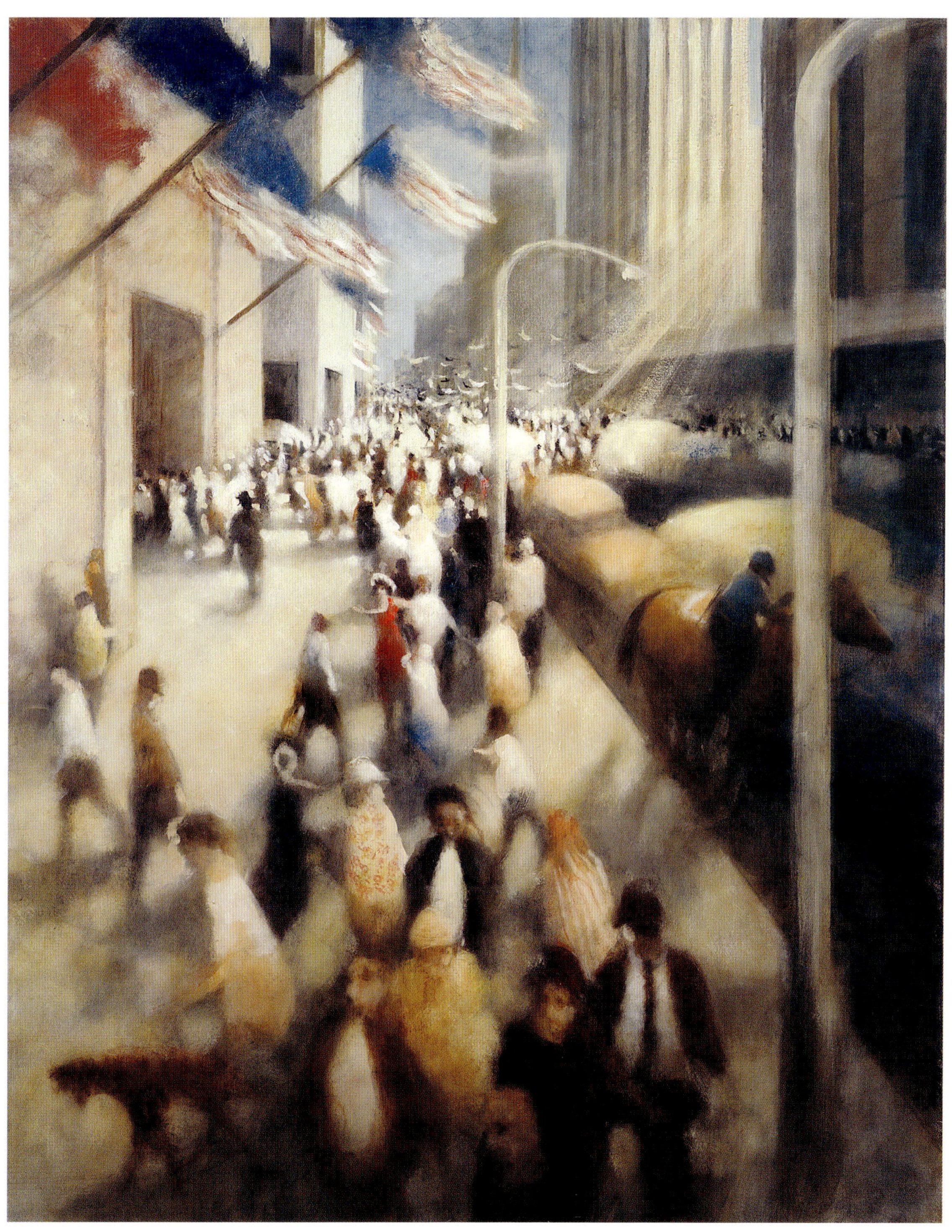

Towards Empire, Fifth Avenue II
2006
Oil on canvas
198.1×152.4 cm.
78×60 in.

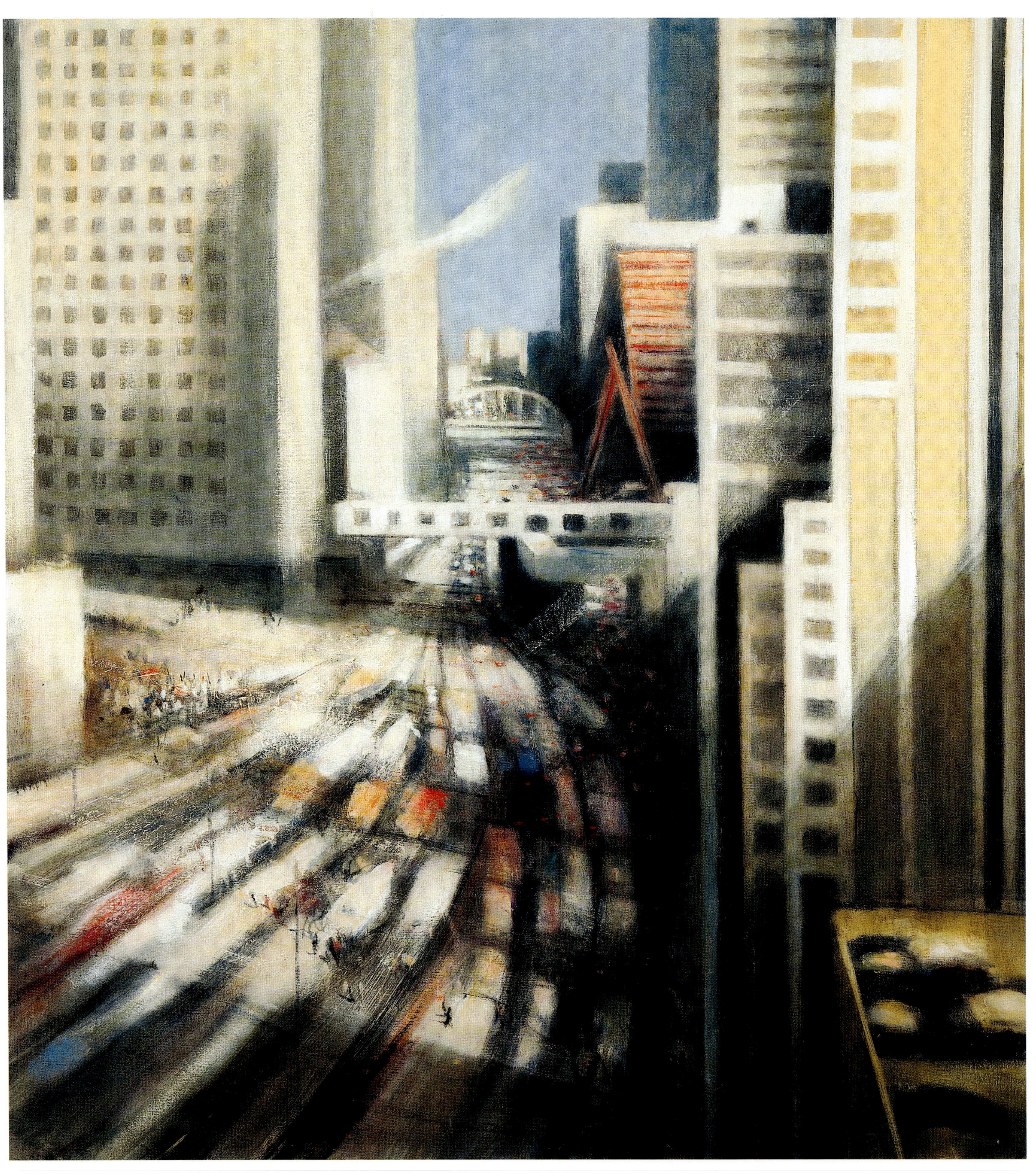

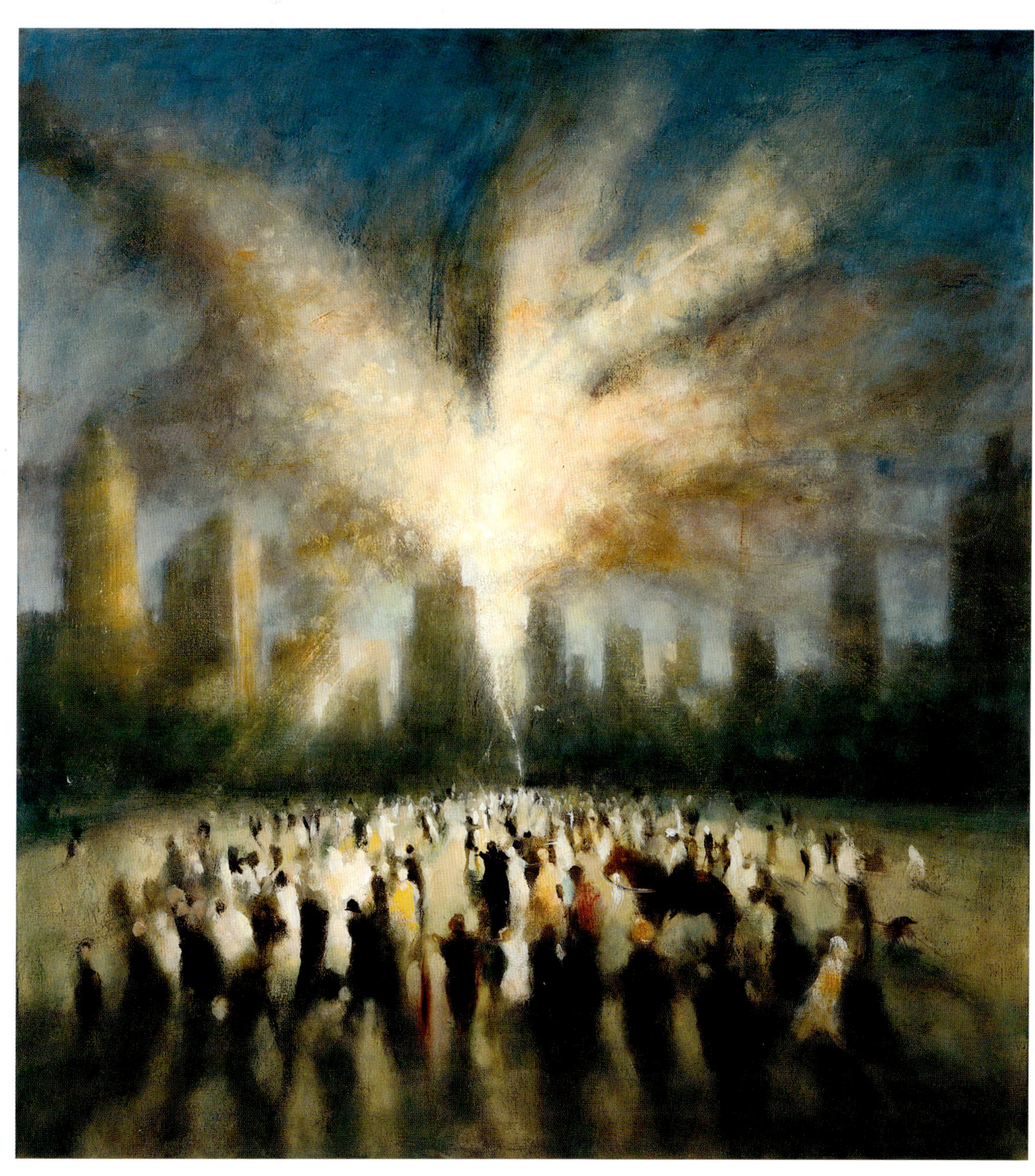

123

West Side Highway

2011

Oil on canvas

137.2×121.9 cm.

54×48 in.

Illumination I

2012–13

Oil on canvas

121.9×106.7 cm.

48×42 in.

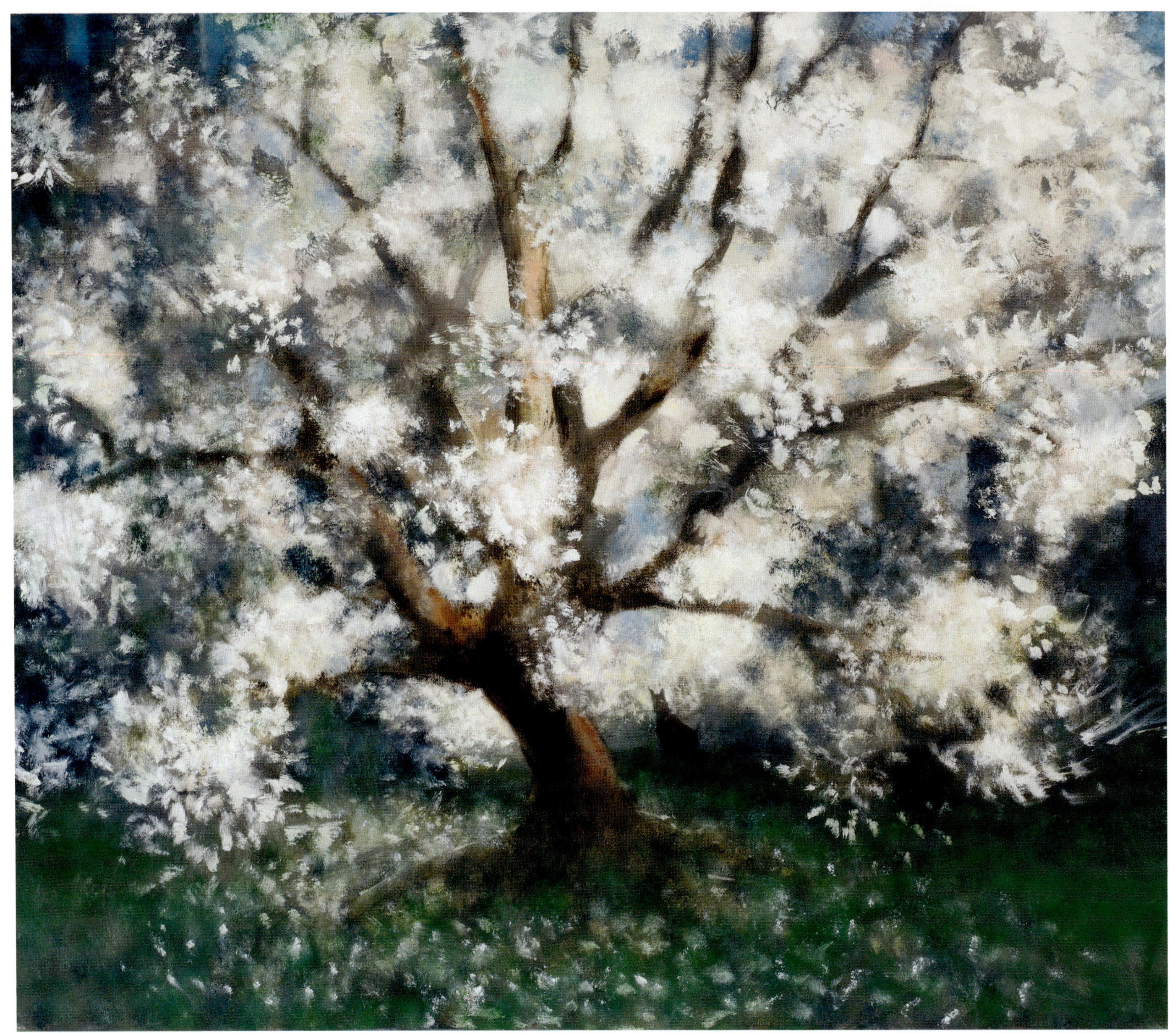

Cherry Tree With Doberman, Central Park

2013
Oil on canvas
106.7×121.9 cm.
42×48 in.

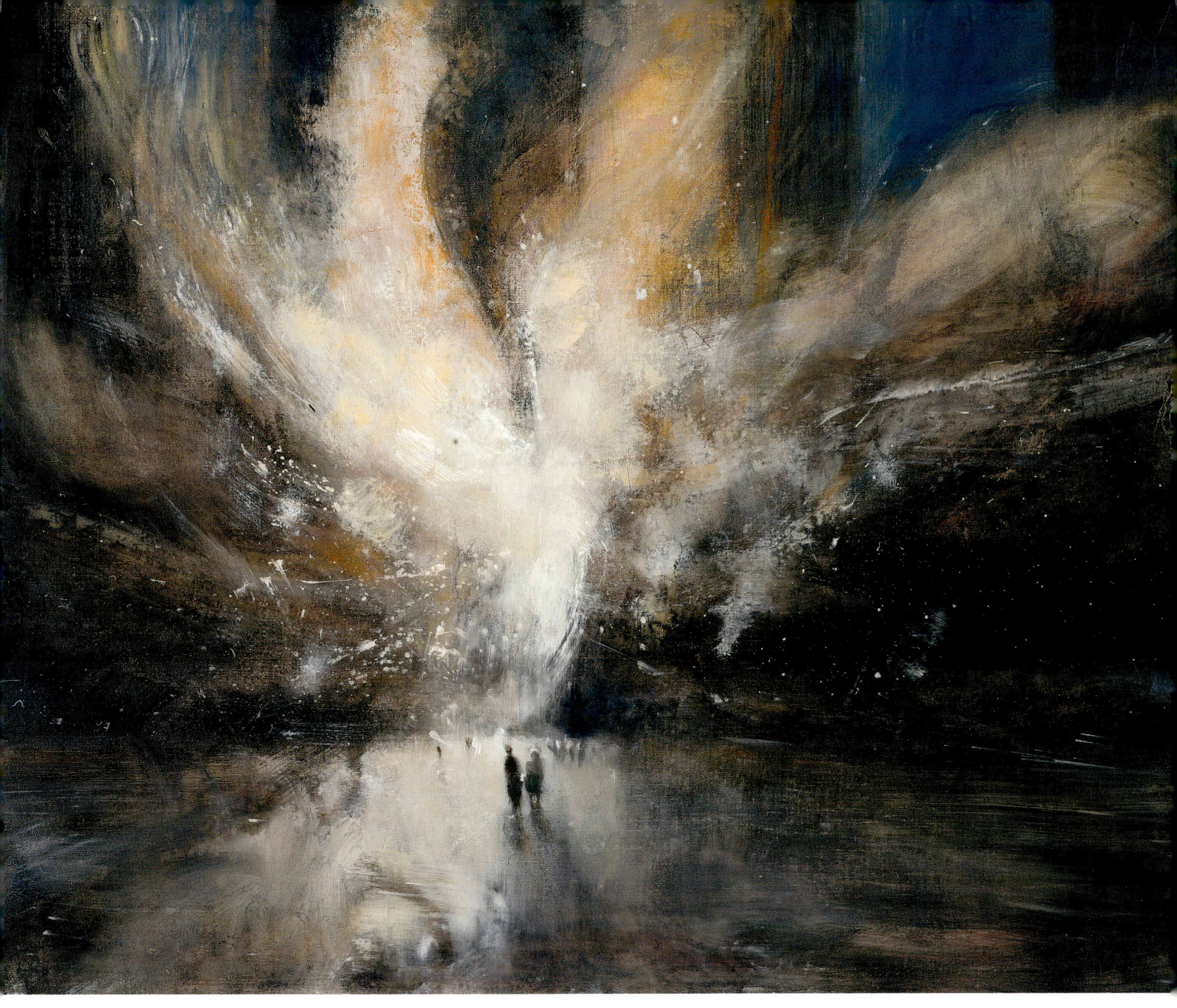

Illumination II
2013
Oil on canvas
76.2×91.4 cm.
30×36 in.

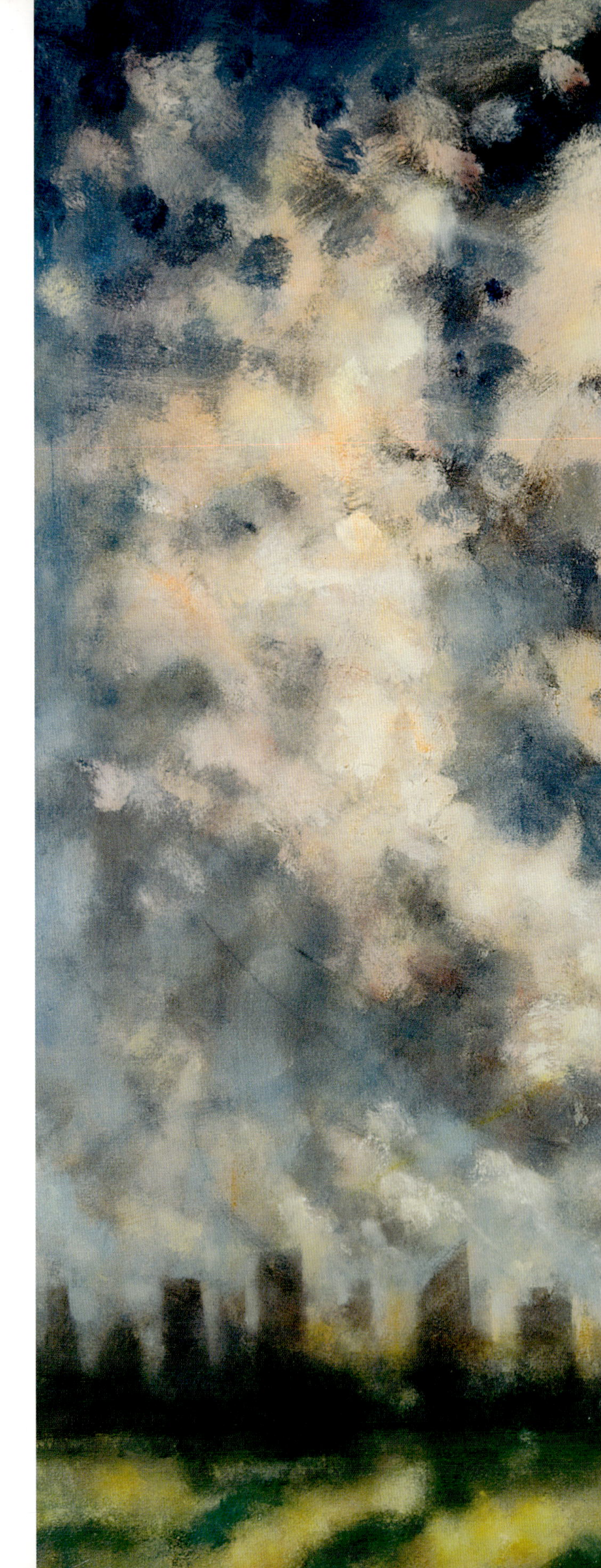

Clouds Over The City I

2013
Oil on canvas
152.4×182.9 cm.
60×72 in.

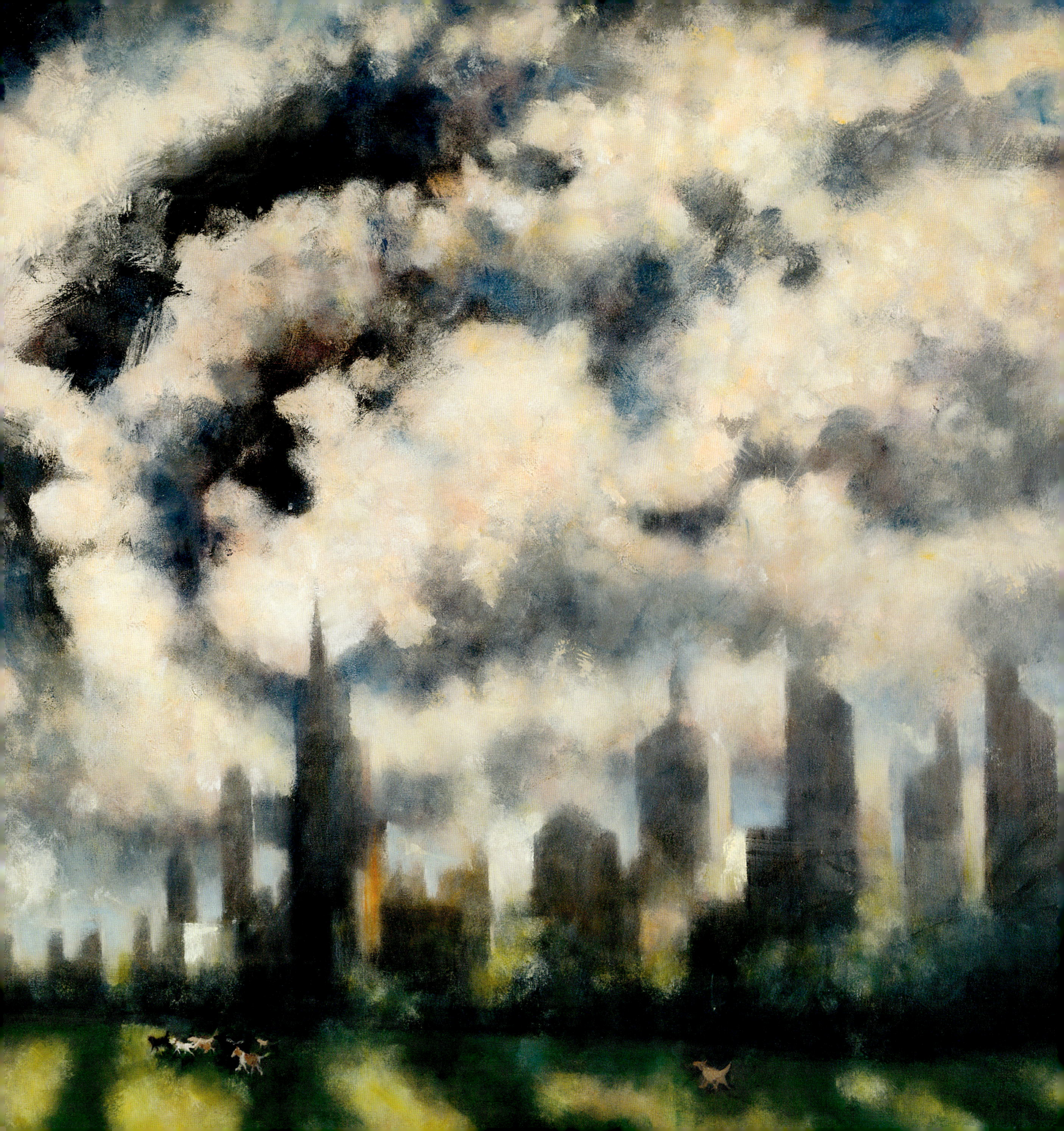

Index of Titles

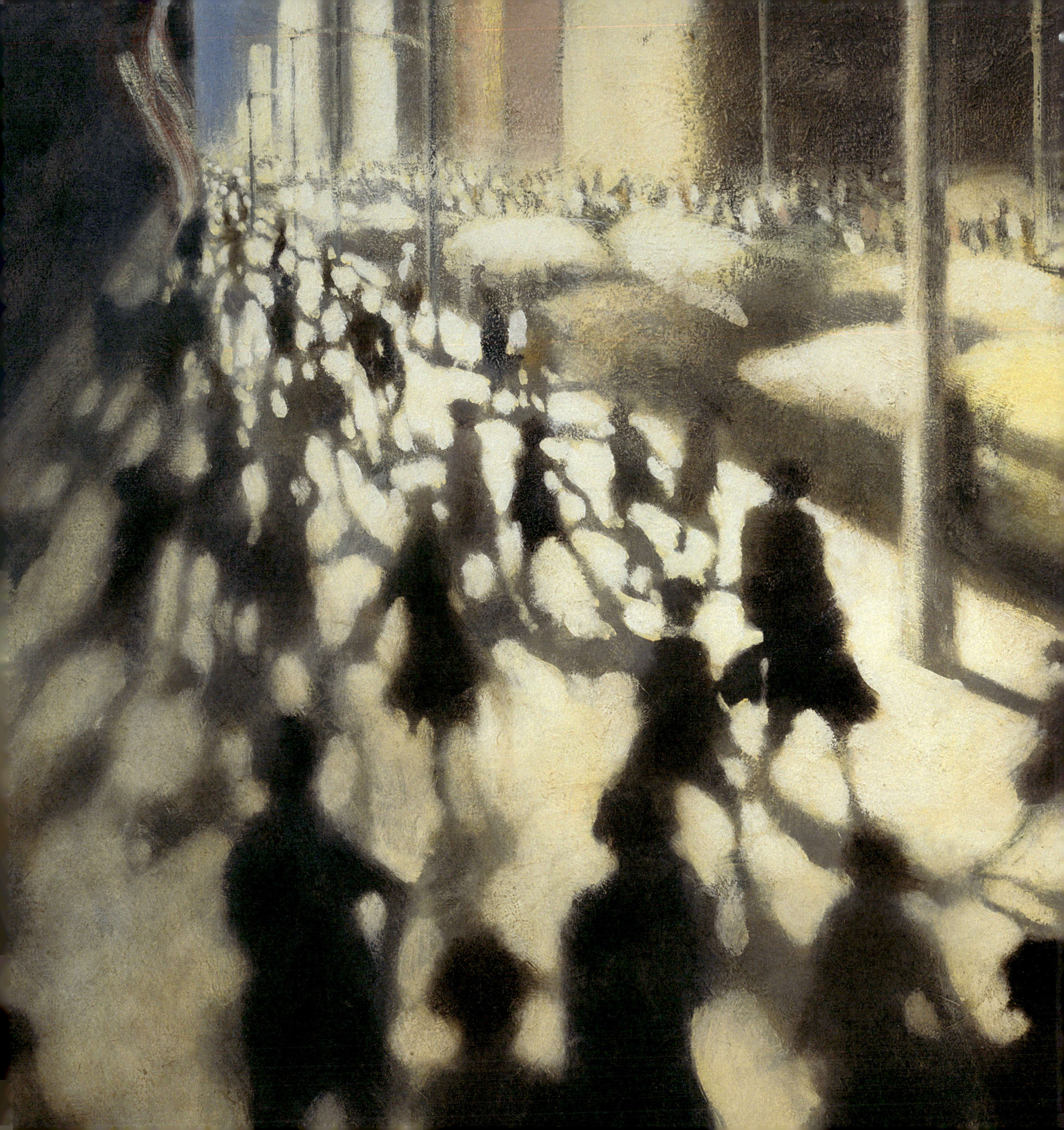